Copyright © 2019

Author Photo by Charles Ho

Cover Painting entitled *Ruptured Soul* by Marianthe Robertson

ISBN: 978-1-7325655-2-4 (sc)
ISBN: 978-1-7325655-3-1(e-Book)

Misguided Love:

Christians and the Rupture of LGBTQI2+ People

Charles Fensham

Table of Contents

ACKNOWLEDGEMENTS

I wish to acknowledge the institutional support of Knox College and the Principal of Knox College, Rev. Professor John Vissers and his predecessor Rev. Dr. Dorcas Gordon. The College has offered me timely support by granting a sabbatical and provided financial support during my sabbatical. This enabled me to respond the invitations of The Faculty of Theology of the University of Stellenbosch and the Faculty of Theology of the University of Western Cape in South Africa to be a visiting professor during 2016. At that time, I had the invaluable experience of exploring the ideas in this book with African Scholars. I am particularly thankful to Professors Ernst Conradie and Xolile Simon who hosted me at their respective institutions and allowed me to discuss important themes raised in this book. Through this exposure I gained valuable insight into pre-colonial African understandings of sexual orientation.

Many have read the manuscript in different versions and provided helpful feedback. Thank you to my colleague Rev. Dr. Harris Athanasiadis for his review of the manuscript and careful comments. I am thankful to Rev. Wes Denyer, my minister, who provided feedback on the manuscript and pastoral support. The congregation of Rosedale Presbyterian Church gave their moral and emotional support. You kept me on my feet and held me up when things were difficult! Thanks to Dr. Wendy Gritter, a former student and friend who has been a champion of the rights of sexual and gender minorities and played a key role in stopping the harm being done by the Christian organizations "Exodus" and "New Directions Ministries." Wendy reviewed the manuscript and helped me improve it significantly. Dr. Albert M. Wolters, although he disagreed with some of my argument, graciously read and critiqued the manuscript and saved me from much embarrassment. Thank you. Special thanks to Brent Hawkes CM, ONB, who reviewed the manuscript and then spent considerable time providing feedback and corrections.

Very special thanks are due to the Journal of Pastoral Care and Counseling and in particular the editor, Rabbi Dr. Terry R. Bard, who recognized the significant harm that religion has inflicted on sexual and gender minority people. Terry Bard worked hard to support this project and to guide it through the peer review and publication process. It goes without saying that none of the good people above can be blamed for the content of this book. I remain solely responsible.

To my extended family, especially to my partner Charlie for loving support, good humor and love. To my family, Alex, with his ideas for the cover, Holly and Andy, Marina, Marianthé and Theresé and their families, thanks for being in my corner and for your caring support and all the fun we are blessed to have together!

Section 1:
Moral Logic, Intuitive Disgust, and Christian Arguments

CHAPTER 1: INTRODUCTION

While walking on a bridge across the Seine, I decided that rather than "give in to temptation," I would kill myself in some kind of "accident" so that no one would ever know. I was tired of the struggle. So I wrote a long suicide note to my family and then stared into the dark waters below-but I just didn't have the courage to end my own life. Thank God I didn't during those long, lonely years. I would have missed so much.[1]

(Rev. Dr. Mel White)

This experience is all too familiar to many sexual and gender minority people who are part of, or grew up in, non-affirming faith communities. Not only can I relate to it personally, but, as a pastor I have witnessed two people take their lives under similar circumstances as described by Mel White. One was a dear friend – a brilliant philosopher – who could not reconcile the non-affirming Christian teaching of his faith community with his sexual orientation. The other was a person under my pastoral care who never had the courage to tell me about his struggle with sexual orientation. Shortly after my denomination, the Presbyterian Church in Canada, issued a statement on human sexuality that took a non-affirming stance, he hung himself from a bridge and left a suicide note. Christian teaching that does not affirm the humanity and the wholeness of sexual and gender minority people does harm. It is not simply a theological debate with different perspectives. It is not simply a matter of gracious disagreement. It is a matter of causing material harm to the point of death. As the conservative Baptist ethicist, David Gushee, recently put it, "You are hurting me with your bible."[2]

The invitation of this book is for my readers who are Christian to consider the dimension of harm in the ongoing debates on affirming or not affirming sexual and gender minority Christians within church communities. Much has been said and much is written on biblical interpretation and Christian traditions of teaching. There are also many arguments on the issue of justice and equality that have been made for and against the affirmation of sexual and gender minorities. Here I bring evidence of the history of harm and the infliction of harm on sexual and gender minority Christians. The history of Christians causing harm through teaching is a long and devastating story. We can think of parallel histories of harm such as the theological defense of slavery and the untold harm caused by "well-meaning" Christians to slaves. The same can be said about the treatment and place of women in Christian communities, the relentless persecution of Jewish people through the ages, and many of us are aware of the role of racism and colonial exploitation of racial minorities and indigenous communities in Christian teaching and behavior. My own adoptive country, Canada, has undergone a process of "truth and reconciliation" with its aboriginal peoples over the past years, and key to the harm done here was the teaching and abusive role of Christian churches both Protestant and Roman Catholic. In South Africa, my country of origin, I lived through the apartheid era and experienced first-hand how "biblical teaching" can be used in pious ways to exploit, discriminate, and kill people. Presently and in the past, similar things happen to sexual and gender minority Christians. When we discover that we do harm we must stop.

There has been a history of denial of responsibility for harm done in Christian arguments. When the first major work on Christianity and Homosexuality in the 20th century was published by Derrick Sherwin Bailey (1955), he did not record a single execution of a "homosexual" person in Christian history.[3] Even now, more than 60 years later, Western Christians, both Roman Catholic and Protestant, have yet to begin to face the witness of history about Christian instigation and participation in extreme violence. This violence involved torture, abuse and brutal killing. At some critical points, such as in the Dutch Republic during the 18th century, this behavior included drowning teenage boys in barrels of water and hanging boys as young as 14. Live burning has been the preferred form of execution. In Protestant Geneva hanging, drowning and burning was used, but the preferred method was "breaking on the wheel." This involved tying the victim to a large wooden wheel and then systematically beating them with clubs until their bones broke and they died. My hope is that this history and its terrifying witness will no longer be ignored when Christians conduct theological debates on the place and role of sexual and gender minorities in Christian communities. The argument here is simple. Non-affirming Christian teaching and behavior has caused and still cause great harm to sexual and gender minority people. There is no unambiguous Christian scriptural base for maintaining Christian non-affirming attitudes and teaching. This, as we will see in the second chapter, is particularly important in the light of the Gospel witness to Jesus' teaching about the central interpretive principal of the scriptures – love God and neighbor. There is no Christian scriptural basis for causing harm to our neighbors inside or outside Christian communities. Therefore, we need to find a way of repentance, and a new path of ethical discernment in relation to sexual and gender minorities.

This was a very hard book to write. Throughout the writing process I have had a picture in my mind that sustained me to continue. Some years back I was involved as a volunteer with the Ecumenical Chaplaincy at the University of Toronto. This ministry ran a special bible study group for young Christians who were struggling to come to terms with their sexual orientation. At our major fundraiser a young Korean man rose to speak. He told the story of the darkness and rejection he experienced in his church context. Most of all, he spoke of how, as a first-year student, he found himself in a place where he was ready to commit suicide. This wonderful child of God was driven to the edge of self-destruction by Christian teaching and attitudes encountered in his home congregation. It was only after he discovered this bible study group that he could find a place where he could trust the acceptance of God. His agonized face haunts me. Many teens who end up living on the streets of Toronto come from a context where the attitudes of derision and abuse of sexual and gender minority people is still considered a good thing, even a holy thing. Social research, that I will discuss later, has now shown the powerful role non-affirming Christian teaching plays in these contexts. The abuses of history continue in many ways. Despite dramatic changes in society and culture in North America many religious communities still harbor deep disgust and act in ways unworthy of the gospel of Jesus Christ. Even in a country like Canada, considered to be socially progressive in relation to sexual and gender minorities, Statistics Canada reports that most violent hate crimes are directed at sexual and gender minorities. If only some people will cease to act and speak harmfully, this book would be worth it.

This book makes an argument for a process of positive moral discernment for the support of covenanted erotic relationships among sexual and gender minority Christians. By sexual and gender minority persons I mean people who identify as LGBTQI2+. What does this acronym mean? Acronyms, and particularly those applied to sexual orientation and gender identity, have a way of growing and changing as the complexity of human experience unfolds in our understanding. I will use this acronym as meaning Lesbian, Gay, Bisexual, Transgender, Gender Queer and Questioning, Intersex and "Two Spirited" (a cultural concept in some aboriginal communities) plus other forms of human experience yet to be discerned.[4] This acronym covers a wide spectrum of human experience and identity. Beside the specific definitions of these experiences and identities, it is important to note one particular distinction. That distinction is between sexual orientation and gender identity. Sexual orientation speaks of an inherent, enduring emotional, romantic and sexual attraction which for lesbian women may be to another woman or for gay males to another male. In the case of bisexual individuals, it is an orientation that is indifferent to the person being male or female. Gender identity speaks of an innermost concept off self as male or female, or a form of identity not limited by the cultural constructs of male or female, that may be the same or different from the sex assigned at birth. Gender expression speaks of the way we express ourselves in socio-cultural ways that may be the same or different from the sex we are assigned at birth. Transgender refers to people whose gender expression differs from the cultural expectations of the sex assigned at birth. Most Christian churches have struggled with the acceptance or rejection of all these forms of human experience. Later we will look briefly at contemporary arguments about gender and gender identity as socially constructed. It is undeniable that gender, in any cultural context, has a strong socially constructed dimension, but, as Margaret Farley wisely points out, even strong advocates for ideas of social gender construction recognize that our bodies are not simply passive slates on which society imprints.[5] Many of the disturbing stories from Christian history that you will encounter in this book will encompass some combination of constructions and experiences of sexual orientation and gender. Often our only access to such historic examples is through the lens of sexual behavior with someone of the same sex as oneself. It is important to remember that this simplified historic lens obscures the deeper struggles and complex experiences of the people we will encounter. There is no simplistic way to unpack these stories. We also face the large gap between our present understandings of gender and sexuality and the way such experiences and cultural phenomena were understood and engaged in other historical and cultural contexts. Similarly, research in cultural anthropology has shown a great diversity of cultural perspectives on gender and sexuality.[6]

Because I suspect that some readers may jump to conclusions, I need to make clear that I do not use the term sexual and gender minorities to relay an idea that all erotic sexual practices are simply to be affirmed without discernment or responsibility. As the reader will discover, I will argue for wise boundaries, arising out of the gospel and the Christian Scriptures, in our moral discernment of Christian erotic expression. What I will argue is that, in the complexity of sexualities we encounter, we as Christians, should find a fresh gospel inspired way of discerning the boundaries of healthy sexual expression.[7]

Contemporary acronyms therefore raise the thorny problem of terminology. What are we talking about when we refer to sexual practices understood in different ways throughout the history of Judaism and Christianity? The word homosexual, which I will use occasionally, was first used in the 19th century. It is a word that followed on the more common earlier use of the word sodomite. The 19th century use of this word evolved out of the perception that "homosexuality" was a mental disease. At that time, it was understood as the attraction and expression of erotic love between people with the same sexual organs. This 19th century shift moved sodomy out of the realm of religious sanction to homosexuality in the realm of treatment in penal and mental institutions. Within Christian circles, both liberal and conservative Protestantism followed these secular processes of renaming and reframing same-sex relationships. In a powerful account Heather White demonstrates how a pastoral model of "healing the homosexual" evolved out of these changes in Christian perspective in North America.[8] She also shows how this development influenced mid-twentieth century English Bible translations. Today, homosexuality is no longer considered a psychological or psychiatric disorder. It has lost most of its pejorative quality but is still somewhat tainted by it. When I use this term, I will use it in a neutral way, not intending any pejorative meaning. In some ways, by inference, one could sometimes apply the word homosexual to specific practices in the distant past. Even some of the sexual orientation concepts in the acronym LGBTQI2+ can with some caution be applied in some cases. So, for example, we could, from our perspective, probably describe the great founder of Western Christianity, Saint Augustine as bisexual. By his own confession he had an intense relationship with another boy in his youth. Later he lived with a concubine and fathered a son. This could certainly qualify him as bisexual. Some men executed as "sodomites" could likely also be understood as transgender in today's terms. The rare mention of women in same-sex erotic relationships could also apply the word lesbian, such as Saint Augustine's comment on nuns "playing" with each other.[9] However, the cultural differences between ancient Israel, first century Palestine, and medieval Europe are so vast that descriptive terms such as "people in homoerotic relationships" or "sexual and gender minorities" are more appropriate. I will use the phrase sexual and gender minorities most often because it allows for a flexible and open-ended understanding of sexual diversity. Although Christian traditions occasionally addressed gender expression when different from cultural expectations, most of the cases we will encounter have to do with male homoerotic relationships and Christian sanctions against them. All the nuances of gender identity and sexual orientation require gentle loving gospel moral discernment in community. Consistently, Christian traditions have struggled most with male homoerotic expressions of these experiences. Ecclesial debates today often use contemporary terms like homosexual in relation to ancient Christian texts in ways that are not academically sound. This is true for the use of homosexual in some 20th century translations of the bible, but it is also true for the use of that same word for something called "the sin of sodomy" in Christian tradition. The "sin of sodomy," as we will see has a long history and has meant different things and reflected different practices at different times in church history. Mark Jordan describes that process as "a long process of thinning and condensing."[10] When Christians, in their rhetoric, call "homosexuality" a sin and claim that this is what Christian Scripture and tradition always taught, they are oversimplifying in an untruthful way. In fact, there is a long history of different meanings and social constructions attached to both the biblical texts referred to and the concept of "sodomy" developed later in church history. The personal experience and content of homoerotic relationships in Christian history is mostly inaccessible to us. What we do have a clear record of is how people accused of "sodomy" were treated. It is this Christian practice of evil revealed in history that that should lead us to repentance.

The reader also needs to know that my description of brutal executions and torture of people accused of sodomy does not imply that all such people were always without any fault. As it is today, both heterosexual erotic passion and homosexual erotic passion take many forms and some of it is potentially exploitative, damaging, abusive, and deeply harmful. The point of the historical description is to focus on the excessive and wicked behavior on behalf of the church and civil authorities. Without a doubt, some of those executed acted badly. We know that many victims of the church were poor teenage boys who prostituted themselves under desperate circumstances. Today, in compassion, we would consider such children victims. We also have evidence of deep loving relationships through some of the court records, which suggest that committed loving same-sex relationships also existed throughout history. We do not know how many of those executed fitted these descriptions.

I assume here that sexual orientation is a reality experienced in people's lives. Every reader has a sexual orientation situated somewhere on a spectrum of possibilities. For those primarily oriented heterosexually their experience is simply a given, and, because this is the normative experience of our cultures we often unconsciously judge and act out of the privilege of that experience and cultural affirmation. I am personally aware of the power of such "normative privilege" as a South African white man who grew up under the apartheid system in South Africa. Today I understand much of my early experience and cultural bias in the light of the "white privilege" in which I was raised and from which I benefited. White South African Christians have had to learn through hard struggle and much inner resistance of our own moral culpability in the exploitation, torture, and killing that happened in that situation. Some churches, including the Dutch Reformed Church, in which I was raised, even developed sophisticated biblical arguments to support the system of exploitation. Ultimately, we have had to learn the importance of repentance as the fundamental posture of moral discernment. In the Reformed Church community, the call for that repentance was most powerfully expressed in the Belhar Confession.[11] In my own journey from internalized homophobia, with which I will deal later, to struggling with the pastoral challenge of suicide of gay men in my ministry, to facing my own awareness of sexual orientation, I have become convinced that Christians today need a new repentant way of engaging Christian sexual and gender minorities.

We will look briefly at the Christian debates on "born this way" or "God made me like this" later. However, when I assume sexual orientation, I understand the shaping of this human experience of sexuality as a process that involves both biology and socio-cultural factors.

These play on each other. I do not assume a complete determinism; neither do I believe that sexual orientation for most people is a choice of "lifestyle." Of course, research, such as the famous work of the Kinseys, showed that sexual orientation must also be seen from the perspective of a continuum or spectrum of experiences. This means that for most people their experienced orientation is not something they can change. Years of attempts at "reparative therapy" also called "conversion therapy," has demonstrated that these attempts at changing sexual orientation are fruitless for most people. Even though some people seem able to live for periods of time in a sexual orientation mode other than the dominant one in their experience, they end up eventually not being able to maintain it. Reparative therapy in such cases has also turned out to be psychologically harmful. This disparity is the main reason the conservative Christian ex-gay organization "Exodus" issued an apology and closed down. In some cases, when people's orientation is more to the middle of the continuum, they might be able to choose one way or the other. Nevertheless, the experience of most gay men is that, from their earliest awareness of sexuality, they realized that they were different from the norm. Many women report a more fluid sense of awareness of orientation. Transgender people also testify to early childhood awareness gender identity that did not fit with their apparent biological gender.

This book will focus on the erotic dimension of sexuality. However, there are many more questions that deserve equally careful Christian communal moral discernment. What to do if a young child seems to identify with the opposite gender from their biological reality? How do we navigate age, development, hormonal treatment and the other psychosocial complexities? How do we connect graciously with intersex people? Often some kind of gender-assignment is presently done by the medical system. Is this the right approach? Should we decide early if someone is a boy or a girl, and do we have the right to decide? None of these questions have simple answers, and the larger moral logic of gospel and Scripture discussed later in this book may be helpful, but discernment in such circumstances will require deep compassion and wisdom, not facile judgment and set rules. This book will not focus on such questions as important as they are.

Celibacy remains a real possibility for some people. However, the New Testament and Protestant tradition has emphasized that celibacy is a gift and a choice that is not appropriate for many people. This is equally true no matter sexual orientation. Some people choose not to be in intimate erotic relationships. We should have no problem with that. However, when we require celibacy in a discriminatory way based on sexual orientation, such a requirement is both unjust and harmful.

I will sometimes use the word homophobia. This is a modern word that presents many problems. First, it seems to ignore discrimination and anger directed at sexual orientations such as transgender people. It is also a word that can be compared in similar ways to racism or xenophobia. There is a shaming element to the use of this term. The reader needs to know that I always strive to examine myself for homophobia in bias, shame, judgment, and discrimination against people. When I use homophobia, it expresses a certain level of pejorative visceral disgust. I am disturbed and moved to disgust when I read about torture, the abuse of children, live burnings, breaking people on the wheel, public hangings, the use of the pillory against people accused of sodomy or buggery. As a Christian my conscience is moved by these stories. I hope the Spirit will also awake you as a reader to these realities and their implications. I therefore never intend to use the word homophobic or homophobe against an individual in this book or against you as a reader. Please do not take it in that way.

Homophobia has three major dimensions. The first can be identified as institutional homophobia. In that case it speaks of institutions that are consistently and systemically biased against sexual and gender minority people, treat them with discrimination, and blame them in unjust ways. In this book the institutional homophobia of non-affirming denominations should become abundantly clear. Homophobia also addresses personal disgust, discrimination, bias and unjust blaming directed at sexual and gender minority people. It can be as subtle as the assumption that homosexual equals child-abuse. At other times it can be as blatant as violent attacks against sexual and gender minorities. In Chapter 3 I address the role of homophobia in myself and others as we make intuitive judgments against sexual and gender minorities. A third level of homophobia is known as the psychological phenomenon of internalized homophobia. Chapter 3 discusses internalized homophobia and its role in the larger process of homophobia. Internalized homophobia is often present within people who identify as sexual and gender minorities. The shame they have experienced by being branded as disgusting, abominable, and unacceptable often migrate inside creating profound psychological distress and inner alienation. We will see that the research shows that internalized homophobia is common among sexual and gender minority people who are in non-affirming Christian communities. Sometimes, when closeted, such people can be overtly homophobic towards others. Perhaps some of the pastoral disasters of conservative evangelical leaders who preached against "'homosexuals" and are caught with gay prostitutes represent this painful and sad condition most dramatically. Such painful situations should not make us judge and gloat, but rather, should invite us to morally discern the role of church and community in the institutional homophobia that creates such alienation.

As the bibliography at the end of this book will demonstrate, there is a large body of historical research on Christian faith and homophobia. Sadly, this history of largely unknown and unacknowledged in Christian theological conversations about sexual and gender minority people. My intention with this book is to gather together the research evidence from history and social science and bring it into conversation with our ethical and moral discernment as Christians. The reader will see that my research relies heavily on the thoughts and analysis of many other authors. I stand on their shoulders but bear sole responsibility for my interpretation of their work and contribution to the conversation. My hope is to offer a different perspective from the regular Christian controversies between affirming and non-affirming Christians. Even though I will touch on the classic Biblical passages often cited in clashing Christian rhetorics, I will not make them my main focus. In fact, even as I think it is important to consider Leviticus, Romans and Genesis, I think we need a wider biblical perspective. It is this perspective for moral discernment that will be the main focus. Personally, I read the "classic" anti-homosexual texts differently from the more conservative interpretations. Biblical scholars like James Brownson, Renato K. Lings, Dale Martin, David T. Stewart and Rabbi Jacob Milgrom have made credible and coherent cases for alternative readings that take interpretation history and cultural context into consideration. However, I respect and recognize that those contrary perspectives represent plausible readings of Scripture and Christian traditions. Nevertheless, I will argue that in no way are any of those interpretations unequivocally clear in a complete prohibition of all forms of same-sex erotic relationships. Given this lack of clarity and diversity of interpretive possibilities, and most importantly, given the harm done and being done, I will argue that the logic of gospel and Scripture needs to guide us as we make moral discernment. I believe there are two faithful ways of responding to the Scriptural traditions in Christianity. One is to respond to the harm done and being done by means of gracious pastoral exception. In this way Christians make clear that, despite a long tradition of rejecting sexual and gender minority practices in Christianity, our insight into history, social science and psychology leads us to find new affirming pastoral ways to welcome and affirm sexual and gender minority people. The second faithful way, and my preference, is to find ways to read through the traditions, and particularly the interpretation history of our Christian texts, as well as the impact of those texts through time, to find new and life-giving ways to help sexual and gender minority Christians thrive within Christian communities and society.[12] What we cannot and should not do is to continue to do harm.

At this point it would be clear that this book addresses a Christian audience from the Western perspective and particularly a Christian audience in North America – Turtle Island.[13] This does not mean that the implications of the argument may not resonate with Eastern Orthodox Christians or people following other religious traditions. There is much to be learned from interfaith dialogue on the potential harm that different religious traditions can do to sexual and gender minority people. Historically, Christianity shares some of its homophobic assumptions with the Greco-Roman world out of which it emerged as well as the Judaism of that time. Conclusions and responses to the potential harm we might do, however, is most appropriately the domain of people who stand in their own religious traditions. The best I can do from the side lines is to beg my friends in other religions to seek not to do harm. Where appropriate through the book I will make the case for a need for further interfaith reflection.

The book will unfold in three sections. The first section sets the stage for moral, social and Christian discernment. Chapter 2 engages the question of the process of moral discernment in relation to sexual and gender minority people. Chapter 3 examines the psychological and social factors that influence our process of decision making in moral discernment. Chapter 4 applies these insights more particularly to the broader Christian controversies on the place and role of sexual and gender minority people in Christian churches.

The second section of the book will deal with the history of the treatment of sexual and gender minority people in Christian tradition. Chapter 5 focuses on the developments in the first three centuries of Christianity, some of the lessons we can learn from early Christianity, as well as the emerging trends towards a rejection of all forms of erotic sexuality. Chapter 6 details the story of the pivotal influence of the Jewish Scholar Philo of Alexandria on the emerging 4th and 5th century understanding of sexuality and homoerotic relationships in Christianity. This occurs as the Christian faith becomes the faith of the declining Roman Empire. This chapter also examines the parallel development of Roman conceptions of manliness and the new emerging Christian conception of manliness in relation to homoerotic relationships during the 4th and 5th centuries. Chapter 7 explores the emergence of "confessional manuals" and their role in the development of a profoundly homophobic Christian culture where the sin of sodomy ascends to becoming the most heinous sin against God and nature. These developments set the stage for the emergence of extreme violence in the treatment of those accused of sodomy. Chapter 8 details legal developments in canon and civil law and how these merged with corruption. Through this process sodomy accusations and executions became key to the confiscation of property by those in power to enrich their coffers. Chapter 9 explores disturbing examples of the human implications of church law and civil action in the torture, abuse and execution of those accused of sodomy and buggery. The chapter shows how the rising Christian brutality grows exponentially out of the doctrinal and canon law developments of the 13th century onwards. Chapter 10 tells the story of the Reformation and its abuse of children, execution of slaves, public hangings, and drownings, pillorying and the consequences of the export of anti-sodomy laws around the world. It also makes the connection between these developments, the role of churches, and the Nazi execution of homosexuals in concentration camps and Northern Front death squads.

The final section of the book examines the Christian response. Chapter 11 examines the evolution of the Gay Rights Movement and the way Protestant Christianity, both Evangelical and Mainline, adopted the modernist psychiatric view of homosexuality as a disease. It shows how both these Protestant traditions synchronized with the new sexual freedom movement and then developed their own heterosexist responses. Out of this discussion the chapter argues that confession, repentance and the seeking of reconciliation and healing is the way for Christians to begin to respond. Chapter 12 develops a conclusion on moral discernment. It makes an argument for a broad erotic Christian Scriptural logic that incorporates holy, committed, erotic relationships for sexual and gender minority people.

CHAPTER 2: MORAL DISCERNMENT

I will open the LIA (Love in Action Ex-Gay Therapy) handbook, read a few sentences, and feel the old shame wash over me until I can no longer focus. Once again, Smid's voice will swallow my own before I have a chance to say anything. I'll face doubt, distrust my memories, spend hours trying to reconstruct scenes so charged with emotion they'll seem impossible to pin down. (Garrard Conley, *Boy Erased* - Epilogue)[14]

I was surprised when I read these words in Garrard Conley's powerful memoir of his experience of 'ex gay therapy.' Not surprised by the pain or the struggle he experiences but surprised by how much of it reflects my own experience as someone never subjected to 'ex gay' or 'reparative' therapy. I would sit in church and suddenly be overwhelmed by shame. The God I love and embrace, God, whom I believe is a loving and gracious God, would suddenly seem remote, stern and angry. There would not be any particular triggers save for being in a place of worship. Even in my home congregation where I am welcomed, embraced, and loved, it would happen at unexpected moments. This experience is shaped by the dark cloud of Christian tradition and hurt by a thousand comments that colors every day of my life. Official statements by my own denomination and appeals to the "good tradition" that condemns "sodomites" will continuously turn the knife of inner rupture. This dissonance, and the heavy burden of many years of spiritual abuse rests heavily in my heart. It rests so heavily that some years ago my suicidal ideation became unbearable and I had to seek medical help. As recently as a few months ago a colleague told me that people like me could never delight the heart of God. I take this broken shame as a gift - a call from the God of Jesus Christ - reminding me never to forget my fellow sexual and gender minority Christian pilgrims who are so profoundly harmed by the teaching of their churches and the behavior of some fellow Christians.

This chapter does not attempt to develop comprehensive Christian ethics or finalize arguments about sexual morality. Rather, it attempts to wrestle with the phenomenon of ongoing harm done by Christians who often see themselves as gracious and loving people. Kind and gentle smiles and neat theological arguments backed up by handy biblical texts serve as the weapons of their warfare. Their work penetrates deep. So, deep that there is an epidemic of suicides particularly among sexual and gender minority youth. So pernicious are these claims of "loving teaching" that the rate of depression and substance abuse among sexual and gender minority people is staggering.[15] So hidden the hatred behind smiles and pious prayers that such Christians will ascribe these phenomena of suffering and pain as consequences of sin. Blame the victim is the *modus operandi*. Not only is this true for fundamentalists or conservative evangelical Christians; it is true for a large swath of more traditional Christianity that camouflages its judgment in theological arguments.

Behind this behavior of Christian harm lies a naïve version of "Divine Command Theory." In the world of Christian ethics today, there are two main approaches. One is rooted in the idea that good is defined and determined by God's command, the other approach relies on the ancient Greek idea of human virtue to define what is good. This second view, called virtue ethics, is focused on the outcome of the larger good of God's creation based in human virtue and the ultimate end of the flourishing of all creation. These are complex ideas, and I do not presume to settle the debates between a Divine command ethic and a virtue ethic in this chapter. I suspect that both these approaches hold truth and should probably be held in tension with each other.

When it comes to the Christian treatment of sexual and gender minorities, the problem does not lie with a "Divine command" approach versus a "virtue" approach, but rather with a profoundly naïve form of a Divine command approach. The argument goes something like this: "The Bible says it is wrong, therefore God says it is wrong, therefore you are wrong and sinful for not obeying God's command." In many institutions, such as my own denomination, the Presbyterian Church in Canada, this naïve logic is applied particularly to sexual and gender minority people. However, almost every other case, moral and ethical judgments, including judgments about sexual ethics, is handled with much greater nuance and care. This tendency of the discriminatory treatment of sexual and gender minority people in Christianity, as we will see later, has a very long history in Christian official behavior. In this chapter I attempt to chart a course that might be helpful to those who read this book and are willing to listen to the pain and its sources throughout history. As I seek an ethical and moral compass that does not simply want to judge others based on a superficial reading of proof-texts, I propose a way of moral discernment in community.

It is telling that in all the passionate debates occurring in North America and globally, the consideration of the harm done to sexual and gender minority people seldom appears as part of the debate. Conversations tend to focus on the Bible, the anticipated disastrous schisms that may occur in denominations that dare to treat sexual and gender minorities with inclusive love, or how to give an out to people who insist it is their moral right to condemn others. Most of all, the debate centers around the presumed terrible sinfulness of same sex erotic relationships and how then might or might not be a moral outrage forbidden by God. By minimizing harm for the sake of unity such debates ignore the integral relationship between love, justice and unity.

In contrast, I invite readers here to consider the moral failure of a Christian faith that claims that it pleases God while being indifferent to harming others. Surely, now that we have a tide of evidence that Christian teaching can do harm. Now that we know that sexual and gender minority people are being alienated from God. Now that it is demonstrated to be a significant contributor to the despair that leads to depression and suicide, we might want to consider our own moral culpability in teaching and behavior that causes harm? I include myself in the "we" in the preceding question. I am a Christian committed to the church and therefore responsible for its behavior.

In this chapter, I argue for including the reality of the infliction of harm in our process of moral discernment as Christians. To find a way forward, I propose a paradigm for discerning Christian moral decisions and actions. This approach is necessary because, first and foremost, all Christian moral decisions happen in community in its widest sense.[16] It is a complex task and this chapter offers a biblically based proposal. I draw on the work of Reformed ethicists James M. Gustafson and Nicholas Wolterstorff. Additionally, I draw on the important and influential work of the Roman Catholic ethicist, Margaret Farley in her book "Just Love" which develops a credible Christian sexual ethic in an ecumenical spirit.[17] Although Farley applies her ethical concept of just love to same-sex relationships, it is not the core of her focus in her book. Farley's concept of "just love" is very helpful in our reflection on all forms of sexual ethics today. An additional author that has provided a provocative reflection on contemporary Christian sexual ethics is the Southern Baptist Theologian Miguel De La Torre in his book *A Lily Among the Thorns*.[18]

When it comes to sexual and gender minority people, the concept of justice in the wider Christian community, deserves more reflection. So, for example, the ongoing vocal political opposition of many Christian denominations against equal civil marriage rights in many jurisdictions around the world casts serious doubt on Christian conceptions of civil justice. Christians do not oppose the right of people who follow other religions and vastly different concepts of marriage to marry civilly and to receive the same legal rights. Wherein lies justification for denying equal marriage rights to sexual and gender minorities?

Because so much of the harm and condemnation in Christianity is based on a naïve use of Scripture, I wrestle with our personal engagement with Scripture in our communal process of moral discernment. I highlight blind spots to equality, justice and concern for well-being when it comes to sexual and gender minorities. In my tradition, and for me personally, Scripture is paramount for the way I make theological arguments. This effort is an exercise in drawing together ethical traditions in my wrestling with moral discernment. In so doing, I invite you, as part of the greater community, to wrestle with me and to consider this contribution prayerfully.

False Dualism

What happened to me has made it impossible to speak with God, to believe in a version of Him that isn't charged with self-loathing. (Garrard Conley, *Boy Erased.* Epilogue)[19]

The inner fracture experienced by Christian people who are sexual and gender minorities is rooted in the lie of false dualisms. It starts with the dualism of us and them. The "us" of the heterosexual world is good while the "them" of the others is shameful. Sexuality is presumed to be a matter of "straight," which equals right and blessed by God, and "gay," which equals God's judgment and displeasure. The scientific evidence that sexual orientation is complex and is better represented on a scale between two ends is simply ignored or considered irrelevant in the light of God's judgment on anything not heterosexual. The false dualism continues in theological and biblical debates. One is either a Christian who follows "tradition"– which is considered to be good and blessed by God and uncompromisingly heterosexual – or, one is a Christian who is a "revisionist" – which is considered unfaithful to God and the Bible. Gender is presumed to be a duality. If one experiences attraction to the same gender as oneself, that person is presumed to be twisted and shamefully sinful caused by a psychiatric disorder. Anything non-heterosexual is to be "fixed" in the case of those supporting reparative therapy. For many other traditional Christian denominations, who are skittish about the bad press reparative therapy has received, these non-heterosexual attractions are to be sublimated. Most people who are sexual and gender minorities will echo Garrard Conley's observation, "I came to therapy thinking that my sexuality didn't matter, but it turned out that every part of my personality was intimately connected. Cutting one piece damaged the rest" (*Boy Erased,* Monday June 14).[20] The fact of the matter is that the "traditional" approach, whether it prescribes reparative therapy or legalistic abstinence, leads to profound psychological harm and spiritual abuse that leads to depression and suicidal ideation. Historian Heather White has shown how twentieth century Protestantism, both Mainline and Evangelical adopted the medicalized psychiatric view of same-sex attraction as an "inversion" and therefore a disorder to be treated.[21] Even though the psychiatric profession has since changed its mind, many Christian institutions still hold to this therapeutically biased synthesis between outdated psychiatry and therapeutic psychology. Sexual orientation is not a piece that can be cut out without dissecting the very spirit and soul of the person. Christian moral and ethical considerations cannot simply ignore the clear evidence of the harm done. Ignoring harm is in itself a moral failure.

Christian ethical considerations cannot be framed simplistically by a contrast between God's command and Christian virtue, nor in the contrast between a contextual ethic as opposed to a principled ethic. In 1965, James Gustafson wrote a seminal paper in the *Harvard Theological Review* that pointed out that such a contrast is simply not tenable.[22] Gustafson showed how the proponents of these different approaches end up also having to answer the same questions. Moreover, someone like Karl Barth associated with the "context" side ends up having to assume "principles."[23] I accept Gustafson's argument. A resolute focus on Christian Scriptures requires a recognition that Scripture is always interpreted by people. The people who interpret live in and are influenced by context, history, tradition and experience. No wonder then, when it comes to the matter at hand, we are dealing with dueling interpretations of specific texts assumed to speak about homoerotic relationships. We end up with arguments that simply say, "my interpretation trumps yours." Often these interpretational battles focus on the few biblical texts that are identified as speaking about homoerotic relationships. Our moral decisions get bogged down in the crossfire of such interpretive arguments which are further complicated by the context of the arguers and the psychological dimensions of human moral decision making. As Christians, we are caught in a Gordian Knot. I believe there is a way through this conundrum. It is the way of honest discernment.

Towards Honest Self-Awareness

Being honestly self-aware is a good place to start. For me this means that I need to be aware that I start with a personal and contextual influence of having become an advocate for the welcome and affirmation of sexual and gender minority Christians in Christian communities.[24] At the same time, I also must be clear that, for me, moral discernment on all matters, including matters sexual, requires some wise boundaries. When we deal with profound human passion that is relational, we inevitably deal with the potential of harming and hurting others. Moral discernment is therefore about setting healthy Christian boundaries within our communities. Erotic sexual relationships have a long tradition of being associated with sin in both Eastern Orthodox and Western Christianities. In our current context, almost all Christians see the erotic in sexuality different than the Christianity of the 4th century.[25] Because the erotic sexual drive is both part of our biology and part of our humanness, and because it is relational, it always offers the potential for great joy and human affirmation. It also may become destructive, alienating and dehumanizing.[26] This down side also highlights the potential for the erotic to alienate us from others and God - sin. The objective of honest discernment is to help find the boundaries that will protect against sin.

Honest discernment will also have to come to terms with the realization that our current Christian context will follow a different cultural logic than that of patriarchal Israel or honor-shame Roman patriarchy. It is therefore wise to listen carefully to those Christian authors such as Pamela Dickey Young and Jay Emmerson Johnson who argue for a positive recovery of erotic love in Christian tradition. Young makes a strong and persuasive case that *eros* can and should be recovered as a positive form of embodied love while shedding the Greco-Roman baggage of *eros* as lust.[27] Jay Johnson demonstrates the importance of *eros* and embodiment and the recognition of sexual intimacy as part of the Eucharistic spirituality of Christian faith.[28] The Episcopal queer theologian Patrick Cheng argues that Jesus is the embodiment of his vision of radical Christian love.[29] There is in Cheng's theology, as well as in the work of the ground-breaking Queer theologian Robert Goss, a focus on the transgressive or boundary-challenging dimensions of Jesus' ministry and how this focus may inform Queer conceptions of theology and sexuality.[30] Jesus, particularly in his incarnated boundary-challenging life and ministry, defines and demonstrates love. What I will argue below echoes these perspectives. The reality of the embodied incarnated life of Jesus provides a lens for our reading and interpretation of Scripture. What we know of that life is captured in a very specific way in the memory of the early Christianity recorded in four Gospels of the New Testament. There is no simplistic path from the memory of the church to our concrete situations today. There never was. David Bosch points out that the Gospel writers faced the task of taking the memory of Jesus and then "prolonging the logic of Jesus' ministry into their historical circumstances…[31] That is our task and our challenge.

Uncovering the Process of Discernment

Before moving to the matter of being moral we need to clarify the idea of discernment. Discernment, James Gustafson argues, is critical in our process of moral decision-making. Discernment is a dynamic process.[32] Gustafson states that it is simply seeing what is there. However, it includes a deeper process of discrimination that takes place that seeks to determine the accuracy of our perceptions. Thus, a good process of discernment requires perception, discrimination, observation, and critical judgment. It's not just a matter of data presented to us, but also how we interpret them.[33] This is the sense in which I mean to use the concept of discernment. To discern spiritually is to interpret, exercise evaluative judgment and, ultimately, to do so responsibly before God. Rather than naïve judgment, discernment seeks to exercise "rational discrimination as well as a sensible response."[34] To discern spiritually is also to pray. Christian rational sensibility grows out of prayerful community. This prayerful discernment is to be inspired by reflection on the gospel and the Gospels as I note later in this chapter.

Many things pull us away from prayerful and rational discernment. We need to think carefully about our pre-rational motivations. The next chapter will deal with some of those factors and motivations. Rational discernment requires Christians, "to be sensitive to oppression and injustice, to physical and mental suffering."[35] I attend to oppression and suffering as I tell the story of the treatment sexual and gender minorities in the historical section of this book. At the heart of a process of moral discernment is having the right posture. This posture is best described as walking the way of Christ.

Walking the Way of Christ

Embedded in the New Testament we find a witness of the earliest process of Christian discernment. It is important to distinguish between process and content as we discuss the role of Scripture in shaping our moral discernment. A naïve command theory would argue that Christians have traditionally judged and discerned things in a certain way and therefore it should not change. The naiveté lies in an unwillingness to be honest about how dramatically Christian discernment on moral and ethical issues has changed on many topics over 2000 years. Slavery is a case in point. The Bible and Early Christian writings challenged dehumanizing ways of treating slaves, but these did not challenge the institution. It is only in the late 18th to early 19th century that careful and prayerful moral discernment led to the rejection of slavery. In the chapter on the Gospel of Love and Charity later in this book, I describe how some early Christians engaged in many admirable practices in relation to slaves. In some cases, early Christians bought the freedom of some Christian slaves, but they never advocated to stop taking slaves.

The key lies in prolonging the logic of the teachings of Jesus of Nazareth into a process of moral discernment. Biblical texts cannot be simplistically interpreted as determinants of God's will. For responsible Christian discernment we need to consider the content as well as the spirit of Jesus' teaching as handed to us in the New Testament. Margaret Farley shows the complications of culture, particularly in relation to gender justice in sexual relations embedded in the biblical texts if read naively.[36] Simplistically citing texts written in different cultural contexts and believing that these can be applied directly to the present, is untenable. Discernment requires prayerful reflection on the implications of the whole story of Jesus including his teaching for sexual ethics and moral discernment.

An example of attending to the process of discernment reflected in Scripture can be found in Philippians 1:27[37] and Philippians 2.[38] The author addresses a pastoral issue in the community and provides his response to recall and demonstrate the attitude or posture of Jesus.[39] First, we learn that discernment in community arises out of living, thinking, and acting in a way worthy of and reflective of the self-giving way of Jesus Christ. Particularly, the section that follows Phil 2:5 clarifies the perspective that the whole story of Jesus is paradigmatic for our own process of discernment. Phil 2:2[40] dramatically amplifies the spirit and attitude of those who work together in moral discernment. It describes this attitude as one of kindness and compassion for one another. Such kindness and compassion echo the "fruit of the Spirit" that in turn provides the frame for the spirit by which we are to conduct moral discernment. In short, the process of moral discernment is linked to Christ and to the fruits that flow from being in Christ and Christ being in us by means of the Holy Spirit. Those fruits will bias us towards kindness and compassion rather than rejection and judgment. It will bias us towards being sensitive to oppression, justice, physical and mental suffering. Our process of moral discernment is therefore to be shaped by a prayerful piety seeking to walk in this way of justice.

Both the reflection of Margaret Farley on "just love" and Nicholas Wolterstorff on "care" demonstrate how this New Testament process might transfer to our moral discernment today. Nicholas Wolterstorff describes how the biblical theme of love and justice can best be represented in our English word "care."[41] Wolterstorff's concept of "care" compliments and enhances Farley's framing of "just love" for sexual ethics. When Farley argues that "just love" requires the truthful affirmation of the "concrete reality of the beloved,"[42] she builds a similar norm to "care." For both Wolterstorff and Farley, the important ethical consideration is the coming together of the biblical concepts of love and justice in our erotic relationship with the beloved. The concepts of "care" and "just love" require that Christians affirm the concrete reality of sexual and gender minority people, particularly the reality of their experience of harm. To hold the posture of Jesus, to follow the way of kindness and compassion, and to discern in the fruit of the Spirit require treating people as whole people. Sexual and gender minorities are not an issue, problem, or a shameful embarrassment; they are neighbors to be loved.

Gospel, Gospels and Scriptures

The reflection on Philippians begs the further question, how does all this relate to the four Gospels in the New Testament, to the gospel of Jesus Christ, and ultimately to the Scriptures as a whole? In the Reformed-Evangelical tradition this concern is known as the question of making our moral discernment with "gospel glasses." Gustafson argues that the Gospel of Jesus Christ is to shape our "characteristic orientation towards God, the world and others."[43] By Gospel we mean nothing less than the whole story of Jesus. By the Gospels we mean the four books of the New Testament that tells the story of Jesus from four different perspectives for four different contexts. As such, Christ, his whole story, his life, actions, teachings, death, resurrection and ascension, becomes our paradigm of life. He becomes the inspiration for our bearing or posture in life. This does not mean that we become copies or clones. It certainly does not mean complete uniformity, but the whole story is our baseline.[44] We might end up coming to different contextual responses to sexual and gender minorities, yet the whole witness of the traditions about Jesus in the Gospels constructs a boundary.

20

In the four Gospels of the New Testament we find the reliable witness of early Christian communities to the memory of the inspiring stories of Jesus Christ. As with our range of different responses possible in Christian communities, so the Gospels tell the stories in different ways and even sometimes in ways that seem contradictory. It is no accident that Jesus teaches by means of parables. Such stories invite the hearers to wrestle, discern, question and struggle together to find solutions. Jesus' stories also tend to humanize and contextualize questions that may seem theoretical. Jesus refuses to objectify people as issues; he regards people in their concrete reality. Think, for example, of the story of the "Good Samaritan" (Luke 10:30-35). Those listening to Jesus when he told this story considered Samaritans an abomination because they thought their worship of God was impure. Yet, Jesus' story challenges his listeners to think in new ways about Samaritans as human beings. This invitation to puzzle together and to recognize the "other" as a human being is a characteristic of God's reign as it breaks into the world in Jesus Christ. In short, Jesus's boundary challenging interactions with people who were considered unacceptable such as the Samaritans, prostitutes, tax collectors, the poor, eunuchs and women invite us to think about treating one another in terms of a wide and generous anthropology of well-being. The process of wrestling, reading, debating, and discerning is inspired by the four Gospels in their differences and similarities. They set us on our path and orient us. They call us to seek the fruit of the Spirit that would reflect Jesus Christ himself. This is what Gustafson means when he writes,

The *Gospels*, in their literary unity as well as their variety, provide the engendering provocation, the efficient cause, which brings this new orientation into being...[45]

Jesus' view of the human being invites us to see those who are unacceptable and on the margins through new gospel eyes and behave towards them in a self-giving and compassionate way. It is a process born out of people who walk in the Spirit of God. Where judgments are made that are harmful and where behavior is counselled that harm, it calls into question the very basis of the judgment and counsel. In the historical section of this book I describe just how questionable Christian tradition has been in the treatment of "sodomites." Christians in those times may have considered their harmful actions as "compassionate." They believed that burning someone alive might save their soul or protect the community from God's wrath yet relying on such faulty traditions is no longer tenable for Christians today. Later in this book where I describe the many instances in history in which the fruit of the Spirit was absent from Christian behavior and where profound harm was done to the point of torture and death. This reflection should call us to think carefully and compassionately about our judgments, teaching, and attitudes towards sexual and gender minorities today. The absence of the fruit of the Spirit in our judgment and discernment is still with us in Christian attitudes such as being "welcoming but not affirming," and this harmful spirit in the past has been described by historians as "charitable hatred."

What then of the whole of Scriptures? Reformed Christians have always insisted that all of Scripture is important. Nevertheless, we also insist that the Scriptures, both Hebrew and New Testament, require interpretive discernment – a prolonging of logic. Just as we seek to make moral discernment based in Scripture, so we seek to make gospel discernment of the Scriptures. We stand under Jesus Christ the living present One who leads us together in community. So, for example, we no longer stone people as some Levitical texts require. There are many things in both the New and Old Testament that we have dealt with through a process of community-gospel-discernment. In many Christian communities, as in the infant church of the first two centuries, women are again leaders and ordained pastors because of such a process of discernment. We no longer keep slaves, and we oppose enslavement. Thus, we are always busy discerning as we read and interpret the Scriptures. This process is embedded in the piety or spirituality of a gospel-posture in the community where this posture continues to challenge us to pray, discern and love.

The Glory of God Gives Life – The Law of Love

Biblical scholar, Walter Breuggemann, in his inspiring commentary on the Book of Genesis writes that one of the great themes of Genesis is the following message, "When the facts demand death, God demands life for his creatures."[46] Christian faith, founded in this gracious God, is concretely rooted in the God of love who demonstrated that love in the incarnation of Jesus Christ. Gustafson emphasizes God's gracious intent for humankind this way,

That which restores and brings life and joy is to be preferred to that which destroys and brings death and suffering and pain...[47]

This understanding of God's love reflects the ancient and greatest law of both Judaism and Christianity which is to love God with all we are and to love our neighbors as ourselves. According to the Gospels this is also the summary of the law - the summary of the heart of Christian moral discernment – arising out of the moral teaching of Jesus Christ.[48] Thus, when the Gospel of John records Jesus as saying, "If you love me, you will obey my commandments" it refers to this core posture of loving God and neighbor.[49] The centrality of love, thankfulness and concern for God and neighbor is further underlined in the Gospel of John when Jesus is recorded as clarifying, "If you obey my commandments you will remain in my love..."[50]

How then do we read the Hebrew and Christian Scriptures today? What guides our interpretation? What is our central interpretive-hermeneutical principle? It is nothing short of the simplicity of the love commandment – the inextricably interconnected love of God and neighbor. The Jesus traditions of the Gospels represent this fundamental principle of interpretation in Matthew 22:34-40, and Mark 12:28-33. In Luke's version (Luke 10:25-37), Jesus explains that the love commandment is expressed and interpreted in the form of boundary-challenging loving altruistic behavior by his telling of the parable of the Good Samaritan.[51] So pervasive is this central conception in the early Christianity of the New Testament that it shows up time and again in the Pauline literature including in Romans 13:10 and Gal 5:14. This is not simply a new New Testament idea but an understanding firmly rooted in the law of the Hebrew Scriptures. Jesus is simply citing Deut 6:5, Deut

30:6 and Lev 19:18. He shows that the love of God and neighbor is to qualify all other parts of the law.

Every text we read, and every discernment and judgment we make, and every way we behave towards others, be it about slavery, the role of women, or sexual behavior must be read through the refining lens of the love commandment. It is the love commandment that demands and imposes the love of God and neighbor as inseparable, that is the central moral logic of Christian faith.

This tradition of interpretation is further supported by the famous early Christian leader Irenaeus of Lyon (130-202) who captured this value with his famous formulation, *gloria enim Dei vivens homo*[52] usually translated as "The Glory of God gives life."[53] Love, as conceived in the Scriptural witness and particularly in the teaching of Jesus, is understood as that which brings full, meaningful, and flourishing life through God's grace.[54] Irenaeus establishes a kind of baseline for a Christian understanding of the meaning and purpose of the human being. When humans thrive in relationships of love, mutual respect, equality and just care for one another, in humble thankfulness to God, then God is glorified. These are signs of God's grace working in the Holy Spirit. Christian tradition has often drawn on the simple but profound definition offered by the prophet Micah that essentially says the same thing. "No, the Lord has told us what is good. What he requires of us is this: to do what is just, to show constant love, and to live in humble fellowship with our God."[55] Placing obedience to God in opposition to God's justice in love for people is a false dichotomy. God's love seeks the flourishing of God's people and this is demonstrated in the gospel of Jesus Christ and the Scriptures as a whole. Flourishing, whole, loving human beings give glory to God and express the core of obedience to God's will. God created humans to flourish. Although I cannot speak for Judaism, given that Jesus relies heavily on the Torah in his argument, I wonder if there might be profound ways in which Christians and Jews can agree on this central idea?

Whatever we discern in our moral reasoning as Christians will thus need to give account of how this vision of God as the graceful Life-Giver is reflected in our moral judgment. Where our moral judgment brings pain, death, suffering, and psychological harm, as it often does in relation to sexual and gender minority people, we must ask if this discernment reflects God as we know God in Jesus Christ? God's glory and will does not stand against love and justice, it is love and justice united in one. This is where the fruit of a life of thinking about God's justice by Nicholas Wolterstorff, and the fruit of reflection on sexual ethics as "just love" in Margaret Farley, guides us to understand the importance of care. Wolterstorff disagrees with theologians who argued that love trumps justice. He goes on to show the beauty of the intimate entanglement of love and justice in the logic of the whole biblical witness. Treating one's neighbor justly, Wolterstorff insist, is an example of biblical love.[56]

This awareness brings us to the important topic of sin in Christian moral thinking. Where are the life-giving just boundaries of our sexual relationships? For those who wish to argue that their particular interpretation of biblical passages insists that sexual and gender minority people must be treated as unequal and therefore unjustly, the response must simply be that love and justice cannot be separated. Some might attempt to compare what they consider the biblical illegitimacy of loving same-sex relationships with the biblical rejection of murder, stealing or other kinds of obvious wickedness. They might argue that one still loves the murderer or thief while rejecting their actions. However, the love commandment in its depth of justice requires more than such a simplistic argument. How is it just to condemn and exclude people based on actions that actually demonstrate love and care for others? How is it loving your neighbor to lump loving same-sex relationships that do no harm and bring much relational good together with obviously harmful wickedness?

Discerning Sin and Eros

Later in this book we will see how, in the fourth century, Western Christianity moved to the point where it considered all erotic sexual expressions as lustful and thus basically sinful. It left room for sexual intercourse in marriage only for the purpose of procreation. Such procreative acts were still considered tainted by sin due to erotic passion. For them, erotic experience was considered irrational and therefore not worthy of a Roman man. This development was a long time in coming, especially through the late second and third centuries of the early church. It was a function of the Christian faith seeking to become accepted within higher Roman culture which admired Greek philosophical traditions like stoicism, that considered all forms of erotic sexuality as signs of irrationality.[57] Within the Greco-Roman patriarchal culture, the expression of erotic sexual passion was considered a female "weakness" that should be resisted by rational Roman men. Men who gave in to their erotic passions were considered "soft" and unmanly. By the fourth century, official Western Christianity had become deeply impacted with a profound distrust of any form of erotic passion and the Christian manly ideal was self-denial and withdrawal from the world. We will see later how these developments led to tragic consequences for people in same-sex erotic relationships.[58] Despite these developing anti-erotic theological ideals, ordinary 4th century Christian behavior did not necessarily agree with the theology espoused by their leaders.

Today our Christian understanding of the erotic dimension of our lives is more complex than simply considering it equal to sinful lust. Even in Roman Catholicism, where the ancient tradition of procreation is held in high regard, the "theology of the body"[59] of Pope John Paul II, redefined room for blessed God glorifying erotic relationships that are non-procreative. John Paul II named this space of holy eroticism, the "unitive" function of sexuality in the life of a couple. This view, more affirming of sexual erotic expression beyond procreation, had its Genesis in the 1930's with Pope Pius XI's *Casti Connubii.*[60] Most Christians today understand their sexual desire and the expression of it in covenanted relationship as a gift from God. We have no problem marrying couples who are beyond child-bearing age because we understand that the mutual comfort and help that such couples find in their most intimate relationship is a gift from God. In this way we have already demonstrated how a deeper insight into the human condition can adjust our conceptions of sexuality and moral integrity as a function of prolonging the logic of the ministry and teaching of Jesus.

As one of the stronger biological drives in the human condition, erotic sexual passion also has the potential to be destructive, hurtful, and abusive. There is no doubt about this. Therefore, as with all forms of the human condition, there is potential for not loving our neighbor, not showing due respect, and not glorifying God in our sexual passion, and not approaching our beloved in their concrete reality. We have the potential power to work against the flourishing life God intends for creation and human beings. We can work against such flourishing life by sexually hurting and exploiting. We can also work against it by harming and prohibiting healthy sexual expressions among sexual and gender minority people. How then can we discern the boundaries of erotic love with "care" and "just love?"

In his essay on sexual ethics James Gustafson identifies some of the most seminal parts of Christian moral discernment about sexual erotic passion. We will look more fully at his argument in the final chapter of this book. At this point we simply need to note that he identifies the behaviors of exploitation, harassment, objectification and deception as important markers in our Christian discernment of the boundaries of sexual erotic passion. It is particularly important to note the potential harm raised by the idea of deception in relationships. Deception for erotic self-gratification raises questions of relational trustworthiness and the violation of loyalty which leads to disaffection, resentment and alienation.[61] In short, one of the boundaries indicated in Christian moral discernment is faithfulness in covenanted relationship. Working at being faithful in Christian erotic relationships glorifies God and reflects God's own faithfulness described throughout the Scriptures and demonstrated in Jesus Christ. Therefore, Gustafson describes this boundary with the biblical concept of covenant.[62] Sexual sin, or, to use the language of tradition, lust, is demonstrated in excessive selfish expression of erotic passion that breaks covenant and causes relational destruction. David Jensen rightly points out that norms for erotic sexual life in the church "risks oversimplification and the flattening of the Christian story of redemption into a tidy list."[63] Therefore, all lists of norms, whether mine above, Gustafson's, Farley's (consent, mutuality, equality, commitment, fruitfulness and social justice) or Jensen's (consent, mutuality, covenant and trust, community and joy), must never become disembodied and decontextualized rules that lose sight of the concrete reality of people embodied in a network of relational responsibilities.

James Brownson, in his sensitive Scriptural treatment of sexual erotic passion in relation to sexual and gender minority people, also speaks of the moral logic of the Bible.[64] On this point it is helpful to note that Brownson comes to similar conclusions to Gustafson on the boundaries of blessed Christian erotic relationships. He describes the boundaries as defined by promiscuous behavior (like Gustafson's covenant unfaithfulness), selfish expressions of lust, and the abuse of power.[65] In his recent lecture on Gay and Lesbian Christians and marriage equality, Nicholas Wolterstorff makes essentially the same point when he asks if sexual and gender minority people in loving intimate relationships are transgressing the love commandment? He concludes that covenanted loving same-sex relationships does not transgress this commandment.[66]

The central biblical importance of the Love of God and neighbor in both the Old and New Testament, and particularly in the teaching of Jesus invites us to take this commandment and its application seriously. Brownson, Wolterstorff, Gustafson, Farley and Jensen all contribute to making clear a comprehensive biblical picture of holy sexual expression. I would suggest that their lists of sexual norms need to be understood more as music that resonates with the spirit of the gospel than as sets of rules. When we consider the teaching of Scripture as a whole, we need to read particular texts associated with same-sex relationships against the backdrop of a more complete symphony of biblical teaching. Beside this wider biblical picture of sexual expression, we also need to attend to a final but critical element of the process of moral discernment which is the pastoral dimension. Such pastoral discernment does not only ask what a Christian understanding of flourishing erotic relationships is, it also has to consider the pastoral responsibility for fostering a life-giving and flourishing place for sexual and gender minorities in Christian community.

Pastoral Discernment

It is fairly easy to develop theories about ethics and boundaries about sin. The question becomes more real when we encounter our material world where people struggle and live. As I argue throughout this book, it was often on the level of dealing with these concrete situations that the Christian church and its traditions failed in relation to sexual and gender minorities. Moral discernment, as argued above, is above all a posture of loving humility before God as we encounter our neighbors in community. It also involves accountability for the just treatment of our neighbors. Wolterstorff is correct when he emphasizes that love and justice cannot be separated. Pastoral discernment does not require the suspension of moral boundaries or the just treatment of others. Pastoral discernment does require the careful consideration of specific scriptural texts in relation to the larger moral logic of the Bible and ultimately the gospel of Jesus Christ. It also requires a relentless process of taking the beam out of our own eyes before we pick at the splinter in our neighbor's eye. One of the most ironic aspects about the employment of Paul's first chapter to the Romans in the abuse, torture and killing of those accused of "sodomy" throughout Christian history is that the use of this passage from the New Testament consistently missed Paul's rhetorical point. That point is demonstrated in Chapter 2:1

Do you, my friend, pass judgment on others? You have no excuse at all, whoever you are. For when you judge others and then do the same things which they do, you condemn yourself (Good News Bible).

This statement then builds up to his famous conclusion that all have sinned and fall short of the glory of God.[67]

Throughout history Christians have sinned in their failure to be humble and graceful in their moral judgment of others. Divorce is a case in point. Even though one can argue that divorce represents a clear scriptural moral boundary and can potentially cause harm, many Christian communities, including my own, have slowly and carefully concluded that dealing with the reality of this form of human brokenness by judgment rather than graceful healing is not the way of the gospel. We have also read the response of Jesus to questions about divorce without considering the socio-cultural context. When Jesus makes a pronouncement about divorce according to Matthew 5:31 or the discussion in Matthew 19, the cultural backdrop is the exploitation of married women by men who could easily write a divorce note and thus shed all responsibility for their wife. Justice and the responsibility for care is therefore a key matter to consider when we think about the break-down of relationships today. Even though we might continue to believe that divorce is not God's intention for just relationships, we also recognize that God's grace can move in healing ways and in new God-glorifying relationships in the lives of God's people. In such cases considering justice and mutual responsibility become important dimensions of our relationships. We can call this recognition "graceful pastoral exception." However, it is a pastoral exception that should never be short on either justice or love.

When we discern together, we are never to discern an abstract thing such as "divorce" or "lesbian" or "gay" or "bisexual" or "transgender" or "queer" or "intersex." We are always to discern in relation to embodied people. These are people with hearts, dreams, and love. When we as the church forget the human reality of people, we forget that we are ultimately accountable before God for the love of our neighbors. We owe them respect as carriers of the image of God. Wolterstorff expresses this in terms or rights rooted in the image of God.[68] The process of Christian moral discernment on the place of sexual and gender minority people in the church needs to proceed with a humble caution to seek a gracious pastoral response to a human reality. As Christians together on the road to discernment, our gospel hearts need to seek pastoral behavior that glorifies the God who brought grace to us in Jesus Christ. Such grace is too often absent when it comes to the treatment of sexual and gender minorities.

Where to Now?

I have argued that Christian moral discernment is a process that occurs in Christian community. That community extends beyond the local to the broader Christian world and to the traditions of the past. It is a diverse witness. The process of discernment requires being responsible and rational. We need to attend therefore to our human tendency to make moral judgment on a pre-rational intuitive level, often deeply influenced by socio-cultural context. The process of discernment invites us to walk together in the way of the gospel rooted in the witness of the Gospels of the New Testament and the Scriptures as a whole. We are invited to discern together in this Spirit. That Spirit is manifested in us as it bears fruit in our lives demonstrated by means of love and justice. In this way we seek the glory of God in our moral discernment and we find the boundaries that God's love and glory requires. Such boundaries can never be separated from God's love and justice, which demand that humankind flourish and grow. When we act according to this way of discernment, we will be open to the struggles, pains and psychological suffering of our neighbors and will always invite them to live within moral boundaries with humility and love.

As we continue in this first section of the book, I will begin to use this frame for moral discernment by first examining ourselves and the larger cultural frames of our communities.

How do we make moral decisions and what influences us? As we relate to sexual and gender minority people, how do long Christian traditions of prejudice and judgment impact our discernment? What role does this psychology play and how does it hinder or help us walk together in the fruit of the Spirit? To what extent are we still driven by homophobia and its other expressions such as trans-phobia, disgust, and violent anger to cause harm to others?

CHAPTER 3: THE ROLE OF DISGUST

"Why do people bother to attack a group of people who really do them no harm?" (Stephen Fry)

This part of the book wrestles with Stephen Fry's vexing question raised in his two-part BBC Documentary "Out There" in which he investigated the sources and realities of the hatred, abuse, and persecution of homosexual people in the contemporary world. Fry's documentary work took him to Africa, Russia, Latin America and India, and led him to such despair that he attempted suicide during its filming. The hatred and anger against sexual and gender minorities still seethe across the world and is particularly prevalent in religious communities. As a Christian Theologian, I am interested in how a theology of hatred, violence, torture, abuse and killing became an accepted part of Christian faith and practice? Later in this book we will learn more about the profoundly disturbing practices of the church. We will learn about torture, the cutting off of genitalia and limbs. We will see evidence of live burnings and how teenagers were held under water until they drowned. How did the Gospel of love and charity, embodied by the self-giving Divine-Human person Jesus of Nazareth, become so twisted that it even holds sway in contemporary North American Christianity today? How can Christians still insist on a hate-inducing theology in the light of this terrible, shocking, and evil history? How can Christians, Protestant, Roman Catholic and Orthodox, insist that this is the long-standing teaching of the church despite what we will discover about our history? How did our Christian moral discernment bring us to this place where we seem oblivious to the harm we do to sexual and gender minorities?

A response to these questions is complex. It begs for an exploration into the complicated story of history, social construction of gender and sexuality, cultural anthropology, psychology, and its entanglement with theology. Such exploration is difficult because it involves an effort to understand the gut feelings of people in difficult historical periods and how these feelings drove rationalizations of terrifying behavior. Above all, it becomes important to understand the profound role of human disgust and its role in human moral development within particular cultural contexts. Here, I will focus on the North American context which is most familiar to me. Despite dramatic changes over the last thirty years on the perception and legal position of people who live in same-sex relationships, disgust, hatred and violence are still a daily threat to such people in the United States and Canada. In my own Country, Canada, equal rights of sexual and gender minority people have come a long way yet Statistics Canada notes that most violent hate crimes committed in Canada are still committed against sexual and gender minorities.[69] Even though this violence can no longer be directly laid at the feet of practicing Christians, social research will show that the atmosphere, the judgment, and the deep disgust is still present among Christians and contribute significantly to the atmosphere of homophobia that gives rise to such violence and harm.

Christian Shame

Sometimes individual events evolve to symbolize profoundly disturbing attitudes in society. With reference to torture and violent killing, the 1998 execution of University of Wyoming student Matthew Shepard is such a symbol. Although the idealized version of Matthew Shepherd's story has come under scrutiny in recent times, the fundamental role that his status as a sexual minority played in his death remains as central and critical as before.[70] One of his murderers, McKinney, is on record that Shepard was targeted because of his "weakness" and "frailty." As we will see later, conceptions of manliness and unmanliness represented in ideas of strength and weakness have their genesis in the development of misogynistic conceptions of manliness in late antiquity and early Christianity. What becomes clear is that the torture and violence done to Matthew Shepard is not isolated; it is fundamentally rooted and reflective of Christian behavior through a long period of history. As much as I would wish to be able to say that these were isolated behaviors in the larger good stream of Christian faith, there is nothing isolated or unusual about the Christian history of abuse, torture and killing. After completing his magnum opus on the history of homosexuality, "Homosexuality and Civilization", the North American scholar Louis Crompton writes,

If Christianity was concerned primarily with sinful acts, we must remember that it was sentient human beings who suffered, and acknowledge their flesh and blood reality. The killing, maiming, or torture of homosexuals ranks among humanity's innumerable "hate crimes," crimes encouraged in this instance by the Christian clergy. We must deduct such actions, as we deduct the persecution of heretics, witches, and Jews, from the enormous debt our civilization owes to the religion preached in Jesus' name. (Louis Crompton, 2003)[71]

Crompton's sober reflection should give Christians pause. He does not claim that the Christian faith or message is all bad. Rather, he does point to our deep entanglement with hate crimes. This claim should invite us to repent of the way we have violated the love of our neighbor. However, such careful and humble responses are rare in contemporary Christian communities. In fact, we have not even begun to take responsibility for such actions of our forebears in history. The approach of the Dutch Reformed Church in South Africa represents a recent example of a Christian denomination's statements and acts of repentance.

Not only did the General Synod approve that ministers can officiate at same sex weddings, it also affirmed that all offices of the church are open to sexual and gender minority ministers in married relationships.[72] The Church also issued an apology for the former treatment of sexual and gender minority members and ministers. Perhaps this decision was shaped by the history of that denomination's former implication in apartheid ideology and its hard-won repentance from the Apartheid heresy? Of course, a formal apology is not yet the same as repentance implying a profound change of heart.

The Role of Disgust I

Currently, there is a vigorous debate afoot in the United States in response to Federal directives re: public school washroom use for people who identify as transgender. This debate hearkens back to days before formal racial integration in the US, Canada and South Africa, when "separate but equal" characterized social attitudes in some regions. By May 2016 eleven states have sued the Federal Government over the directive. Some Christians in the United States are at the center of the advocacy against the Federal directive. If we read the arguments, such as the statement issued by Franklin Graham, we find a strong link with a sense of disgust when it comes to sexual and gender minority people. Mr. Graham is president and CEO of the Christian charity, The Samaritan's purse. He is a fellow Christian who is associated with global efforts to do good. It is therefore surprising to find a very different attitude when it comes to sexual and gender minorities. On February 5, 2016 he posted the following on his Facebook page,

LGBT activists are trying to hook their caboose to the "freedom train" and drag their immoral agenda into our communities by claiming that this is a civil rights issue. Civil rights issues are very real and important—but don't be fooled, this isn't one of them. I heard one African-American minister say recently that "the freedom train doesn't stop at Sodom and Gomorrah."[73]

The language is a rhetoric of disgust. It seems to emerge out of a gut reaction against sexual and gender minority people. At best it is misinformed, confusing a transgender orientation with homosexuality, and then considering the story of Sodom and Gomorrah as the basis for the universal rejection of all same-sex relationships. The majority of biblical scholars today agree that the story of Sodom and Gomorrah is about gang rape and not a story about homosexual orientation. In fact, the association with Sodom and the idea of the sin of sodomy and references to being a "Sodomite" is largely a medieval development. Clearly, the story has nothing to do with people who have the experience of being transgender. Why then the vehement disgust about a small number of people and the insistence that they do not have a right to equality? I cite this example not as a condemnation of Mr. Graham, but rather as an example of how quickly an inner sense of disgust might thwart a careful reading of the Bible and gracious gospel discernment.

In his 1974 essay on moral discernment, James Gustafson wrote prophetically, "Not enough work has yet been done by either philosophers or theologians on just how people actually make moral judgments…"[74] It seems that social scientists have beaten the theologians and philosophers to it. There is a solid body of social science research in North America on how humans make moral judgments. Issues of sexuality and gender diversity and their impact on human psychology, perhaps rooted in our evolution, can be linked to human moral judgment based in disgust. In short moral judgments often happen on a pre-rational intuitive level.

Social Theories about Moral Decisions and Disgust

Recent conversations on gender identity have brought to our attention how the delicate dance between the social world and our experience of gender identity are interlinked. In short, we understand today that an overarching factor in gender is its cultural construction and its performance in rituals and discourses over time. This reality of speech-act performance lies at the heart of the idea of the social construction of gender in culture and society. In turn it intersects in important ways with the way power functions in our lived experience. Judith Butler writes,

Performative acts are forms of authoritative speech: most performatives, for instance, are statements that, in the uttering, also performs a certain action and exercise a binding power.[75]

Christian communities intuitively understand the formative power of the performative act of worship and the way that the language of worship through liturgy shapes how we make meaning of experience. The idea of social construction of gender points to the way our conceptions of gender and sexuality is shaped through the larger societal forces of repeated speech-acts. Even when we transgress such boundaries protected by language and ritual, we tend to further enforce the evocative power of those boundaries. When, in a marriage ceremony, a pastor or civil magistrate declares, "now I pronounce you man and wife," the performative power is enforced and enacted. How deeply this performative social power, and, in this case, its assumption of a gender binary, reaches into our psyche and unconscious remains a matter of ongoing debate. Nevertheless, we cannot think about the place and role of sexual and gender minority people and the way they are understood and treated within our specific cultural world, without attending to these powerful performative forces. We know today that gender, gender roles, the concept marriage, and sexual orientation hold very different meanings and function in different ways in different cultural contexts throughout the world. In her inter-cultural survey, Margaret Farley records how diverse understandings of sexuality function in different cultural contexts.[76] This diversity is not only true of sex; it is also holds true for the way we understand something as unacceptable or disgusting. For example, Western people are often disgusted by the idea of eating insects. Yet insects are delicacies in other parts of the world. Even though we can make rational arguments for the high protein content of insects and how important these insects are as a food source in a world increasingly overpopulated, our inner sense of disgust may remain powerful and may be reignited and enforced through speech-act social responses. When it comes to sexual and gender minorities in North American society, we face a changing cultural landscape that introduces new affirming responses mixed in with a very long Western socio-cultural history rooted in ever evolving and changing Christian teaching that carries a deep sense of discomfort and disgust. The different constructions of sexuality and gender coexist in a complex network off discourses enforced by repeated speech acts. "A man shall not lie with a man," Leviticus (18:22), takes on a powerful performative power for many. The use of the word "sodomy," ensconced in legal tradition and re-invoked over time, exercises a similar power. In the historical section of this book I will unpack the history of binding speech-acts and performance of violent actions that has shaped our Western consciousness against sexual and gender diversity.

The Anthropologist Mary Douglas produced seminal work on how the experience of purity and taboo functions across cultures. In her ground-breaking cultural-anthropology classic study published in 1966, "Purity and Danger: An Analysis of Concepts of Pollution and Taboo," Douglas writes on sexual taboos about body fluids and how they are conceived to present danger of the female to the male or vice versa:

It is implausible to interpret them (bodily fluid taboos) as expressing something about the actual relation of the sexes. I suggest that many ideas about sexual dangers are better interpreted as symbols of the relation between parts of society, as mirroring designs of hierarchy or symmetry which apply in the larger social system.[77]

Douglas, who is usually associated with the structuralist school of cultural anthropology, here begins to develop a sense of the way that our socio-cultural world and the performance of its speech-acts reach into our understanding and experience of matters of gender and sexuality.[78] Later we will refer briefly to the work of Julia Kristeva, who builds on Douglas' work, to explore the human experience of abjection-disgust. At this point I am interested in a larger question: how does the larger frame of our cultural performance and context shape our experience and response to sexuality and gender? Later I will pay closer attention to individual responses. When we try to understand why Christians and others in Western culture wish to judge and reject sexual and gender diversity, we need to recognize the profound social power still acting on them.

Jonathan Haidt has popularized the process of intuitive moral decision making with his 2012 best-selling book, "The Righteous Mind: Why Good People are Divided by Politics and Religion." He argues persuasively that human moral decision making is a complex process that requires an understanding of evolutionary psychology, brain function, and cultural anthropology. Haidt's key puzzle is to figure out the difference in motivation between "conservative" and "liberal" Americans in their political and moral decision making and arguments. Haidt develops a sophisticated explanation moving away from equating Republicans and Democrats with the categories "conservative" and "liberal." What he shows, through evidence-based research, is that there is a non-determinative predisposition in some people to lean toward a more conservative perspective in the sense of being more cautious about change, suspicious of those who are different, and more averse to risk. In others, a non-determinative predisposition leans towards new experience, risk and the acceptance of difference. Haidt argues that all people share a deeply rooted intuitive reaction shaping moral decisions and judgment. I add to Haidt's argument that these "predispositions" are also shaped by the performative powers of our cultural context. Even as decisions originate on the intuitive level, they are followed up by finding arguments to support such decisions. That decisive intuitional decision is shaped by larger cultural powers. Haidt demonstrates that people tend to assume positions while tending to ignore persuasive counter arguments. People tend to look for arguments to embrace that will support their position. It is also important to remember that Haidt emphasizes that people of all dispositions can have different outcomes based in culture, life history, and experience. People can change their perspective whether they are cautiously pre-disposed or risk pre-disposed. An example he cites is the change in "liberal" and Democratic sentiment towards a more vigorous patriotism after 9/11. It is here that Haidt's work challenges a kind of complete social constructivist determinism. As Margaret Farley so rightly argues, social construction does not have to be deterministic,

Even social constructionists like Butler argue that human bodies are not passive slates on which society imprints meaning. There are enough gaps in socialization that questions can arise and we can shape our bodies anew.[79]

We can therefore conclude that many factors play a role in shaping our bodies, sexuality and gender identity. Although Haidt's research focuses more on the internal psychological construction of moral formation, he too recognizes that many factors play a role. It is therefore important to remember that the larger social frame in North American culture deeply influences the prevailing anti-homoerotic sentiment.

Haidt argues that there are six "foundations" for morality that include: care/harm, fairness/cheating, loyalty/betrayal, authority/subversion, sanctity/degradation, and liberty/oppression.[80] He presents research evidence for each of these foundations arguing that the adaptive challenges in human development and evolution led to original triggers that making these moral structures important. Haidt also describes how current issues trigger emotional responses. His work is mainly descriptive. In his attempt to make sense of the data and the emerging theories about how human beings make moral decisions. Haidt does not claim anything normative for his description. He does not state that this is the way it ought to be or even always is. Rather he simply notes this is the larger observed patterns of moral decision making that may inform our understanding of human behavior. In fact, Haidt is adamant that there is nothing completely deterministic in what he describes and observes.[81] It is also in this non-normative descriptive way that I wish to engage Haidt's argument.

Because Haidt's research is describing the way our moral decision making is constructed within North American cultures, it casts light on the puzzling presence of anti-homoerotic bias in North American society. It may also explain why we might end up making decisions out of an intuitive sense of disgust. The disgust of sexual and gender minorities still present in North American society thus has many layers. One important layer is the role and place and history of Christian rejection and persecution of sexual and gender minorities and the rhetorical repetition of phrases and texts considered to be normative. I maintain that the harm caused is aided by the churches.

The Role of Disgust II

Haidt is not writing specifically about sexual and gender minority people and attitudes towards them, but he does refer in a few cases to attitudes and discrimination faced by this community. His argument is helpful in discerning why people's positions become so easily entrenched when it comes to the acceptance and affirmation of sexual and gender minorities. He also discusses the increased volume of research on the human response of disgust. He argues that our ability to be disgusted is rooted and partially shaped by our status as omnivores and it serves as protection against ingesting dangerous or poisonous food. However, in the adaptation through culture and time, disgust has also become associated with our acceptance of or fear of outsiders or people who are different. All of us have different levels of tolerance when facing such challenges. In part, we can conclude from Haidt's argument that disgust expressed towards sexual and gender minorities arises out of the tension between things considered sacred and things considered degrading. This tension in turn reflects Mary Douglas' conclusions about the role of some societal rules about sexual purity and taboo that really serve the purpose of enforcing the social order.[82] An example of enforcement of social order through performative speech-acts in Christian theological arguments is the use of the word "abomination" when it comes to two verses in Leviticus that seem to reject male same sex sexual intercourse (Lev 18:22 & Lev 20:13). In fact, one possible translation of the Hebrew word translated as "abomination" is "disgusting."[83] It is also the word commonly used in the Hebrew law to indicate idolatrous practices which in part forms the background to these Hebrew prohibitions. In terms of Haidt's moral foundations, we are dealing here with a classic matter of perceptions of sanctity and degradation. Even though our culture or theology no longer believe and argue from the perspective of traditional patriarchal kinship conceptions, a perspective that underlay notions of purity and degradation, many in contemporary North American culture are still moved to a feeling of disgust. We no longer follow the patriarchal assumption that male seed is something that rightfully only belongs to a wife. Yet, a feeling of degradation is still in many when seeing two women or men kiss passionately. When Christians seek to make moral discernment about the place and role of sexual and gender minority people, awareness of the role of inner disgust is critical. Such disgust emerges out of a broader social context in which the performative-acts of Christian theological traditions play a key role.

Rationalizing Disgust

The rationalization of theologies critical of homosexual relationships today employs significantly different arguments than those raised in early Christianity and Medieval Christianity. For example, fifth century Christianity did not appeal to Romans 1:26 to argue against homosexual relationships. In fact, much of the rationalization of the rejection of homosexual relationships by Christians at that time appealed to Roman cultural conceptions of manliness. This difference suggests that, in part an intuitive gut level response leads to arguments that would then rationalize a response. The reasons for these intuitive gut level feelings are many. It is logical to assume that the history of Christian behavior and thought does present a major component in shaping a culture of disgust – a kind of historically shaped consciousness or a "horizon" that influences us. Later we will explore this long and painful history. For now, it is sufficient to note the importance of the intuitive gut response of disgust that many people still feel in relation to sexual and gender minority people. This discomfort is often expressed in protestations that people should not flaunt their sexuality. Of course, the same measure is not applied to heterosexual couples. For many such people this is not a religious matter, and yet they feel intuitively that something sacred is being violated and that such behavior is disgusting or gross. It is telling that people who have no personal commitment to Christian communities still invoke the bible and tropes such as "a man shall not lie with a man," in their arguments.

Disgust, A Freudian Perspective

There is also a second avenue of exploring the human response of disgust. This is rooted in the Freudian tradition of psychology. It must be observed that Freudian theories of disgust, notwithstanding their ongoing popularity among some psychologists, have a much more speculative and philosophical basis than Haidt's descriptive-empirical approach. Nevertheless, Freudian traditions draw on insights gained from the treasures of Western myths, dramas, religious concepts and stories collected in literature. In addition, they are tested and reflected upon from clinical practice. In some way we can assume that such myths, dramas, religious concepts and stories reflect a level of human self-insight into reality. Its challenge is that such stories require interpretation which suggests the need for an ongoing caveat not to make a particular interpretation, including Freudian perspectives, normative or absolute.

I propose to engage the Freudian tradition here by seeking ways to see if additional insight can be gained into the human disgust directed at sexual and gender minorities. One of the creative and interesting Freudian scholars and philosopher, Julia Kristeva has contributed to a growing Freudian understanding of disgust in her book *Powers of Horror: An Essay in Abjection*.[84] Drawing on the works of Mary Douglas', Jacques Lacan's, post-structuralist theory, along with an understanding of developmental psychology, Kristeva re-describes the concept of abjection in human experience. Whereas the word abjection literally means "to cast off" it has come to denote baseness or meanness of spirit and is also associated with degradation. We should note the convergence of the idea of abjection with Haidt's moral category of sanctity/degradation. Regardless of the somewhat different theoretical orientations of Douglas (structuralist), Haidt (evolutionary psychology) and Kristeva (Freudian-post-structuralist), there is also an interesting convergence of ideas about abjection-disgust as a human reaction. Kristeva adds to our understanding of horror, disgust and degradation by positing the experience of horror or disgust as located in the space between the object and the taboo elements of self. For Kristeva this sense of abjection is not so much about degradation as a lack of cleanliness or health, but, rather, as with Mary Douglas, it is about a disturbance of identity and social order. For Kristeva there is a deeply internalized process of self-horror linked to abjection and experiences of abjection.

It is not difficult to see how these Freudian and Lacanian insights of Kristeva can be linked to Haidt's argument from the point of view of evolutionary psychology. An inner sense of self-disgust-abjection can rise out of our own struggles with sexual orientation. Kristeva's work, and particularly her arguments about women's sexuality and the "casting off of the mother" is not without controversy and she has been accused of developing her own form of homophobia.[85] However, one does not have to accept all of Kristeva's argument to grasp how her theory makes sense of disgust of sexual and gender minority experience. Horror and disgust towards sexual and gender minority people is socially embedded, yet it is also deeply rooted in a struggle with our own inner sexual identity. In the shaping of our sexual identity there is the potential for a deep alienation – abjection – of that part of ourselves. For a long time, psychologists have noted a phenomenon they have labelled "internalized homophobia." Some of the earliest studies of such a psychological phenomenon go back to Sandor Ferenczi's argument first published in 1914.[86] "Internalized homophobia" is described thus, "The term *internalized homophobia* has been used by clinicians to refer to the internalization of societal antihomosexual attitudes (e.g., Malyon, 1982)."[87] As we come to terms with our own fluid sexual orientations, Kristeva may cast light on how these inner alienations may lead to internalized homophobia. To what degree does this phenomenon contribute to disgust against and even self-disgust among sexual and gender minorities? To what degree do our Christian traditions play a role in shaping the inner fractures that lead to internalized homophobia and the painful reality of high suicide rates among sexual and gender minority teens? How might it shape our conversations of moral discernment in Christian communities? It is to these questions that we now turn.

Disgust and Internalized Homophobia

Critical to our consideration of Christian attitudes towards sexual and gender minority people, we note that the well documented psychological phenomenon of internalized homophobia essentially feeds on negative cultural attitudes and stereotypes. In her provocative exploration of violence against gay men in the United States, Karin Franklin finds that it oversimplifies matters to lay blame at the feet of individual homophobic attitudes. Rather, she finds that in the people she studied, a complex interplay of cultural stereotypes, including forms of male hierarchical gender norms mixed with peer dynamics and youthful thrill seeking, contribute to a more complex pattern of influence towards anti-sexual and gender minority violence.[88] This research supports the arguments above for an interplay of factors between the social construction of gender and sexuality and personal psychology. It might also suggest that sub-cultures play a role in overt harmful actions against sexual and gender minorities.

As discussed in the Introduction, homophobia can take three basic forms. In this case a kind of societal level of systemic homophobia is served by various forms of institutional homophobia. Christian communities continue to contribute to this wider systemic homophobia. Religious and particularly Christian support for hierarchical gender norms and gender binary prejudice is a contributor to cultural matrix combined with internalized attitudes that lead to violence. It is not simply that those who perpetrate violent hate acts are hate filled individuals, nor are they necessarily "Christian." Rather, they are people shaped by cultural stereotypes and motivated by a demonstration in front of their peers of "appropriate maleness" based in strict hierarchical binary norms. When Christian theologians argue that Christians should be "welcoming but not affirming" of sexual and gender minorities they are furthering a cultural matrix that perpetuates the ritual and liturgical social enforcement of attitudes of abjection that contribute to harm and violence. What does non-affirmation mean? How does the moral judgment that the erotic relationships of sexual and gender minority people are by definition always sinful, contribute to an atmosphere of disgust?

In their recent study of religious bias-based bullying of sexual and gender minority youth, Newman, Fantus, Woodford and Rwigema have noted the significant role that religion and particularly Christian teaching plays in that bullying.[89] They note that there are a limited number of empirical studies that explore the role of religion in the harm documented among sexual and gender minority youth. Such studies are notoriously difficult to conduct as subjects are often closeted and inaccessible to researchers until the harm done to them has reached a destructive level. What the increasing number of studies, and particularly the work of Peter Newman, a social work professor at the University of Toronto, provide is empirical evidence of harm done by Christian teaching and Christian communities through both their non-affirming teaching and through the resultant marginalization, victimization, and bullying that such sexual and gender minorities endure within their religious communities. Two other scholars note:

Importantly, religiously based rhetoric endorsing prejudice or condemnation of SGM, in both religious and secular institutions, is often framed as a right to freedom of religious expression (Meyer, 2010; Taylor, 2008).[90]

Further contributing to this harm is the patriarchal and gender binaries in the form of an exclusive theology of gender complementarity that features in some Christian anti-homosexual arguments. Moreover, a theology couched in a kind of presumed kindness as "welcoming" places the sexual and gender minority person in the double bind[91] of pretended kindness while also essentially rejecting the person in their most profound experience of giving and receiving love. We will note later that prohibitions against the positive psychological and biological wellness created by tender and loving human touch can cause potential harm. In another paper Newman and Fantus review the literature and bring evidence that the religious biased bullying of sexual and gender minority youth by Christian communities contribute to a higher risk of depression, sexual risk behavior, substance abuse, and suicide compared to heterosexual youth.[92] As hard as it has been to come by evidence of the role of non-affirming Christian teaching on sexual and gender minorities, the empirical evidence is now strong and published in peer reviewed publications. We, the Christian churches, in as much as we continue to teach and behave in non-affirming ways, are harming people.

Besides the work of Newman and Fantus, the earlier research of Meyer and Dean found a correlation in gay men who were affiliated to non-affirming religious organizations and higher levels of internalized homophobia than those in affirming communities. These findings lend research support to assessing the conflicting messages created by non-affirming Christian theology as psychologically harmful.[93] The research demonstrates that sexual and gender minority people in non-affirming Christian communities are at greater risk of serious mental health problems. This is particularly true of youth who are not only at a higher risk of suicide than their peers but also at a higher risk of living in non-affirming and condemning Christian families. Meyer and Dean put it well:

Our findings have important public health implications for prevention and treatment. The role of internalized homophobia in mental health suggests the need for intervention at the social level to reduce antigay attitudes and prejudice, and at the individual level to help lesbian, gay, and bisexual people to develop healthy sexual identities.[94]

For Christian communities, the current research challenges us to think about our moral responsibility in our process of moral discernment. Can we truly stand before God in love and with a sense of justice in our midst and say with certainty that wholesome loving erotic relationships are not an option for sexual and gender minority Christians? If we are doing harm, the question that emerges is, what will it take for us to stop? Why is it that a matter that receives so little attention in the Hebrew and Christian Scriptures has become the rallying cry for so many Christians, to the point of seeing the anti-sexual and gender minority message as a matter essential to "the gospel"? One classic example of the rhetorical rejection of critiques of Christian harm of is the work of Robert Gagnon. In the introduction to his book on the Bible and homosexual practice he writes

While antihomosexual violence deserves to be vigorously denounced, it does nobody any good to ignore the dangerous way in which isolated and relatively rare incidents of violence against homosexuals have been exploited to stifle freedom of speech and coerce societal endorsement of homosexual practice.[95]

Gagnon describes himself here as an offended Christian discriminated against because of his intolerance. He trivializes real violence done to human bodies by placing it on the same plane as his perceived lack of freedom to express his opinion. He trivializes this real violence by not recognizing its ongoing reality and the statistical fact that most violent hate crimes in North America are committed against sexual and gender minorities. There can be no doubt that our moral discernment here requires a stronger dose of the fruit of the Spirit. It appears that sexual and gender minority people have become a kind of scapegoat for Christian theologians like Gagnon. Any disagreement or critique of their position is rejected as part of a societal conspiracy against the righteous position of "traditional" Christians. For this reason, it is also important to attend to the place and role of scapegoating in the plight of sexual and gender minority people.

Disgust and Scapegoating

One of the most interesting historians, literary critics and social theorists of the 20th century is Rene Girard. Girard was a practicing Roman Catholic Christian who spent his career examining the stories and patterns of scapegoating in human cultures around the world. Most of all, he has focused on Biblical material to illuminate how the Christian message and the Hebrew tradition may inform this pattern and its impact on human societies. In his reflection on the macro patterns of Western culture, Girard developed the concept of mimetic (imitational) desire, as a core principle of the functioning of human communities and the cause of scapegoating and violence. His work has been engaged fruitfully by theologians, psychologists and sociologists. Although critics rightly point to the limitations of his work,[96] particularly the way he seems to make all human desire mimetic, the larger patterns of mimetic desire and its violent outcomes seem self-evident. For Girard, the competition created in a particular community to attain the same thing through mimetic desire creates a level of anxiety and a building pressure towards violence. The key way that communities deal with this anxiety and tendency towards violence is by creating a scapegoat. He sees Jesus as such a scapegoat. For a scapegoat to be effective, that individual, so chosen, must absorb the pressure of the violence of the community. By directing the focus away from the pressures of mimetic desire, the violence perpetrated against the scapegoat, who is often a willing participant, releases the pressure and saves the community from larger self-destructive behavior. Three Christian theologians, Mark Heim (a Baptist), and James Alison (a Queer Roman Catholic), Anthony Bartlett (an Independent Christian Community with Anglican roots) have developed Girard's insights into full-fledged theologies of redemption that examine the role of Jesus as scapegoat in his crucifixion.[97]

Girard's theory helps to make some sense of the vehement way in which some Christian communities condemn, judge and oppose sexual and gender minority people. This small and vulnerable group of people in society provides easy targets, as scapegoats that can focus those communities away from their internal controversies and mimetic desire. Most sexual and gender minority people in these communities are deeply closeted and already racked by internal guilt and self-hatred due to the teaching of such communities. So, they hide as they struggle with psychosocial pain. When they are outed, they become even more vulnerable to both subtle and overt forms of homophobia. The overwhelming force of community disgust combined with internalized homophobia creates an unbearable burden. Often such people become willing scapegoats confessing their sexual identity as sinful and seeking "reparative" therapies that become harmful to their psychological health. For short periods of time they become poster children for the idea that appropriate sexuality is exclusively heterosexual. They may speak at conventions, or services to convince others that they too can change. However, as time progresses, research shows that for many such people change simply is a long-term impossibility. Sadly, some are driven to suicide. It is worth observing that the dimensions of sin identified in the previous chapter including alienation, objectification, and abuse, become sins committed not by the sexual and gender minorities but by the non-affirming Christian community itself.

Some Christian communities rightly reject such radical "reparative" therapies as harmful. However, these communities may then demand that sexual and gender minorities remain celibate if they want to identify as Christian. By thus declaring a person's most intimate being as "disordered" or "sinful," such communities do harm not only by enforcing a fundamental internal rejection but also by denying that person the gift of full human intimacy.

Given Girard's theory of scapegoating, it is no surprise then that much of the more conservative Christian discussion of sexual and gender minorities focuses on a perceived threat from the outside. The Franklin Graham Facebook post referred to earlier is a classic example of this phenomenon. Graham claims in response to the US Federal Nondiscrimination Ordinance, "In reality, this type of so-called 'non-discrimination' law is being used to discriminate against Christians." The "discrimination" he claims against Christians has to do with such Christian business people being inhospitable to sexual and gender minority people. When their lack of hospitality for others, hardly Christian a virtue, is challenged as discrimination they claim to be discriminated against. Paradoxically, by attempting to be morally upright such Christian behaviors risk becoming immoral in leaving behind the just treatment of others. Christian history is filled with examples of this in its extreme as theologically inspired violence.

In the light of Christian moral discernment, the role of the fruit of the Spirit, the need for accountability before the God of love and justice, it becomes clear that a more profoundly centered Christian Scriptural moral logic needs to be generated. The kind of argument that Franklin Graham makes on his Facebook page, referred to earlier, points to an "us against them" attitude which leads to scapegoating. It amounts to a kind of bullying. Within traditional Christian communities that remain resistant to the affirmation of sexual and gender minority people, there is often the threat of a declining membership and financial base. It appears that fear of decline might influence such communities away from compassion and love. They move towards strategies of survival in the midst of fear that they will lose members and money if they welcome and affirm. In such a case the sexual and gender minority scapegoating becomes expedient for the survival of the community.

Conclusion

Why do people then bother to attack a group of people who really do them no harm? In response to Stephen Fry's question, I have argued that the reasons and motivations are complex and intertwined. It is situated within the larger structures of social construction of gender and the performative powers that shapes society for the enforcement of social order. It also finds its roots in the human experience of disgust that Jonathan Haidt relates to the process of human evolution. Disgust, shaped by social factors and a disposition in some to be less open to difference, leads to a gut level formation of moral decisions. Thus this chapter has outlined how Freudian theories, including the work of Julia Kristeva on horror and abjection, helps us understand the location of the personal psychological process of being disgusted at an alienated part of ourselves. Such personal psychology makes responses to sexual difference and diversity particularly fraught with a tendency towards deep discomfort with difference in gender identity.

It is now evident that psychologists, in sympathy with such theories, have studied the harmful effects of internalized homophobia and how social scientists have shown a strong correlation between non-affirming Christian teaching and harm done to sexual and gender minority people. Behind the increased level of violence against sexual and gender minorities, researchers have found a complex set of factors that include a set hierarchical view of a gender complementarity together with a need to demonstrate toxic hyper masculinity to a peer group and the desire for thrill seeking. Researchers have also shown how non-affirming religious communities marginalize and harm sexual and gender minority youth. Too often such youth are driven to the point of suicide. The research concludes that the cultural shaping of strong gender hierarchy and gender binary plays a key role. Non-affirming Christian religious communities contribute to the support of a culture of harm. The studies cited studies suggest that sexual and gender minority people involved with non-affirming religious communities are more deeply affected by internalized homophobia including shameful self-hatred and suicidal ideation. The approaches of Christian communities vary from hardline approaches that require harmful "reparative" therapy to subtle forms of rejection such as the requirement that people to remain celibate. The so called "welcoming but not affirming" approach also presents problems. It places sexual and gender minority people in the distress of an emotional double bind. Research findings demonstrate that the fundamental rejection of the person's identity is harmful to a person's mental health, in some cases, to the point of suicide.

We have also explored the mimetic and scapegoat theories of Rene Girard and argued that contemporary Christian communities that make sexual and gender minorities a target of attack and rejection are finding in this minority group an easy target as a scapegoat. This process of scapegoating, according to Girard's theory, enables these communities to leave behind their internal conflicts and anxieties by uniting against a common target. For all these reasons, it becomes expedient for such Christian communities to maintain positions of rejection, judgment, and, in some cases, outright attack against sexual and gender minorities. For other traditional Christian communities that are experiencing decline in membership and income, finding grace and love for sexual and gender minority people becomes difficult as the community anxiously fret about the loss of members and income that may ensue if they become fully affirming.

Given the theories discussed and the research evidence offered earlier, I conclude that non-affirming Christian communities contribute significantly to the cultural atmosphere of harm. In particular, the mental health of sexual and gender minority people is compromised. Given these severe and harmful consequences, one would assume that Christians who contribute to such harm would have an incontrovertible Scriptural warrant for their actions. However, as we have already seen in the previous chapter, our process of moral decision making suggests otherwise. Moreover, the next chapter will detail how the arguments from the Christian Scriptures that lead to such harmful ways have been challenged both on the interpretation of the texts and on the way these texts are privileged in moral discernment. It seems that our moral decisions about the affirmation or non-affirmation of sexual and gender minorities have a significant level of intuitive gut level influence. Although the argument in this chapter focused on Christian communities and its activities, much of the logic of the research and theories discussed might also be of help to communities of faith other than Christianity. We all share the human condition. As we discern the harm done, it is time for serious reflection and soul searching.

CHAPTER 4: THE PARADOX OF CHRISTIAN MORAL LOGIC

"Why do people bother to attack a group of people who really do them no harm?" (Stephen Fry)

Stephen Fry's asks, "why?" Why do Christians teach and act in ways that cause harm to sexual and gender minorities? As described in the previous chapter, moral decision-making is a complex process. I have argued that social context, Christian teaching and its impact on the construction of sexuality and gender as well as the experience of disgust at sexual otherness, is a significant factor. I have also pointed to Jonathan Haidt's research which suggests that all people make moral decisions on an intuitive level. Then, after feeling our way to a position, we proceed to find evidence that supports our position. Insights from Freudian psychology, research on perpetrators of violence against sexual and gender minorities, the role of internalized homophobia, as well as the tendency in communities to deal with conflict by means of a scapegoating have all been explored. It is safe to assume that these processes play a role in the affirmation or non-affirmation of sexual and gender minorities for Christian communities. I have also demonstrated that non-affirming Christian positions contribute towards harm. In this chapter I examine some of the core disputes among Christian theological thinkers around sexual and gender minority affirmation. I maintain that the theological, moral, and ethical conclusions reached by those engaged in this debate are by no means self-evident. I invite you as reader is to explore with me whether there might be a way of respectful Christian moral discernment that could balance respect for Scripture and tradition without doing harm?

For Protestants, which is my own tradition, the Bible represents the basis of all theological arguments. It is therefore not surprising that in Protestant circles the debates focus on the Biblical text and, in most cases, on specific texts deemed to articulate about the matter of same-sex sexual behavior. I suggest that this way of using the Bible is inherently problematic. For the last fourty years Protestants of a more centrist persuasion tended to argue for a nuanced and open consideration of sexual minorities. Over the last twenty years these arguments have become sophisticated, looking at the impact on the plight of transgender, gender queer and intersex people. In my own country, Canada, the largest Protestant denomination, the United Church of Canada moved to the ordination of gay and lesbian people in 1988. Most other traditional protestant denominations maintained a negative theological stance while maintaining a kind of "don't ask don't tell" attitude towards members and in some cases clergy who might identify as sexual or gender minorities. Recently Lutherans, Anglicans and some Mennonites have moved to create space for the affirmation of intimate sexual and gender minority relationships by making it an option in particular contexts. In contrast, the global denomination, the United Methodist Church voted not to move to an affirming stance in 2019.

On the evangelical side of the denominational spectrum in North America, until recently, there was an almost universal rejection of all forms of affirmation while many claimed to follow a position described as "welcoming but not affirming." That position is represented by the Canadian theologian Stanley Grenz in his book, "Welcoming but not Affirming: An Evangelical Response to Homosexuality."[98] Since 2009 many evangelicals started to change their minds. Perhaps the earliest signal of this change is represented by Jack Rogers' book "Jesus, the Bible, and Homosexuality: Exploding the Myths, Heal the Church."[99] There were of course precursors such as the Pentecostal preacher Troy Perry who started the sexual minority affirming denomination, *Metropolitan Community Churches*, in 1968. As a gay man and a Pentecostal evangelical preacher, he had to come to terms with his identity and Christian faith which led him on this journey. In 1970, within Roman Catholicism, Fr. Pat Nidorf founded an affirming movement called *Dignity* in Los Angeles. Jack Rogers represents someone with strong evangelical credentials who changed his mind. Rogers is a former professor of the prominent evangelical seminary, Fuller Theological Seminary, and an ordained Presbyterian minister.[100]

Other faith communities have been more inclusive. In a city such as Toronto, there is an all-inclusive synagogue, *Shir Libeynu* along with other synagogues that follow policies of welcoming and affirming sexual and gender minorities in Judaism. *Mashid el-Tawid – Unity Mosque,* an Islamic community, is also welcoming and affirming towards sexual and gender minorities.

Since the appearance of Rogers' book, a steady number of leaders, identified with North American Evangelicalism, have moved to affirming positions. Disturbingly, little change in rhetoric has taken place on the more fundamentalist side of the movement. A poster child for the conservative evangelical side was the organization "Exodus" that supported "reparative" or conversion therapy to attempt to change people's sexual orientation. This movement was also identified with the term ex-gay that claimed that they were having success in "curing" people of same sex sexual attractions. However, a critical moment came with the very public confession of the president of Exodus USA, Alan Chambers, in 2013, that accompanied the decision to close down the organization. The New York Times reported Mr. Chamber's apology as,

I am sorry for the pain and hurt many of you have experienced. I am sorry that some of you spent years working through the shame and guilt you felt when your attractions didn't change. I am sorry we promoted sexual orientation change efforts and reparative theories about sexual orientation that stigmatized parents.[101]

This apology was prompted by a process generated by Wendy Gritter's speech at the Exodus convention in 2008.[102] Dr. Gritter is Director of the evangelical Canadian organization "New Directions Ministries" now called "Generous Space Ministries," that eventually withdrew from Exodus because they concluded that "reparative" therapies were harmful.[103] Through such interventions even more conservative evangelicals started rethinking their position on inclusion. Two of the most recent evangelical representatives who spoke up are the conservative ethicist David Gushee[104] and Tony Campolo.[105] In October 2016, Nicholas

Wolterstorff, the highly respected evangelical-Reformed theologian and former Professor at Calvin College and Yale, gave a lecture in Grand Rapids Michigan in which he explained his support for same-sex marriage and the affirmation of same-sex Christian couples in covenanted relationships.[106] Within Roman Catholicism the well-known conservative journalist Michael Coren changed his own position as he explained in his recent book *"Epiphany: A Christian's Change of Heart and Mind over Same-Sex Marriage."*[107] What these changes among leaders, and particularly intellectual leaders in the evangelical and conservative Roman Catholic movements mean is that the affirmation and support of sexual minorities in Christian communities is no longer simply a matter of claiming a liberal versus conservative argument in which one group can easily dismiss the other. Rather, this is now a matter of vigorous debate among people who consider themselves on the same side. How is this possible? Is it not true that Christianity has always maintained a rejecting stance towards homosexuality? To quote one of the strongest proponents of a Christian rejection of all forms of homoeroticism Robert Gagnon,

However, on this issue, as on any other, if a clear, unequivocal, and pervasive stance in the Bible can be shown to exist-across the Testaments and accepted for nearly two millennia of the church's existence-then the burden of proof lies with those in the church who take a radically different approach to the issue.[108]

In essence this statement lies at the heart on contemporary debates about sexual minority people in the church. Does the Bible not clearly reject "homosexuality" and that is the sum of its perspective? Has the church not always clearly taught this? Is homosexual sexual activity not by definition a sin? Is the teaching not clear and unequivocal across the Testaments? Responses to these questions require acknowledging the problem and bracketing the human tendency to make pre-rational intuitive moral judgments. We must tread carefully and thoughtfully. If we have the proverbial hammer, everything in the Bible might look like a nail to us! To make good Christian moral decisions we need to start by acknowledging our biases. We also need to be prepared to find a mixed picture if we go to such a rich tradition as the complex Biblical material produced over thousands of years and in vastly different cultural contexts. Acknowledging that Christians long assumed a clear unequivocal Biblical stance across the Testaments on the acceptability of slavery is an important step. It was only during the late 18th and early 19th century that the Spirit led us to new moral discernment on this issue. So, the matter is not quite as simple as Gagnon suggests. In addition, we also need to seek communal discernment as we walk in the way of the gospel. We need to do so responsibly before God and in accountability to our sexual and gender minority neighbors and the harm they experience.

I have observed this reality in moral decision making within my own spiritual journey. As a young pastor I was first confronted with a close friend, a gay man, a devout Roman Catholic, and a brilliant artist and professor of philosophy who committed suicide. For my friend the dissonance between Roman Catholic official teaching which described him as "disordered" and his own experience as a gay man became unbearable. His suicide challenged my own traditional Christian position which sought to be gracious while not being affirming. I also started a journey ultimately identifying my own internalized homophobia. I am sure that this journey is endless. Over time, this life changing tragedy became more fully experienced in my pastoral practice when a man in my pastoral care committed suicide. He was the object of a former colleague's attempts at reparative therapy by prescribing a mixed orientation marriage. The consequences were disastrous for this man, the wife he married to "cure" his homosexuality, as well as his stepchildren. The tragedy of his death became profoundly harmful to the whole family. I am sure that my philosopher friend's suicide set the stage for all that came after in my own convictions, but, these experiences shaped me in a direction away from a simplistic traditional approach to a place where I had to ask more complex questions about the teaching and example of Jesus Christ and the implications for sexual and gender minority people. These experiences challenged me to struggle with my own inner biases, my own comfort with my sexuality, my own sexual orientation, and my own personal moral discernment as a person committed to walk the way of Jesus Christ.

The Bible and Same-Sex Relationships

The first challenge when we consider the Bible is that we are dealing with terms and concepts that are historical and determined by cultural context. The Biblical texts speak to cultural worlds over thousands of years that were fundamentally different from our own. For instance, as we look at current book titles, we often read some association between the Bible and "homosexuality." In fact, in some sense, we can argue that the Bible has absolutely nothing to say about the contemporary sexual orientation described as "homosexuality" or the sexual orientation described as being attracted to people of the same gender. Heather White has shown how the history of the modern term "homosexuality" is linked to the medicalization of sexuality which in turn influenced the language of churches and modern bible translators.[109] Moreover, poems, texts and stories in the Bible do not seem to address negatively same-sex sexual attraction between women unless one reads Romans chapter 1 in a specific way. There seems to be little material on other forms of sexual diversity described today as transgender, queer, and questioning, and intersex.[110] Connections between the contemporary identities of sexual and gender minorities and biblical stories or texts need to be inferred in some way, and these inferences have to be made based on interpretive decisions, and hermeneutic assumptions.

It is often claimed that Jesus has nothing to say about anything related to sexual orientation except to affirm the gender binary physiology of man and woman in marriage. However, this perspective is also a matter of opinion, debate and interpretation because Jesus names three kinds of eunuchs according to the Gospel of Matthew that calls simplistic gender categories into question. There is also an intense discussion of Jesus' as homoerotic example.[111] Many of us might feel uncomfortable with such a suggestion. Why might we feel uncomfortable? Perhaps because we cannot associate Jesus with sexual desire. Perhaps, even more so, we carry within us a disgust at such a suggestion?

Recent scholarship has shown that Jesus' description of the three kinds of eunuchs probably is the closest example we have in the Bible to finding a cultural bridge between sexual diversity then and now. Jesus defines three kinds of eunuchs, those born that way, those made that way by others, and those who chose that way for the sake of the Kingdom (Mt 19:12). Jesus' threefold classification of eunuchs is also reflective of common Greco-Roman cultural conceptions of the time with one key difference; Jesus affirms rather than ridicules eunuchs, thus challenging Roman ideas of manliness and gender bias. The idea that Jesus reflects a kind of understanding of sexual diversity in his time is further supported by Clement of Alexandria's (150-215) interpretation of the Mt 19:12 text. He claims that the kind of eunuch, described by Jesus as "so born" has a "natural repulsion of a woman" and he counsels such men not to marry.[112] For Roman men, particularly those under the influence of stoic philosophy, eunuchs were considered unmanly. In the next section of the book we will see that this cultural belief lies at the heart of the 4th century rejection of all forms of homo-eroticism by the Christianity of that time.[113]

As we explore the debate among authors today, we can see how seemingly pre-determined moral intuition shapes responses to gender diversity inclusion. If one is convinced that "homosexuality is an abomination or a sin," one will reject interpretations that question the direct link between the two texts in Leviticus seeming to condemn same-sex sexual intercourse and all forms of same-sex relationships. One could also be more prone to argue that the meaning of these texts should be universalized beyond their biblical context and must be expanded to include sexual diversity in general. Even though most early Christian arguments against homoerotic relationships did not proceed in the same way as theologians would argue today but rather were based on Greco-Roman conceptions of "manliness", our intuitive moral position might make us claim that we are making the "traditional" argument.

A more fundamental question for me becomes how to use the Bible as our measure as we explore the place and treatment of sexual and gender minority people in Christian communities. Should we not rather start by asking about a broader scriptural and gospel logic as discussed in Chapter 2 before we read the proof texts? Should we not rather ensure that we are rooted in the spirituality of walking the way of the gospel with one another in our consideration of the Bible? Where is our attention to the difficult and responsible work of making moral discernment together? Of course, we need to look at Leviticus and Romans 1, and we have to debate the arguments about strong gender complementarity. Yet, as I contended, we need the attitude of gospel posture as we engage the message of the Scriptures. Ultimately our discernment has to regard people as concrete human beings in the light of the great law of love. Any responsible interpretation of Leviticus 18, 20, Romans 1 or Genesis 1 and 2 requires this larger responsibility as basis.

The most consistent Protestant argument made for a traditional rejection of same-sex sexual relationships is contained in Robert Gagnon's book "The Bible and Homosexual Practice." Since its publication in 2001, this book has become an important text for those who argue for a welcoming but not affirming position in Christian churches. It is instructive to consider the endorsements this book received when first published. Those who endorsed the book are mostly associated with a particular movement in biblical studies described as the biblical theology movement of which Brevard Childs is one of the key architects. He was also one of the key endorsers. Many reviews of the book noted its strong basis in scholarship and argued that this is an important text to consider in debates about sexual and gender minority people in Christian communities (although most reviewers at the time referred to "gays" or "homosexuals").

Robert Gagnon's analysis is an example of a key problem we face in having debates about the place of sexual and gender minority people in the church. The problem is not in the first place with his arguments about biblical texts and the discussion of scholarship in them, but rather, with the assumptions that drive him to make judgments based on these texts. He is candid about those assumptions in his introduction. Rather than claiming that he makes a case for a particular position, he claims to present biblical, and thus Divine authority. It becomes clear that his own moral judgments are shaped by his experiences that include anecdotes that he acknowledges are largely non-representative of the experience of most sexual and gender minority Christians. To quote:

First there is clear, strong, and credible evidence that the Bible unequivocally defines same-sex intercourse as sin. Second, there exists no valid hermeneutical arguments, derived from either general principles or biblical interpretation or contemporary scientific knowledge and experience, for overriding the Bible's authority on this matter.[114]

From this point on Gagnon takes special care to argue text by text that "homosexuality" as in genital relations between men is consistently rejected by the bible. This he does, even in the case of the story of Sodom and Gomorrah, despite the considerable academic consensus that the homosexual interpretation of these text is post biblical.[115] Thus the question we are confronted with as we reflect on Gagnon's argument is this: to what extent has his pre-determined moral judgment determined his interpretive arguments? To what extent is he truly speaking for the testimony of the gospel? Any rational reader can see that Gagnon makes strong arguments for his claim. It is also clear that his interpretation is not the only possible one. It is an argument without the careful moral consideration of the impact on real people. It is an argument of judgment without the humble consideration that one particular interpretation might just be wrong. Most of all, it is a series of arguments that don't ask about the pastoral consequences of his claims. There is little consideration of possible harm done. Some supportive reviews of his work pointed to this problem in gentle ways. So, for example, Gabriel Fackre, professor Emeritus at Andover Newton Seminary, after a positive review wrote,

However, the church has a history of wrestling with controverted questions, and as a company of forgiven sinners knows of a divine grace that may translate into an exception to a rule as well as to its upholding.[116]

Here Fackre gently, and in the spirit of the gospel, points to the difficult communal task of moral discernment lacking in Gagnon's book. Fackre could be considered here as suggesting that, notwithstanding Gagnon's "biblical" arguments, it might be important also to consider a gracious approach of pastoral exception. In contrast, Gagnon's introduction suggests that he finds himself in the difficult area of moral decision making which relate to Haidt's moral category of sanctity and degradation (abjection or disgust). He invokes the Divine authority of sanctity against same-sex erotic love. He does so in a way that assumes that "the Bible speaks unequivocally and forcefully to this issue of homosexuality."[117]

Careful and humble rational discernment in the gospel will invite us to be cautious about such universalized and decisive claims. Is the Gagnon interpretation truly equal to something clear and unequivocal? Below I will show that a claim for complete unequivocal clarity on the rejection and judgment of "homosexuality" is at best overstated. Claiming such clarity would require us to ignore the cultural context of the Hebrew Bible as well as the Greco-Roman Hellenistic context of the New Testament and the early church. We also have to ignore the profound difference between patriarchal constructions of sexuality and gender and our understanding today. In addition, each of the texts invoked by Gagnon and others have contested interpretations and interpretation histories.

Why is it important to establish the lack of clarity and unequivocal interpretation? Because interpretation is the proverbial elephant in the room. Neither complete clarity nor an unequivocal position is possible based on the texts discussed. Even the use of the word homosexual presents a range of meanings that first need to be examined and critiqued in order to come to responsible moral discernment. With potential harm being inflicted on sexual and gender minority neighbors, we would need a greater burden of proof if we want to act responsibly in our moral discernment. This safeguard is particularly true in the light of the larger biblical frame of the love commandment "care" and "just love" developed in Chapter 2. As pointed out earlier, potential and real harm goes as far as psychological harm, and includes the negative effects of denying physical intimacy, greater suicide risk for sexual and gender minority youth, family break-down, unequal treatment of people, and sometimes incites extreme violence. Moreover, the behavior that is being denigrated is not in itself harmful to other human beings. We know today that loving same-sex relationships can be life-promoting and lead to great comfort joy and health. Does this kind of judgment and blanket rejection bring justice, healing and love to people? Are we making moral discernment through gospel eyes as we look at the Scriptures? These questions do not simply identify an interesting debate. People are being harmed.

Gagnon's argument is unconvincing and overreaching. I also question the moral implications of his judgments that generate harm to others. We all share the ability to be fallible human beings who have made our own gut level moral judgments while conversing with the Bible. However, we will need more solid ground to make an informed moral decision than this Gagnon's example. As William Stacey Johnson pointed out in his twin review of Jack Rogers' and Robert Gagnon's books, Rogers provides a credible theological framework for engaging the Bible while Gagnon does not.[118] At its heart, the issue here is about the naïve assumption that the Bible speaks and that we as Christians simply have to listen. Dale Martin writes about this assumption,

For me, this is not only a point about literary theory. It is also an ethical issue. I believe that one of the most serious impediments to the ethical use of Scripture, especially with regard to issues of gender and sexuality has been the myth of textual agency. ... People throughout history, therefore, have committed grave ethical offenses-supporting slavery, oppressing women, fighting unjust wars, killing, torturing and harming their fellow human beings-under cover of "the Bible says."[119]

Gagnon's claim that "Bible unequivocally defines same-sex intercourse as sin" is an example of such an assumption of textual agency. In fact, there are some very strong arguments to challenge such a reading of Scripture, particularly in the light of the harm it is doing. Examples of such interpretive challenges are represented in the work of Dale Martin, K. Renato Lings and James Brownson.[120] Brownson offers a strong over-all systematic challenge to most of Gagnon's arguments. Like Rogers, he goes further by seeking to discern a Biblical moral logic that will help us assess the moral questions involved for sexual and gender minority people today. In short, Brownson begins the work of careful responsible moral discernment of the moral logic of the Scriptures on erotic sexuality. Lings follows a different pattern. He uses 13 different English translations of the Bible and examines their translation decisions philologically and grammatically. This approach involves looking at words and patterns in the original text and comparing them to similar words and patterns in the rest of the Bible. His study is meticulous. Lings also draws from a much wider field of research to study the history of interpretation of specific texts and illuminates many misconceptions commonly accepted even by modern Bible translators and Hebrew and Greek Lexicons. He relays the arguments of contemporary theologians who write from a Feminist, Womanist and Queer perspective. Lings refers to Martin's detailed and persuasive work and meticulously examines specific arguments around the texts that are often cited by non-affirming authors.

It is important to remember here that my argument is not that Martin's, Brownson's or Lings' scholarship and interpretive arguments are incontestable. I maintain that their research demonstrates that Gagnon's conclusion about clarity and unequivocality is not sustainable. Christians who value the Bible will always offer different interpretations of the Bible. Given the interpretive ambiguity demonstrated by the scholars named above, when some interpretations are demonstrated to have generated harm, we have fundamental ethical responsibility to be open to question those interpretations in the light of the larger gospel witness. Open and ongoing debate is part of building omit insight into the riches of the Bible. What Martin, Brownson and Lings demonstrate is that Gagnon's claim for complete clarity and an unequivocal position in the Bible against all forms of erotic "homosexual practice" is unsupportable. These three authors bring a different spirit in approaching their arguments. None of them claim a kind of final authority for interpretation. They offer their scholarship for reflection and discussion in the spirit of a process of moral discernment. For example, rather than claiming a final authority on the matter, Brownson gently, starts to question his own previously traditional and conservative position and struggles to find a Biblical moral logic. Along with Fackre he asks if the biblical arguments should necessarily lead to the conclusion of a complete and universal non-affirmation of all sexual minority relationships?

My intention in the section that follows is not to give a full-fledged discussion of the texts that will be cited. Instead I focus on harm and the ethical and moral responsibility not to harm others. However, as a Reformed-Presbyterian Christian I do take the Bible very seriously. I regard it important to show that reaching interpretive conclusions based on the Biblical text has a strong and credible basis. The intent of the following section is thus to introduce the reader to some alternative interpretive approaches to the classical biblical texts associated with a non-affirming Christian stance. Much more needs to be said to further flesh out these biblical discussions. My hope is that, for the interested reader, the following section offers a primer to encourage readers to read further and follow up on sources cited.

What follows will look at the role of the creation narrative in Genesis 1 and 2 in dictating universal divinely required gender complementarity, the prohibitions of Leviticus 18 and 20, "a man shall not lie with a man...", the interpretation of Romans 1, and two sets of vice lists in 1 Corinthians and 2 Timothy. These texts are presented as specifically hostile to homoerotic relationships and make up the core argument of authors such as Gagnon.

Genesis and the Gender Binary

Non-affirming Arguments in the Reformed tradition often start with an interpretation of the creation story. In the Reformed tradition the story of the Bible is often told in terms of the scheme of creation-fall(sin)-redemption. There is nothing specifically in the texts that says that two women or men could not love each other. The argument is rather a theological-interpretive one that states that God created the woman as companion for the man and that a man shall leave his father and mother and cleave to his wife. I cite two extracts from the two creation stories in Genesis 1 and 2 like this,

Gen 1:26 – 27. Then God said, "And now we will make human beings; they will be like us and resemble us. They will have power over the fish, the birds, and all animals, domestic and wild, large and small." So God created human beings, making them to be like himself. He created them male and female,... (GNB)

Gen 2:21 -24. Then the LORD God made the man fall into a deep sleep, and while he was sleeping, he took out one of the man's ribs and closed up the flesh. He formed a woman out of the rib and brought her to him. Then the man said, "At last, here is one of my own kind--- Bone taken from my bone, and flesh from my flesh. 'Woman' is her name because she was taken out of man." That is why a man leaves his father and mother and is united with his wife, and they become one. (GNB)

 The "being united with his wife" often translated as "cleaving to," is taken as a sexual relationship and therefore other forms of sexual relationships are considered fundamentally against God's creative intent and covenant with humankind. The argument is that God made man and woman in this gender-binary way and that other forms of gender identity and sexual orientation is thus part of sin and "the Fall." This interpretation, which is supported by the Reformed theologian Karl Barth, is often read back into the Genesis stories in the light of New Testament texts. In modern contemporary discussions this argument is often connected to Paul's statement in Romans 1:26-27 that behavior, interpreted as homoerotic behavior, is "against nature"[121] In Matthew 19:4-6, the complementary camp argues that

Jesus explicitly enforces this conception of the gender complementarity in his response to questions about divorce.

There are many potential problems with this interpretation of Genesis 1 and 2. To begin, the use of Genesis 1 and 2 in a dogmatic way rather than a metaphorical way must be questioned in the light of the poetic and narrative styles of the stories. Most non-fundamentalist Christians don't read these Biblical chapters in literal ways, divorced from their original context and genre, to make scientific conclusions about reality. Why then employ these texts in that way when it comes to sexuality and gender? Another problem is the patriarchal cultural bias embedded in the text. A reading of a kind of binary sexual complementarity and a primacy of male over female poses many problematic questions in Christian communities that strive for gender equality as a gospel principle. In addition, Brownson discusses Genesis 1 and 2 in great detail and points to the well-known problem of patriarchal cultural assumptions in the text. He also describes the problem with interpreting "cling to his wife" as a statement on sex and sexuality. Brownson points to some very good historical-cultural reasons to see this biblical expression as a statement on the formation of a new kinship bond.[122] Lings also points to the problem with interpreting "united with" or "cleaving to" as representative of sexual union. He shows how the similar Hebrew expression is used for the relationship between Naomi and Ruth for their relationship. Moreover, Lings discusses the problems created by the erroneous translation of the Hebrew word for "side" by using the English word rib.[123] In fact, it seems that, pre-Eve, Adam, in the Hebrew text, is actually a being that contains both sexes. He specifically explores how the text employs singulars and plurals to emphasize this reality. Thus, the challenge with the argument from Genesis 1 and 2 is the many problems of language, translations, cultural context and then the inference of a moral message in a text which is poetry. Deducing a potentially harmful moral boundary from the beautiful poem of creation raises disturbing questions. To what extent are these stories, which probably took their final form during the exile, intended to shape moral guidance? Even if one accepts a strong emphasis on gender complementarity in the interpretation of Genesis 2, does this mean the outright and universal rejection of homosexual erotic companionship within the boundaries of faithfulness?

This text is often the key text for arguing that those who experience same-sex erotic attraction suffer from a disorder of God's creation. I ask, is there enough in these passages to reach such a strong and clear conclusion? Nicholas Wolterstorff does not believe so.[124] In fact he argues that, rather than seeing same-sex attraction as a disorder, we could understand it as a "creational variance." Doing so makes particular sense in the light of our growing knowledge of the complex factors that create a spectrum of sexual orientation. The creation stories thus do not offer unequivocal evidence that Christians should not affirm erotic relationships among people of the same sex. These stories provide an inspiring poetic vision of humans created to flourish in intimate relationships and in community. They do not provide definitive moral guidance for sexual relationships.

The laws of Leviticus

Lev 18:22 No man is to have sexual relations with another man; God hates that.

Lev 20:13 If a man has sexual relations with another man, they have done a disgusting thing, and both shall be put to death. They are responsible for their own death. (GNB)

Perhaps the most often cited texts by Christians to prove a very specific Divine disapproval of homoerotic relationships are Leviticus 18:22 and Leviticus 20:13. In some translations, these texts clearly state: "a man shall not lie with a man as with a woman," or as explicitly noted in the Good News Bible translation above, "no man is to have sexual relations with another man." Such translations make it seem like the original text makes an unequivocal and universal statement. The argument is that all same-sex sexual intercourse is so despicable, so disgusting, that it deserves the death penalty according to Lev 20:13. It is telling that Gagnon emphasizes the high degree of revulsion against same-sex sexual intercourse implied in the text.[125] Gagnon assumes that "a man who lies with a male as though lying with a woman" is equal to what he deems "homosexual intercourse."[126] Christians who have sought to affirm sexual and gender minority people today have recognized that these texts are experienced as "texts of terror," particularly the injunction of death which some claim is echoed by Paul in Romans 1:32 (They know that God's law says that people who live in this way deserve death. GNB) and the ensuing frightening torture and executions that occurred through the history of Christendom in the employment of the text as warrant for the death penalty later in church history and in civil law.

One contrary argument often made is that the contemporary application of this Levitical law for Christians is to take it out of context. According to this approach, many other injunctions in the law are not taken literally anymore, why pull this one out? In rebuttal it is argued that Paul obviously considered this law still in force due to his statements in Romans 1. Actually, there is little evidence that Paul was referring to Leviticus in Romans 1. The closest the text gets to Leviticus 20:13 is the injunction of death, but that injunction in the Romans text addresses a wide range of wickedness. A more sophisticated argument of context is advanced by Wolterstorff. He argues that the universalization of these two prohibitions to all forms of same-sex erotic relationship is moving these texts beyond their original intent and context.[127] The arguments from the biblical scholarship of Rabbi Jacob Milgrom, Lings and Brownson further adds credence to Wolterstorff's perspective. Jacob Milgrom, in his influential commentary on Leviticus writes,

Thus since illicit carnal relations are implied by the term *miskiibe 'isso*, it may be plausibly suggested that homosexuality is herewith forbidden for only the equivalent degree of forbidden heterosexual relations, namely, those enumerated in the preceding verses (D. Stewart). However, sexual liaisons occurring with males outside these relations would not be forbidden. And since the same term *miskebe 'isso* is used in the list containing sanctions (20:13), it would mean that sexual liaisons with males, falling outside the control of the paterfamilias, would be neither condemnable nor punishable. Thus *miskiibe 'isso*, referring to illicit male-female relations, is applied to illicit male-male relations, and the **literal meaning of our verse is: do not have sex with a male with whose widow sex is forbidden**. In effect, this means that the homosexual prohibition applies to Ego with father, son, and brother (subsumed in v. 6) and to grandfather grandson, uncle-nephew, and stepfather-stepson, but not to any other male .[128]

Milgrom concludes that these texts, read in their context in the law, do not represent a universal condemnation of same-sex male erotic relationships. What they do represent is a prohibition of male-male sexual intercourse for married Jewish men under specific circumstances. It is therefore instructive that within Judaism today the simplistic application of these texts to same-sex relationships is not necessarily a given. Moreover, it does not come from a "liberal" source but from a highly respected conservative Rabbi and biblical scholar.

Another consideration is that most non-affirming arguments that universalize these texts as unequivocal rejection of all male same-sex erotic relationships have devoted little discussion of the text itself and the bias in its English translation. The problem is that the original Hebrew simply does not say what the English translations make it say. Many translations interpolate two words "as" and "with" and then interpret a Hebrew word which literally means "lyings" in a particular way. It also translates a word that most commonly means "wife" as "woman." As a Hebrew scholar, Lings argue that a literal translation of Lev 18:22 should read, *"With (a) male you shall not lie (the) lyings (of a) woman. (an) abomination (is) that."* The interpretive rendering of the texts, as in most modern English translations, makes it look deceptively straight forward. As Lings points out, if there was an intention in the holiness code of Leviticus to make a clear and unequivocal statement against all forms of homoerotic behavior, the law could simply say, "you (as a man) shall not lie with a man."[129] Both Lings and Brownson show the rich literature produced on these texts in both Judaism and Christianity. Some forms of Conservative Judaism have moved to thinking about these texts as prohibiting anal intercourse only, and not necessarily other forms of homoerotic behavior. Some rabbinic scholars emphasize the active role and others the passive role in such intercourse as the real problem. However, David Stewart and Rabbi Jacob Milgrom have each pointed to the importance to consider that these texts are located in the midst of laws against all forms of incest. Lings has taken this idea and has made an argument, particularly based on the odd wording of the text itself and its location in Lev 20:13, that this is a prohibition against incest including male on male incest within the kinship group. In this Lings essentially echoes the important work of Jacob Milgrom. All these arguments underline that these two texts appear in a <u>context</u> in which married Jewish men are addressed in relation to their spouse, family and kinship group. To ignore these dimensions is to pull these texts out of context and simplistically make them speak as a universal prohibition and condemnation, essentially then employing them as proof-texts. It is therefore important for interpreters in both Christianity and Judaism to think deeply about our responsibility in using these texts to create universal judgments on same-sex erotic love.

Questions about the validity of applying these texts to today's context remain important to consider in our gospel shaped moral discernment. The scholarly insights into the original language and its meaning in the Levitical context also demonstrate the lack of unequivocal clarity in interpreting and translating these texts. Such perspectives call into question the long-held assumption that the Hebrew Bible displays revulsion against all forms of homoeroticism. There is no doubt that homosexual rape, adultery by means of a same-sex encounter, and same-sex exploitation of minors are behaviors that clearly violate Scriptural sexual boundaries of "care" and "just love." This does not necessarily mean that all forms of same-sex relationships are scripturally taboo. Perhaps this understanding helps us grasp the positive biblical portrayal of story of the relationship between David in Jonathan, Ruth and Naomi, and Jesus and the beloved disciple?[130] In addition, Lings points out that the family incest context of the texts in Leviticus also solves the puzzle of why these injunctions seem so different from ancient legal codes of other nations with parallel legal codes of that time. He cites examples of other extra-biblical injunctions against male on male incest.[131] Clearly, not even these Levitical texts, so often considered as having self-evident meaning, can simply be considered an unequivocal rejection of all homoerotic relationships. At the very least, as we think of sexual and gender minorities in their concrete humanity, we might need to think compassionately of another Scriptural way.

Romans Chapter 1:24-27

Rom 1:24 - 27 And so God has given those people over to do the filthy things their hearts desire, and they do shameful things with each other. They exchange the truth about God for a lie; they worship and serve what God has created instead of the Creator himself, who is to be praised forever! Amen. Because they do this, God has given them over to shameful passions. Even the women pervert the natural use of their sex by unnatural acts. In the same way the men give up natural sexual relations with women and burn with passion for each other. Men do shameful things with each other, and as a result they bring upon themselves the punishment they deserve for their wrongdoing. (GNB)

One of the most important passages debated today is the reading and interpretation of the second half of Romans 1:26-27. This passage seems to present a clear revulsion and condemnation of all forms of homoerotic behavior including lesbian relationships. In fact, this is the only place in the Bible where there seems to be a comment on lesbian relationships. This passage could be considered the "piece de resistance" for those who argue strongly for a blanket rejection of all forms of homoeroticism. In modern translation it seems to speak very clearly against both male homosexuality and lesbianism. It also seems to declare such behavior as "against nature."[132] The gender complementarity theology based in Genesis 2 also relies on the corroboration of this text.

Interestingly, the early church very seldom interpreted Romans 1:26 as a reference to lesbian homoerotic expression. Most early Christians saw this text as speaking strongly and fiercely against forms of excessive and illicit heterosexual behavior. In fact, the first time a lesbian association with this text is made is by John Chrysostom (349-407) and his interpretation is not followed by anyone else until the 12th century scholar Pierre le Chantre and then followed by Thomas of Aquinas (1225-1274). Aquinas picks up the lesbian reading of Romans 1 and makes lesbianism into a serious form of sinful behavior.[133] Given these factors, it is unlikely that Paul meant this verse to point to lesbian forms of homoeroticism.

But, what about men? Some affirming interpreters have read the seeming allusion to the behavior of the men Paul describes in verse 27 as "against nature," and tried to make the argument that for those for whom homoerotic desire is "natural or inborn" this does not apply. However, the use of the idea of what is "natural" has a specific historical context in the Greco-Roman and particularly Stoic context.

Wolterstorff observes that the kind of behavior described in the context of the whole chapter 1 of Romans, is that of excessively wicked people. The charges of wickedness such as "greed, jealousy, malice, deceit and gossip (Rom 1:29) can not in any just way simply be attributed to contemporary sexual and gender minority Christians. He argues that it would constitute an offense against Christian justice to generalize judgment on such wickedness to all forms of same-sex relationships.[134] I argue later that the "born this way" approach also presents problems. However, I submit that Wolterstorff's argument is very important to consider. After all, we are not to bear false witness against our sexual and gender minority neighbors.

As mentioned above, there are cultural dimensions of the concept "nature" in the Greco-Roman culture of the time that deserves consideration. Byrne Fone demonstrates persuasively how Greco-Roman belief in the moral virtue of same-sex love shifted to a belief that such homo-erotic love is "against nature" in the period directly preceding the Christian era. He shows how Neo-Platonic thought and Stoic philosophy, drawing on Plato's *Laws*, Plutarch's *Erotikos* as well as *Erotes*, a document with an unknown author, all move towards understanding "nature" in terms of a new Roman social convention that censured forms of homo-eroticism that involved a passive male.[135] Medieval theology that declared "sodomy" as an act and sin "against nature," is thus problematic because of the influence of documents such as *Laws, Erotikos,* and *Erotes* on medieval thinking. It appears that cultural social convention played a role in Pauline conceptions of same-sex relationships as did some of the cultural misogyny that considered women inferior. The cultural patriarchal misogyny of that time played a decisive role in establishing a growing anti-homoerotic sentiment. As it was assumed that men were superior to women, so it was assumed that it is "unnatural" for a man to behave sexually like a woman. These ideas were commonly accepted in Paul's world and is highly likely to have shaped his thinking.

The Roman cultural understanding of "nature" also raises serious questions about the interpretation of "natural" in the New Testament texts in arguments today that often glosses "against nature" as against God's created order. There is a logical circularity to modern arguments that connects a blanket anti-homoerotic interpretation of Romans 1 with an anti-homoerotic interpretation of Genesis 1 and 2. The hermeneutic move is to absolutize creation of male and female in the creation stories as a Divine natural law for gender complementarity. "Nature" in Romans 1 is then glossed as "God's natural law of gender complementarity. This is then connected with Jesus' statement on divorce in Matthew 19:4-6, which is taken as further support for gender complementarity. Furthermore, assuming from this complementarity argument appropriate sexual intimacy is then associated with procreation. As, it is argued that homoerotic intimacy does not have the potential of biological procreation and is thus "against nature" which the circular argument relates back to Romans 1.

In addition to the cultural meaning of "nature" at the time of Paul's writing of the Letter to the Romans, scholars have pointed out that the reading and interpretation of "against nature" in both its Scriptural and its cultural context is much more complex and problematic than simply projecting a Divine natural law or a theology of the orders of creation on the use of "nature" in Romans 1.. Considering the Greco-Roman culture of the time and the use of the phrases, "nature," and "natural," "Against nature" in Pauline literature, and the cultural context of the time, most likely refer to "what is culturally unacceptable." So, for example, in Romans 11:24 Paul claims that God acts "against nature" grafting the gentiles into the olive tree of the people of God. Wolterstorff points also to Paul's use of the same root word in 1 Corinthians 11:14. There Paul argues that men with long hair are acting against nature. All these uses of "nature" suggests that Paul uses this concept in the commonly understood Greco-Roman way of his time. When John Calvin comments on 1 Cor. 11:14 in his commentary on Corinthian he makes clear that Paul's use of nature is about what is the custom of the time.[136]

There are also the other culturally contextual factors to consider in relation to this letter specifically addressed to the Roman church. Brownson points to the rule of Emperor Gaius (Caligula) and how the excesses that Paul describes almost exactly matches the scandalous behavior of sexual excess in the court of Gaius.[137] Thus we have here a potential Scriptural rejection of a form of excessive selfish sexual lust expressed in abusive ways by particularly wicked people. Brownson makes a strong case for reading Paul's censure as a censure against excessive desire rather than a blanket rejection of all forms of homoerotic love. I accept that Richard Hays, in his response to John Boswell's arguments on the Romans text, is correct in identifying Paul's mention of sexual behavior simply as an example of the larger problem of human rebellion against God.[138] In fact, Hays argument parallels and reflects the tension between the exegesis of the passage and a responsible hermeneutic of moral discernment. Paul and most of his listeners probably did consider homoerotic relationships as he understood it as signs of rebellion against God in a more general way. In this they were representative of a particularly Roman cultural conception of manliness as we will explore later. However, for Paul those behaviors were perceived as being practiced in the context of extreme wickedness and occasionally within the context of Greco-Roman religious ritual practices. It is therefore much less credible to employ the Pauline statements in Romans 1 to apply it to faithful Christians who are sexual and gender minorities today.

Hays' argument for an obvious connection with the creation stories in Genesis 1 and 2 is much less convincing. Because Hays reads those stories in ways that simplistically projects later theological traditions about procreation and manliness on those texts. The dark and disturbing history of Christian traditions on the interpretation of the expression "against nature" is not without bearing on how we read and interpret Romans 1 today.[139]

We will explore the development of those traditions more fully in the next section of the book. In response to Hays, Dale Martin has argued that a clear and distinct heterosexist bias is evident in Hays' exegesis.[140] By that he means that Hays reads Romans through his own experience as a heterosexual man. Martin raises some interesting points which bear consideration as we think about the way the later Christian bias against homoerotic relationships and sex in general has shaped a culture within Christianity that assumed heterosexual orientation as morally normative. Nevertheless, it is Brownson's argument, supported by Wolterstorff's ethical observations, about the key role of excessive sexual behavior in the Romans text that appears to be the most important insights. From the perspective of moral discernment, we have a problem if we make committed covenantal Christian erotic male same-sex relationships equal to what is described in Romans 1:27 and what follows. Ignoring our ethical and moral responsibility to speak truth about our neighbors and to be just and loving in our discernment risks practicing the same evils Paul denounces in Romans 1:29. The excess and selfish behaviors described simply do not fit.

Lings points to a striking similarity uncovered in the work of the Jesuit scholar James Alison of Paul's language here in Romans 1:26-17 with the apocryphal work, "The Book of Wisdom" also called "The Wisdom of Solomon." This text from the Septuagint (Greek translation of the Hebrew Bible) casts light on the emphasis on idolatry in Romans. Allison and Lings also refer to the changed context in which Paul comments on idolatry and the practices that would be common in Tarsus, Corinth (where he probably penned this letter) and Rome.[141] There were different forms of Greek religion that included practices such as Paul describes as part of their worship. These contextual and cultural factors suggest a more cautious approach than reading this text as a blanket rejection of all homoerotic expression. In fact, the later association with such behaviors as "unrighteousness, wickedness, covetousness, maliciousness; full of envy, murder, strife, deceit, malignity; whisperers, backbiters, hateful to God, insolent, haughty, boastful, inventors of evil things, disobedient to parents, without understanding, covenant-breakers, without natural affection, unmerciful" bear no relationship to contemporary committed relationships of sexual and gender minority Christians.[142]

Another important challenge in interpreting Romans 1 is the rhetorical structure of the whole chapter and its connection with what follows. Douglas Atchison Campbell has advanced an argument for paying more attention to the rhetorical structure of Romans and the false teacher Paul is addressing.[143] Many scholars have noted that Paul is actually constructing a rhetorical trap for his readers in Romans 1. He describes practices that those in the Church of Rome will find unacceptable. There is also allusion to a false teacher in the community that Paul is opposing with his letter. It is likely that Paul is echoing some of that false teacher's argument to get the enthusiastic agreement of his hearers (readers), which is then followed by his stunning accusation in Romans 2:1. The Good News Bible states it like this,

Do you, my friend, pass judgment on others? You have no excuse at all, whoever you are. For when you judge others and then do the same things which they do, you condemn yourself.

All Paul's readers and hearers including us, and including people who quickly move to condemn, attack and exclude sexual and gender minorities today. Thereby, all become implicated in Paul's masterful argument that, "all have sinned and fall short of the glory of God"(Romans 3:23).[144] It is interesting that Richard Hays approvingly notes this argument suggesting that any moral discernment about homoerotic relationships should be made with humility and with a deep sense of gravity.[145] The expressions of disgust by Christians against sexual and gender minority people today seems to play exactly into the Apostle's canny rhetorical strategy to confront all of us with our own sin rather than condemn others. It might very well be that Paul had a contextually shaped bias against same-sex erotic relationships. However, what must be considered, based on the questions raised above, is that, this view was rooted in a particular cultural context and practices that do not simplistically implicate same-sex relationships in loving commitment today. In addition, the simplistic association between homoerotic relationships today and the wickedness described in Romans 1 is both untruthful and harmful. It is most likely that what Paul was offended by in erotic same-sex relationships was colored by cultural behaviors in his time that did not reflect "care" or "just love." Given all these factors a claim for reading Romans 1:24-27 as an unequivocal biblical sanction against all erotic same-sex relationships is not persuasive.

The Vice Lists of 1 Corinthians 6:9: and 1 Timothy 1:10

1Co 6:9 Surely you know that the wicked will not possess God's Kingdom. Do not fool yourselves; people who are immoral or who worship idols or are adulterers or homosexual perverts… (GNB)

1Tim 1:10 for the immoral, for sexual perverts, for kidnappers, for those who lie and give false testimony or who do anything else contrary to sound doctrine. (GNB)

The two texts cited above contain lists of vices that Paul describes as unacceptable within the Christian community. The careful reader will immediately note how inappropriate and ambiguous the use of "homosexual perverts" in the Good News Bible translation is. Homosexual as a modernist (late 19th century) medical term simply does not fit the original Greek text. Furthermore, does this translation mean to imply that all homosexuals are perverts or that there are certain kind of homosexuals that are perverts? The 1 Corinthians text contains two words in the original Greek that are considered a sanction against all homoerotic relationships by some.[146] The 1 Timothy text contains one of these words. The first contested word in 1 Corinthians is *malakoi* and the word that occurs in both 1 Corinthians and 1 Timothy is *arsenokoitai(s)*. Some modern translations have chosen to translate *arsenokoitai(s)* in both these texts as "homosexual." It is very clear that this translation is simply wrong. It is wrong in the first place because it projects in 19th and 20th century medical concept on an ancient text. Secondly, this particular word in Greek has a contested meaning. Literally the word means a combination of man and bed. More than that literal translation we do not know for sure. What we do know is that this word has only been found in these two texts and in other Christian texts that seem to repeat them at a later time. There are no decisive parallels in the Greek language of the time to illuminate its meaning.[147] What we can deduce with some confidence is that this word speaks of sexual impropriety of some kind and most likely, given the other vices outlined, exploitative sexual behavior. I footnoted Gagnon's discussion above: he is convinced that both *malakoi* and *arsenokoitai(s)* denote "homosexual practice." However, his premise is based on his reading the other biblical texts which he believes reject homoerotic expression of any kind. That is to say, because Gagnon reads other biblical texts as rejecting all forms of homoerotic intimacy, he finds these texts to confirm his perspective. It is a circular argument and therefore, in the light of the discussion of other texts above, an exceptionally weak one. Contemporary scholarship continues to debate the meaning of *arsenokoitai(s)* and will likely do so for some time to come. Already in 1986, Richard Hays noted that, though he did not agree with Boswell's arguments on this word, the interpretation of it needs ongoing work.[148] One of the strongest challenges to Gagnon's reading of these words can be found in the work of Dale Martin.[149] Both Brownson and Lings give detailed attention to the problems presented by translating *malakoi* and *arsenokoitai(s)*.

The word *malakoi* is somewhat easier to translate. This word literally means "soft". In early Christian thinking this word was understood as someone who lacked moral courage and who sought to indulge in extravagance of dress, food and drink. Following our knowledge of Greco-Roman conceptions of manliness, Gagnon believes the word denotes the passive ("woman like" in his thinking) partner in a sexual encounter. This would lead to a translation of this word as "effeminate". Some modern Bible translations follow that line of thinking. Of course, this particular interpretation confronts us with Paul seemingly reifying a misogynistic cultural assumption! There are actually many theories about the interpretation of both *malakoi* and *arsenokoitai(s)* most of which do not support Gagnon's interpretation. Unfortunately, and likely due to bias against sexual and gender minorities, many modern Bible translations choose a similar position to Gagnon's questionable interpretation. Lings points out that if Paul wanted to condemn all forms of homoerotic practices or homosexual prostitution in particular, he would have had other very clear Greek words at his disposal.[150] Jerome's Latin translation of the Bible (382) simply translates *malakoi* as *molles* which means "soft ones." It is thus likely that *malakos* refers to a lack of moral courage - a "softness" of resolve.[151]

So far, we have dealt with the word *malakos,* but what about the second term, *arsenokoitai(s)* which occurs both in the 1 Cor 6:9 and 1 Tim 1:10? Could this word be the only place in the Bible where all forms of same-sex intimate relationships are clearly and unequivocally rejected as wicked? Robert Gangon makes a case for reading *arsenokoitai* as a rejection of active same-sex sexual activity. He bases his argument in reference to Lev 18:22, particularly in its Greek translation in the Septuagint version of the Old Testament.[152] The translation of this word is one of the most difficult puzzles of biblical translation. The problem is that this word does not occur in general Greek literature of that time. The only extra biblical references in Greek to this word occur as references to its use in 1 Cor 6:9 and I Tim 1:10. The word could be translated literally as "male-liers" (not liars!). But the part of the word translated with liers could also mean "beds." Clearly this word has something to do with illicit sexual behavior of men in beds. In Romans 13:13 the word for "liers" (*koite*) is usually translated with something like "promiscuity" (for example see the ISV). The fact is that we simply don't know what this word means exactly.[153] The best we can do is to deduct that Paul and the author of 1 Timothy are referring to some kind of abusive or exploitative male sexual activity.[154]   Scholars like Harrell have noted that in 1 Tim 1:10 *arsenokoitais* is placed between "fornicators" and "slave traders" suggesting some form of abusive sexual behaviour.[155] Perhaps, following the tradition of translation of Rom 13:13 we could say with some confidence that this word refers to promiscuous exploitative males. The fairly common tendency to move away from the wisdom of Tyndale and KJV translation which emphasize male sexual abuse (abusers of themselves with mankind) towards translating *arsenokoitai(s)* as sodomite or homosexual, says more about the bias of the translators than the actual text.   Regardless of what the hidden agendas behind the translations may be, claiming with certainty that *arsenokoitai(s)* indicate all sexual minority people who are in erotic same-sex relationships is not sustainable.[156]

At this point it is important to remember that my argument here is that none of these often-cited biblical texts offer clear unequivocal and unambiguous condemnation of contemporary forms of same-sex relationships, particularly those that reflect "care" and "just love." If we were to assume a universal Christian sanction against all forms of erotic same-sex relationships, it would require that we also assume the validity of socio-cultural patriarchal and Roman cultural customs and conviction of the time.   Even if some of us as Christian interpreters choose to read these texts in that way, we have to face the reality of the larger biblical logic of the love of God and neighbor weighed against the harm being done to people of sexual and gender minorities. There is no biblical warrant for doing harm.

The Use of Science

Some people who identify as sexual and gender minorities emphasize that they are born the way they are. Those who are Christian sometimes argue that God made them this way and that rejecting their sexual identity is also rejecting God's creative act in making them who they are.   Those who reject all forms of homoerotic expression as sinful have tried to respond to this argument. In the area of science, however, all of us who are not scientists often flounder. This is particularly true of Gagnon's attempts to discredit the idea of "born this way" scientifically.   Before we explore the implications of the "born this way" argument, whether it helpful or unhelpful in determining Christian moral decisions, it is worth attending to a strong critique of Gagnon's work by a scientist.

The respected Penn State University scientist Carl S. Keener delivers a destructive review of Gagnon's engagement with science.[157]   Keener points to Gagnon's selective use of studies and misunderstanding of scientific data. He points out that Gagnon charges the scientist Dean Hamer with complaints that are not documented and does not tell his readers that Hamer was exonerated after a complaint was made against his research. Gagnon also cites one study by Bailey and ignores several others that contradicts Gagnon's favored conclusion. Of course, all these discussions of biology, genetics, and brain chemistry, wade into the tension between nature and nurture along with (1) the social construction of sexuality and gender identity; and (2) the philosophical difference between extreme social constructivism (which assumes that sexual identity is a complete human and culturally conditioned construction); and (3) biological determinism (which assumes that biology absolutely determines sexual orientation). Keener points out that in his view this dichotomy is false. Sometimes things simply are a certain way in the biological world, but this reality is not necessarily totally deterministic. There is an interplay between socio-cultural factors, human development and biological reality. However, he maintains that biological factors play a large and essential role in the formation of sexual orientation. I think that we can and should forgive Gagnon for misunderstanding scientific studies or for missing key data because he is not a scientist. The real challenge lies in the way Gagnon is trying to use the data he presents. Simply put, what we engage with as arm-chair scientists, and how we engage it, is often shaped by our pre-determined intuitive moral decisions. Gagnon is no different in that regard. Unfortunately, this particular example of arm-chair science leads to harm.

Since the publication of Gagnon's book there has been increasing interest in the role of biology in sexual orientation. As already mentioned, there has been a respectable volume of literature establishing the harm done to sexual and gender minority people through religious rejection and the abusive "double bind" of imposed celibacy. How are we to engage these scientific developments as Christians, and how can they help inform our moral decisions in relation to sexual and gender minority people? The final section of this book addresses the question of building a Biblically and theologically based framework of our moral discernment. At this time, it might be helpful to identify what is helpful and what is unhelpful in the "born this way" argument as we try to make moral sense of nature and nurture as Christians.

First, claiming that someone is born in a certain way is not an adequate argument for moral acceptance. For example, a simplistic argument that a pedophile or a psychopath can also claim a genetic basis for their behavior would be insufficient. As Christians we need more than genetic and biologically determined data to make a good moral decision. We need to ask additional questions, theological questions, about human flourishing, the way people function in community, and how the central command of Christ to love God and one another is lived out in practice. We also have to ask about harm, rights and dignity. In fact, one of today's most important concerns is whether Christians are honoring the dignity and rights of our neighbors who are sexual and gender minorities. We must face the data we now have about the harm we are doing to people. Even though the "born this way" claim is not decisive for reasons given above, it remains relevant to our moral discernment. The reasons why we would disapprove of pedophilia or psychopathy are because these kinds of biologically influenced dispositions are potentially harmful to others and violate "care" and "just love." Simply put, these behaviors violate the love commandment. Covenanted loving same-sex relationships do not violate the love commandment. To the extent that sexual orientation is partly a biological pre-disposition, perhaps a creational variance, in concert with our development and growth as human beings in a wider socio-cultural world, we need to take seriously our growing understanding of this reality and the potentially harmful impact on people when we deny such a reality. Because our erotic sexual dimension contributes significantly to our sense of well-being, this pre-disposition, today described as sexual orientation, becomes an important factor in our process of moral discernment.

To reprise, the biblical analysis so far it is helpful to return to Robert Gagnon's claim cited earlier,

However, on this issue, as on any other, if a clear, unequivocal, and pervasive stance in the Bible can be shown to exist-across the Testaments and accepted for nearly two millennia of the church's existence-then the burden of proof lies with those in the church who take a radically different approach to the issue.[158]

At first read, there might be something quite convincing about Gagnon's statement. Of course, if our collective Christian wisdom, our Bible, and our history support something as fundamentally important to our faith we should handle it with great care and preservation. There is also something very wrong with this statement. Consider that Christians in relatively recent times (the last 200 years) have rejected slavery and, more recently, discrimination against women, and apartheid. These changes challenged 2000 years of Christian tradition and Biblical teaching and turned it on its head. We needed no less than a new Biblical moral vision to lead us through thoughtful, sophisticated, and profound reflection on the meaning and intent of the life, ministry, death and resurrection of Christ.

Christians have now concluded that slavery is out of step with the heart of Christ's teaching on the love of our neighbor and God's intent for humankind to flourish in their living before God. This conclusion remains affirmed despite the fact that a strong, clear, and seemingly unequivocal Biblical case can be made for slavery by citing specific biblical texts. The same can be said for many Christian communities in their consideration of male/female gender discrimination, male hierarchical dominance, and even the ownership of women and daughters by their husbands. After all, all these abhorrent practices can also be said to be ensconced in the Levitical law. Rightly so, many Christians have concluded that the old Hebraic patriarchal codes, the Greco-Roman forms of patriarchy and their offshoots, did not reflect well, the teaching of Christ and God's intent for human flourishing. We learned from science about the equality of women. In this case too, people could make a clear, and seemingly unequivocal, Biblical case for gender inequality, as some still do. However, many Christian communities rejected this approach and are, albeit imperfectly, seeking to bring gender equity into our communities.

In the chapters that are to follow, I continue developing the thesis that there is a very good basis for questioning the 1600 years of destructive and harmful teaching by the church in relation to sexual and gender minorities. History bears witness to the wounds of torture, live burnings, and child abuse instigated by the Christian church in the name of biblical teaching. In fact, the moral question of inflicting harm will loom large in the following chapters as we explore how Christians misbehaved in the name of this teaching of the church. People who practiced some form of homoerotic behavior, and others simply accused of this without proof, faced, persecution, torture, live burning, and other forms of extreme violent execution. All of this have been done in the name of Christ and the teaching of the church. On this matter, rather than an illustrious history of good teaching, the historical evidence suggests a dark and sordid and immoral picture when it comes to the treatment of real people.

Conclusion

Why then are some Christians so "hell-bent" on condemning, judging, and rejecting sexual and gender minority people today? Why the extreme disgust and hot rhetoric? Why do others insist on a welcoming and loving approach to sexual and gender minority people while also presenting them with the double bind of not affirming them in their relational identity? In contrast, why do an increasing number of North American evangelical Christians now argue for marriage equality, equal human rights, and the welcome and affirmation of sexual and gender minority people within Christian communities? As I have argued so far and will continue to do so, the answers emerge out of a complex interplay of cultural social construction, evolutionary, psychological, and experiential factors.

Behind the non-affirming approaches there might also be a sense of a long history of a "historically shaped consciousness," or as German theologians described it the "Wirkungsgeschichte" (historical function) of texts. By this I mean and assume that biblical texts in Christian history take on a power and influence of their own that change over time. The "Wirkungsgeschichte" of a text can be loosely translated as "the working out of a text through history." I do not use the ideas of "historically shaped consciousness" or "Wirkungsgeschichte" slavishly in the way that the philosopher Hans-Georg Gadamer developed them, but rather as an attempt to recognize that the evolution of interpretations and meanings attached the biblical texts have real material consequences in history. The prejudices of the past and the legally and religiously sanctioned violence against sexual minorities of the past 1100 years still linger in our consciousness. The Pauline claim that, "They know that God's law says that people who live in this way deserve death" (Rom 1:32), may not have been intended to lead to the torture and live burning of those accused of sodomy in the medieval period, but that text took on a meaning and interpretation that was employed to abusively physically harm people. Another case in point is how the story of the possible attempted rape of angelic visitors in the city of Sodom told in Genesis 19 became "sodomy" over time. The conjunction of Roman 1:32 and Genesis 19 led, over time, to civil laws against "sodomy" and the prosecution of "sodomites" associated with the heinous "sin against nature" that spread through the British Empire and still exerts power in jurisdictions such as Uganda where attempts remain to enact the death penalty against "sodomites." So powerful are the forces of these ideas that the state minister of "ethics and integrity" of Uganda, the Right Reverend Father Simon Lokodo, claimed, in an interview with Stephen Fry in 2013, that the rape of young girls is natural and is morally preferable to consensual homosexual sex.[159] The texts we have examined above are all subject to this process of condensing and thinning of meaning with real harmful material consequences for sexual and gender minority people. As I have done so far, I do not necessarily make conclusions for other religious traditions and the ways they do ethical and moral reasoning. However, I hope that the discussion above could be helpful for reflection in diverse religious contexts.

For this reason, we are forced to look the historical record squarely in the face. In the next section of this book I endeavor to do that. I will begin by considering the message of early Christianity and the unprecedented spread of the Christian message over the Roman Empire and beyond. The 19th century historian and missiologist, Adolf Von Harnack described the characteristics of this message and the behavior of early Christians as "the gospel of love and charity." That early period contained its beautiful and laudable moments of Christian love in action. That period also contained some dark times and questionable developments that led to the violence that would ensue against people who engage in same-sex relationships during the medieval period.

The next section of the book tells the story of the shaping of Christian gender and sexual conceptions out of the cauldron of the Greco-Roman world and Greek philosophical assumptions. This story is followed by dark and painful medieval developments, the Inquisition, and Protestant forms of extreme violence against people accused of homoerotic behavior. It will become clear that the myth of the sin of sodomy evolved over time and described vastly different practices. Its evolution is shaped by misogynistic bias in the Greco Roman world, mistranslation of texts, and popular myths of time. During much of its history it was not specifically focused on same-sex activity but rather on sexual acts that were considered against what was considered natural within specific cultural contexts. Sodomy became a foil for different forms of exploitation, abuse and church-sanctioned torture and violence. We will also see how the stealing of the assets of people and organizations became a major motivating force for accusations of sodomy or buggery and the entrenchment of violent behavior in law. We will explore the development of doctrine and the creation of the myth of the sin of Sodom as a homoerotic sin. We will trace how this theology of the sin against nature would emerge as a frightening frenzy of Christian torture in killing by the 12th and 13th century. What this historical journey will demonstrate is that "the accepted stance of nearly two millennia" of prohibiting and persecuting same-sex sexual behavior is inextricably entangled with violence, murder, torture, child abuse, stealing and hatred in the name of Jesus Christ. Much of its history was not only focused on same-sex acts but also on many heterosexual behaviors considered completely acceptable today. The very assumption that there is an "accepted tradition of two millennia" is itself an inaccurate description of the checkered history. Rather than a long trustworthy and holy tradition, I argue that history challenges us to confess, repent and hang our heads in shame for the treatment of people who were accused of or engaged in homoerotic relationships.

Section 2: The Shame of Traditions and History

CHAPTER 5: INFANT CHRISTIANITY - THE GOSPEL OF LOVE AND CHARITY

The extraordinary spread of the Christian faith during the first three centuries has many causes and explanations. One manuscript that is often used to cast light on this historical missionary spread is the *Letter to Diognetus.*[160] Although dating of this letter is debatable, the consensus places it in the second century. The author and the recipient are not historically identifiable despite many theories. Most likely, this is one of the earliest records of Christian apologetic writing. If so, it casts light on how Christians perceived the expansion of their faith during this nascent period of the Christian movement. David Bosch notes the changing atmosphere in this early period and points to the rise of the idea that Christians were somehow perceived as different and inspiring in their ethical example as represented in the *Letter to Diognetus* and the identification of Christians as a "third race" by Tertullian.[161] In fact, Bosch references Harnack's persuasive argument for the phenomenon of "the gospel of love and charity" in which Christians slowly transformed the Roman Empire. Harnack actually uses the phrase *"Das Evangelium der Liebe und Hilfleistung."* The translation of "charity" used by Moffatt does not capture completely the focus of *"Hilfleistung."* Even though charity in English could mean doing good deeds, it could also relay an idea of simple good will – being charitable. "Hilfleistung" definitely points to action and particularly the will to practically help others.[162] Perhaps it would be more accurate to translate Harnack's famous expression as "The Gospel of Love and Helpfulness." These early Christian examples are instructive in our quest for moral discernment.

Harnack's meticulous analysis of original sources still represents a strong historical rendering of the attitudes, behaviors, beliefs, and sociological conditions that aided the growth of early Christianity. Many more recent studies have enhanced his arguments including the work of Peter Brown, Lane Fox, Alan Kreider, Ramsay MacMullen, and Michael Green.[163] What is surprising about Harnack's study is how contemporary scholarship has continued to support his claims for the loving character of early Christianity. Not the least among these studies is the Sociologist Rodney Stark's work on early Christianity.[164] In this chapter we will explore the movement of Christianity from the first century to late antiquity through the lens of expansion. The following chapter explores this period through the lens of the construction of gender as Empire and Christian faith reshape each other. In describing the best research, we have about the spread of early Christianity I do not wish to idealize or romanticize the movement or to claim that it had a form of purity never again achieved. In fact, all the authors cited above, and particularly Harnack, describe many questionable excesses and exploitations that were part of the early Christian movement. It was a dynamic and sometimes unruly movement, and many rules and principles were not yet determined. Human beings with all their glorious beauty and love as well as their darkest selfishness drove the movement. Nevertheless, there were factors that played key roles in making the movement persuasive over the first three centuries.

There has been much research on the rapid spread of the Christian movement against the backdrop of the decline of the Roman Empire. Amid this process, a helpful question is how Christians behaved and how they related to people who engaged in same-sex relationships? There is still a lot to be learned from Harnack's account. It is also important to keep in mind that Harnack is a product of his time with an agenda rooted in the world of 19th Century German Liberal theology. Harnack's theology fell into disrepute due to his support of the Kaiser during World War I, but not the quality and validity of most of his historical research. If we read critically through his biases, his historical accounts still bring us one of the most vivid reconstructions of the early church and its life. Harnack shows that it was not only the claims of healing and the casting out of demons, but also the lasting power of a people who cared for their own as well as the outsider and the unbelievers around them, that made early Christianity so persuasive. Even as wily and determined an opponent to early Christianity as emperor Julian ended up grudgingly admitting, "These godless Galileans feed not only their own poor but ours…"[165] Harnack is also clear that these pictures of early Christianity and its attractiveness can be over romanticized. Nevertheless, there cannot be any doubt that it was the loving friendship, active help, and hospitality of Christians and the growing perception of this reality that contributed in major ways to the growth of the faith before Constantine.[166] It is therefore quite a contrast to see some of the research on how Christians are currently perceived among those who are not Christian in North America, particularly among today's younger generation. David Kinnaman and Gabe Lyons are two contemporary cutting-edge researchers in this area. They write,

One of the surprising insights from our research is that the growing hostility toward Christians is very much a reflection of what outsiders feel they receive from believers. They say their aggression simply matches the oversized opinions and egos of Christians. One outsider put it this way: "Most people I meet assume that *Christian* means very conservative, entrenched in their thinking, antigay, antichoice, angry, violent, illogical, empire builders; they want to convert everyone, and they generally cannot live peacefully with anyone who doesn't believe what they believe."[167]

The contrast between this perception prompted by the behavior and attitudes of many people who identify as Christian with that of nascent Christianity in the first three centuries is striking. How did things change from a largely compassionate movement to one that tortured and executed people by live burning during the medieval period. Why do some Christians still have no compunction about harming others? How did things go so wrong? How did the Gospel get so distorted?

68

Our present historical accounts tend to be critical of the rise of Christendom and the ways in which the rise of power of the Christian faith in its association with the Roman Empire might have corrupted some of the more laudable characteristics of early Christianity. This "Christendom Critique" is often cited as one reason for the negative track record of contemporary Christian behavior. However, we would do well to remember Lesslie Newbigin and David Bosch's cautions not to judge this history too simplistically.[168] In fact, in some way we have in this early period a transition from outlaw religion to religion of the state which represents two different models of early Christian public theology. Nevertheless, as this chapter and the discussions that follow will show, it is exactly in the 4th century, as Christianity moved to a position of power as the official religion of the Roman Empire that the animosity against homoerotic relationships started to take on such vehemence that the death penalty is recommended by both Chrysostom, the great Patriarch of Eastern Christianity, and Augustine, the Father of theology in Western Christianity. They have antecedents in the first century apocryphal book, "The Epistle of Barnabas", the second century work of Clement of Alexandria, and in Judaism, particularly in the work of the Jewish scholar, Philo of Alexandria. Philo was a contemporary of Jesus and Paul and was influential in the Judaism that shaped Paul's theology. Most importantly, Philo's perspective evolved to become so important in 4th century Christianity that he was mistakenly referred to as a bishop. The arguments given for a hostile attitude in these sources are surprisingly different from arguments that would be made today. In a real way, what was critiqued in sexual behavior back then and the reasons for that critique turn out to be fundamentally different from what those Christians who oppose same-sex relationships today reject as well as the reasons given for that rejection.

What were the attitudes towards early Christians who were in homoerotic relationships? Do they parallel the strong revulsion, rejection and sometimes hatred relayed towards sexual and gender minorities in later history and today? The answer to these questions is shrouded in the uncertain mist of history. We must piece together from what we do know from written sources available. The most concerted effort to do that is captured by the historian John Boswell.[169] Boswell attempts to identify sources that will help provide a sense of early Christian practice. After the earlier work of Bailey, Boswell offers us a more formal attempt to uncover the place and role of people in homoerotic relationships during this period.[170] However, his account is not without controversy, and there is little doubt that, in his haste to affirm sexual and gender minorities today, he might have overstated his case. In his discussion of Boswell's work on early "brother-making" liturgies, Mark Jordan offers his characteristically careful and fair evaluation of Boswell's contribution that cuts through the rhetoric of vehement critics as well as Boswell supporters.[171] Great diversity of practice characterized early Christianity. What constituted "orthodox" or "non-heretical" Christianity was still then in contest. Besides, Boswell's arguments, there are also sociological factors that makes the presence of Christians in homoerotic relationships likely.

Tom Hanks documents a high number of single people in the early church movement as one such factor.[172] The first challenge we face in discerning attitudes in that period is the problem of identifying behaviors at that time with practices of today. No doubt Boswell's choice to use the historically and inaccurate descriptor "gay" in his book as he looked at this period was unfortunate. However, what he describes does give us a picture of an early Christianity which was not an all-out crusade against homoerotic relationships. Not that the general culture was supportive. Even though a form of same-sex "marriages" or unions were an acceptable practice in the Roman Empire of the time, it did not signify that there was general pagan cultural approval. Boswell notes that the ruralization of the empire generated less and less tolerance for diversity in sexual expression.[173] In this process, he claims, Christianity did not seem to stand out as particularly censorious towards homoerotic relationships. The first century apocryphal "Epistle of Barnabas" expresses a negative attitude towards the sexual exploitation of boys and associates this with some very the strange mythical beliefs of the time. Some of these strange beliefs associated animals with certain kinds of sexual behavior. For this reason, the "Epistle of Barnabas" urges Christians to detest hyenas or hares as they are presumed to embody unacceptable same-sex practices.[174]

Most of the first two centuries of the early Christian movement do not contain a lot of material on homoeroticism. There are, however, notable and highly esteemed same-sex love relationships between Christians that are documented. These include the love of Perpetua and Felicitas and their loving embrace as they were martyred. Similarly, there is the famous love of Paulinus, bishop of Nola for Ausonius.[175] There are also stories that are shrouded in myth such as the love of Sergius and Bacchus - two martyred Christian soldiers. We do not know what homoerotic dimensions these real or imagined loves involved, but, we can say that the depth of emotion expressed in these relationships and those that admired them is similar to what we today would understand as romantic love between two women or two men.[176] The problem with modern historical accounts lies both in our use of terminology and in inherent moral bias as discussed earlier. For example, historians often use the 19th century term "homosexual" or "homosexuality" inaccurately in relation to cultural understandings and practices of the past. Thus, Lane Fox claims, "All Orthodox Christians knew that homosexuals went to hell until a modern minority tried to make them forget it."[177] Fox bases this claim on Peter Coleman's book and some bible verses that he cites.[178] Fox is clearly uninformed about early Christian interpretation history of these texts. Our discussion in Chapter 4 refers to this problem. Additionally, the use of the word "homosexuals" simply does not transfer well to the Greco-Roman world. It could certainly be argued that some kinds of sexual activity between men, such as the exploitation of teenage boys, was rightly frowned upon in much of early Christianity. It is telling that there is not much concern about young teenage girls and their "exploitation" in the cultural practices of the time. For early Christianity, as with the surrounding Roman culture, the concern was with the idea that a man could be a "passive partner" in a sexual relationship. Such acts were presumed to be "unmanly" and challenging to the upper-class Roman culture that valued the "rational" male over the "passionate" "soft" female-like man. These ideas accepted the misogyny of its culture and made assumptions about sexual roles. The idea that people would summarily "go to hell" as a universal judgment develops over time coming to full force with the rise of Christendom in the 4th century. Fox argues that the early Christianity's approach to sexuality, as it draws on Judaism, was essentially different from its surrounding culture in its austerity. It is certainly true that there was a somewhat distinct Christian view of sexuality that by the fourth century valued celibacy. However, this perspective remained firmly rooted in Roman cultural assumptions. The research of Mathew Kuefler discussed in Chapter 6, casts serious doubt on the conclusions reached by Fox on same-sex relationships.

As early Christianity entered the Greco-Roman world, it did not only influence this world, but it came under the profound influence of the culture of its time. Amid this process, early Christianity did form an alternative community that was so loving and attractive that it grew with leaps and bounds. During that time frame, the character of this alternative community was very much expressed in terms of cultural forms and movements already present and appreciated in Greco-Roman culture. As Christian faith enculturated in the Greco-Roman context, there was a process of rejection of some elements of Roman culture, but there was also a new fusion or syncretism that emerged.[179] This cultural integration is particularly true of early Christian sexual morality. Boswell rightly points to the growing influence of dualisms, especially characterized in the Manichean religion, the influence of neo-platonic thought, and the influence of stoicism as it shaped Christianity.[180] Some stoic themes can already be detected in the writings of Paul. What these streams of thought contributed to early Christianity was a general evolution in thinking leading to a rejection of erotic sexual expressions of all kinds. This shift stands in contrast to the traditional Hebrew view that affirmed sexual erotic enjoyment within the parameters of acceptable cultural institutions. The book "Song of Songs" in the Hebrew Scriptures provides an example as does the report that Isaac was caught "laughing" with Rebekah in the book of Genesis.[181] It was not so much that some forms of early Christianity were anti-homoerotic. They slowly became suspicious of all forms of sexual enjoyment including sex within marriage.

This anti-erotic tradition developed in the context of a presumed tension between body and soul in which the soul was considered imprisoned by the body and its desires. Healthy sexual desire, which would have been very much part of the Hebrew world, came to be considered something to eschew by the rational male. We see early examples of this in Paul's eschatological urging of Christians not to marry (1 Corinthians 7:38). At this stage Paul still supports voluntary celibacy only. As Christianity evolved into the second century and became further enculturated in the Greco-Roman world, it started to embrace a spirituality that denied the body the natural comforts of food and erotic sexual intimacy. Even married couples were encouraged to strive to remain abstinent. The first monastics emerged in the form of the Desert Fathers, many of whom were admired for their extreme forms of self-denial. Nevertheless, even these early monastics were quite matter of fact about the sexual desires they experienced including homoerotic fantasies about each other. Early Christians were often accused of sexual impropriety by their enemies. Both Tatian (120-180) and Clement of Alexandria (150-215) started to cement a process of anti-eroticism and anti-homoeroticism in early Christianity. Clement established what is called the "Alexandrian Rule[182].", pleasure sought for its own sake, even within the marriage bonds, is a sin and contrary both to law and to reason[183].

Tatian opposed all forms of sexual expression but Clement reluctantly left room for sexual procreation in marriage. Clement's argument against homoerotic relationships relies on the anti-pleasure principle plus the strange mythical beliefs about animals, documented in the Epistle of Barnabas. Thus, the limited picture we do have provides a story of complexity and diversity of acceptable sexual practices in early Christianity.[184]

The strongest opposition against homoerotic relationships developed by the 4th century. Notable here is Chrysostom (347-407). Although it must be assumed that his fiery sermons contained a fair amount of hyperbole, Boswell persuasively points out that his preaching reveals that homoerotic relationships were not only known in the Christian communities of the time but also fairly common. Some may have believed that such people were "going to hell," but a significant number of people in homoerotic relationships must have been in Christian congregations that Chrysostom felt compelled to preach against it. Chrysostom, arguably the most important Patriarch in Orthodox tradition, was a desert monastic, hailing from Antioch, who was called to become Patriarch of Constantinople. His fiery preaching challenged the rich and the powerful. Unfortunately, it also contained violent anti-Semitism, in no small measure responsible for the pogroms that would erupt centuries later in Russia. Chrysostom's theological argument against homoerotic relationships is rooted in culture as he rails particularly against the violation of Greco-Roman gender roles. He also speaks strongly in favor of the death penalty for people in homoerotic relationships.[185] Chrysostom appears to be the first important Christian teacher to associate lesbianism with the text in Romans 1:26-27[186]. In addition, he takes the story of Sodom, based in the ideas of the Jewish scholar Philo of Alexandria and mixes it with popular travelers' tales to create the myth of Sodom's homoerotic "vice" as its principal and grievous sin.[187] By means of a series of sermons preached by Chrysostom in the year 380, the terrifying history of the violent persecution of people in homoerotic relationships in Christianity begins. At the same time, this very event in late-early Christianity, as it moves to become the religion of the Empire, demonstrates how Greco-Roman Patriarchal gender bias plays a critical role in this change in Christianity's sexual ethic. The pressure to be the respectable religion of the Empire becomes part of the many influencing factors. Yet, at the same time, and in a paradoxical way, Chrysostom's preaching themes become evidence that a fair number of Christians at the time were in homoerotic relationships. Chrysostom's anti-homoerotic preaching only makes sense if many in his Christian audience did not reject homoerotic relationships in the way he wished them to.

A similar pattern can be discerned in the contribution of Augustine. If Chrysostom is the great Patriarch of Eastern Christianity, Augustine can certainly be claimed to be the father of Western Christianity including Protestantism. In his "Confessions" Augustine writes about a passionate love he had for a young male friend who subsequently died. He writes about the deep desolation he experienced and his reflection on such love is profound bordering on the erotic.[188] Augustine for a long time also had a concubine and fathered a son. However, he sent his concubine and son away when opportunity for a profitable respectable Roman marriage occurred. Before his conversion he was a follower of the Manichean religion that emphasized abstinence from sexual practice and extreme austerity in food consumption. Before the marriage arrangements could be consummated, Augustine changed his mind and committed to become a celibate Christian monastic. Despite his dramatic conversion to Christianity, he adopted some personal Manichean biases into his theology. Augustine, like Chrysostom, may have drawn on Philo of Alexandria's arguments to associate homoerotic relationships with the story of Sodom. Despite Augustine's brilliant theological thought and nuanced arguments, as a theologian of the Empire, he also supported the death penalty for those engaged in homoerotic relationships.[189] Thus theological teaching of this time begins to set the stage for the horrendous torture and executions of many Christians in the medieval period and harmful behavior to this day. This rising vehement anti-homoerotic "orthodoxy" is squarely rooted in Greco-Roman gender bias, its patriarchal assumptions, its myths about the animal world. In a smaller way it also builds on the contemporary Judaistic tradition that sought to adapt Judaism to the Greco-Roman cultural world as represented in the writings of Philo of Alexandria. The historical shaping of the meaning of biblical texts biased against sexual minorities thus take decisive shape with Chrysostom and Augustine.

The pre-fourth century Christian movement was diverse in its understanding of gender roles and sexual practice while leaning towards censure against homoerotic relationships. An example of such diversity of practice in North Africa is that the upper classes tended to encourage the marriage of siblings. Early Christianity did not take a strong stance against that form of incest, thus suggesting flexible sexual practice.[190] There was an increasing bias against sexual enjoyment of all kinds, but "orthodox Christianity" firmed up into a vehement rejection of homoerotic relationships only by the fourth century when it started serving as an instrument of the Roman Empire. This process was in a significant way influenced by the biases and beliefs of the Greco-Roman world and the attempts of Christianity to fit into it.

Nevertheless, this nascent period of Christianity also contains a lesson in the power of the Christian faith when ordinary Christians engage their world with love and charity. Alan Kreider vividly describes the winsome quality of a faith characterized by patience, catechetic formation, and "gentle ferment." It is to this lesson we now turn with the hope that some of it could inform our own process of moral discernment. To draw on this tradition, we will look at what the core message was that the Christians conveyed in the first 300 years and how they behaved. First, we will Follow Harnack's work which requires discussing the characteristics of early preaching, the content of the Gospel message, the role of the conflict with demonic powers, the living out of the Gospel of love and charity, the seeking of holiness in the power of the Spirit, and the role of authority, reason and mystery during this period. We will also look at some of the theories why Christians were eventually embraced in the once hostile Roman Empire. It is important to note that in none of these themes anti-homoerotic sentiment and teaching take a prominent or even a notable place.

The Characteristics of early preaching

At the heart of early preaching was the invitation to repent for God's kingdom is at hand.[191] This preaching included a fresh approach to the Hebrew Bible which was now read through the lens of Jesus the Savior as Messiah. Further themes included creation and an emphasis on resurrection.[192] Early Christian preaching also focused on the virtues of love and self-control. Kreider describes how these virtues were expressed in a particularly Christian conception of patient trust in God.[193] By the second century this simple preaching became more and more subsumed in the controversies of heresy particularly anti-gnostic preaching along with an increased emphasis on the sacrament of baptism.[194] This message was persuasive, but people became Christians for a complex set of reasons that went well beyond the content of preaching. The promise of resurrection played a strong role, but the experience of healing and being set free from demonic powers as well as the impressive loving lives of Christians became additional motivations for conversion. As the church institutionalized more and the focus shifted to the authority of the clergy. In the third and fourth centuries, the sacraments remained strong elements, but political reasons competed with them for convincing people to be Christians. Nevertheless, early gospel preaching demonstrated a gospel posture that parallels the stances of "just love" and "care" as developed by Wolterstorff, Gustafson, and Farley and described in Chapter 2.

The Content of the Gospel

The content of the Gospel went beyond the standard content of the preached message. The good news for people in the first two centuries was particularly centered on healing. Jesus was seen as a healer and the Good Shepherd who carries his sheep.[195] No strict distinction was made between the healing of body and soul. The enthusiastic witness of healing among early Christians and new converts contributed to the power of the church's outreach.[196] Michael Green describes the process in which early Christians enthusiastically told the story of their own redemption and healing in the town square and market place with the phrase, "gossiping the gospel."[197] Clearly, what was convincing to outsiders was the combination of good and kind words, a wonderful promise of eternal life, the real benefit of healing in body and soul, and the love and acceptance of the Christian community. This message was truly good news, particularly during this uncertain time when daily living became quite difficult and the Roman Empire started to crumble. It is also a positive message rather than a judgmental one. It demonstrates that active deeds of love were at the core of what made the Christian faith attractive. In a fundamental way, this orientation towards healing and well-being in early Christianity can also be related to the contemporary understanding of the importance of human flourishing in all relationships including gender and sexuality.

Conflict with Demonic Powers

For the modern North American reader who is not Pentecostal or Charismatic in tradition, the casting out of demons might seem a puzzling part of the story. The Greco-Roman world of the time was rife with beliefs in all kinds of powers and forces that controlled the world. Many of the religious activities were focused on assuaging the gods or powers. Christianity offered a simple and clear promise of release and protection from such powers. Although beliefs in demons and angelic beings only entered Judaistic thought around the post-exilic period under Egyptian and Persian influence, it had become well established as part of the world view of Judaism as well as Greco-Roman culture by the time of Jesus.[198] A witness to this is the appearance of stories of healing through the casting out of demons in the Gospels and in the Book of Acts. Liberation from demonic forces become particularly prominent from the time of Justin Martyr (100-165) onwards. Irenaeus of Lyon (130-202) also emphasized this ministry and other gifts of the Spirit like prophesying and healing.[199] Harnack provides a citation from Irenaeus that demonstrates the convictions of the time.[200]

At the heart of this ministry was a real and powerful experience of being liberated by God within the context of the Christian community. As Irenaeus indicates, the casting out of demons was part of the healing ministry of the early church. Christians also developed and practiced rituals that strengthened the power of this experience by using the sign of the cross, the sacrament of baptism, sprinkling with holy water, and anointing with oil. Such rituals contributed to the Christian faith as a powerful and mysterious liberating faith rooted in the transcendent. All kinds of ailments and problems could be externalized as demonic and thus decisively addressed in people's lives. In this way the best of early Christianity was characterized by loving liberation rather than censorious judgment of others. This liberative dimensions also points to a strong emphasis on human flourishing.

The Gospel of Love and Charity ("Hilfleistung" - Helpfulness)

The picture of real and committed people as Christians who are there to help draws together this image of a truly attractive faith in the midst of a world of confusion and fear. Not only was there a simple clear message, a promise of resurrection, healing of soul and body, and liberation from evil powers, but there were also people who were practically helpful. Christian communities went to extraordinary lengths to help each other as well as outsiders. Harnack, citing Mt. 25, describes it this way,

I was hungry, and ye fed me; I was thirsty, and ye gave me drink;... These words of Jesus have shone so brilliantly for many generations in his church, and exerted so powerful an influence, that one may further describe the Christian preaching as the preaching of love and charity.[201]

What shape did this charitable helpfulness take for early Christians? Foremost it meant that these early Christians took the stories handed down about Jesus as their model for action. Likely, this is one of the reasons we don't find anti-homoerotic crusades in this early time. The concern of Christians was to act like Jesus. In his letter to the Corinthians in the year 80, Clement of Rome writes of the Corinthians,

You lamented the transgressions of your neighbours and judged their shortcomings to be your own. You never rued an act of kindness, but were ready for every good work.[202]

The contrast with later attitudes, judgments and brutal behavior in Christianity is instructive. It is also helpful to reflect on how these early Christian attitudes reflect the posture for moral discernment as discussed in Chapter 2. These early Christians excelled in alms giving, supporting the widows, orphans, sick, infirm, disabled, sending help to those sentenced to prison or hard labor in mines and sometimes even paying the price to redeem slaves from slavery.[203] Those who were unemployed were given work by fellow Christians, and much of the charity extended beyond the Christian community including feeding poor non-believing neighbors and even paying for their burial. As noted above, this behavior was so outstanding that Emperor Julian complained that they even took care of his people better than he did. When calamities struck, such as a plague in the city of Carthage, Christians, at the risk of their own lives, went in to take care of the sick.[204] The testimonies of the enemies of early Christianity speak the loudest. The great critic of Christians, Celsus (contemporary of Origen of Alexandria), was reported to complain that Christian morality was dull![205] In this humble, loving, and serving way, many, although not all, early Christians distinguished themselves.

Holiness in the Power of the Spirit

Early Christians also set high moral standards for their own behavior. They believed that they were redeemed by Christ and empowered to live a Christian life that is exemplary in their communities. As Greco-Roman ideas and philosophies took root the initial simple, committed and loving lifestyle of early Christians also started to take on some other-worldly dimensions. It is here where the body – soul dualism started to take root. Over time Christianity became more and more austere in its view of all forms of sexual expression. As persecution of Christians lessened and mere survival was less an issue, emphasis started to shift to a spirituality that imagined itself as battling against the sins of the flesh.[206] A kind of spiritual arrogance developed by which some considered their own self-denial superior to those who indulged in marriage and close human relationships.

Eventually, by the third century, the church had to manage tensions between the large majority of Christians who tried to live simple, good, but relational family lives as opposed to those who advocated radical austere withdrawal from the world.[207] This tension was addressed in the theological distinction made between the "two ways" known as the doctrine of "*praecepta or consilia."* The doctrine stated, "if you can bear the whole yoke of the Lord, you will be perfect, but if you can't, do what you can."[208] The 16th century Reformers would reject this approach, but it came to play an important role in early Christianity. The austere rejection of all forms of sexual pleasure in the encratic-monastic (world-denying) side of the church must be read against the backdrop of this much wider circle of early Christians who sought to follow Christ while expressing love to one another in more tangible ways.

Shifts in Authority, Mystery and Reason

A final dimension of early Christianity to be noted is the role of authority and the shift to clerically dominated reasoned arguments. These developments went along with enshrining the sacraments in a more mysterious and mystical dimension. The authority of the earliest Christianity was very much an authority of trust in relationship, word and deed. The persuasive preaching, healing, casting out of demons and acts of love and charity won people over to trust and believe. As the church entered the fourth century it became increasingly institutionalized and clericalized. The Empire needed a united and uniform religion. This led to a shift of authority to the exclusively male clergy and made the sacraments the mystical task of a priestly class. It led to increasingly hostile debates between "orthodox" and "heretical" perspectives and brutal violent suppression of opposition on all sides.

Thus, early Christianity moved from a relatively loose authority structure where integrity, love and humility were supreme values to an authoritarian structure of the episcopate based on reasoned arguments that served political aims as well as theological. There is also emerging evidence that early Christianity accommodated women in leadership roles.[209] By the end of the second century this practice seemed to have diminished including the documented women's diaconate. Under the pressure of Greco-Roman patriarchal assumptions, the church became more focused on gender binary and gender bias in both its suspicion against women in leadership and in the rejection of men that did not fulfil strict misogynistic Greco-Roman gender roles.[210] Later, the 16th century reformation would challenge these authorities but would soon institute its own new structures that mirrored authority in their own way. The dark stories of torture and killing that would follow in the medieval and reformation periods are significantly stamped by the politics and roles of authority. Where does the authority lie to interpret the teaching of the Bible and the teaching of the church in ways that are harmful to others? The authoritarian assumption of "textual agency" (Dale Martin's critique) or, "the Bible as a paper Pope" (Karl Barth's complaint) both highlight how authority is presently invoked to inflict harm. When we deal with very different interpretations of the same text, how do we discern a moral way? It seems that many of the earliest Christians lived with a fair amount of diversity in gracious love in their process of moral discernment.

The Dark Side?

Over-romanticizing early Christianity offers a great temptation. These early Christians were regular people and creatures of their own time and culture just as we are. Are some of these exemplary trends explored above perhaps overstated? No doubt, much of what we know about early Christianity comes from the documents of Christians themselves. For example, everything we know about the great critic of Christianity, Celsus, comes through the lens of Origen of Alexandria's description of Celsus' views. None of us are always completely scrupulous in describing our opponents. We should therefore be careful when we idealize early Christianity too much. Harnack points out that there were plenty of charlatans, claiming to do miracles, healings, and prophecies in Jesus' name, who gave Christianity a bad name. The early Christian document *Didache* comments on exploitative itinerant preachers, and the New Testament itself testifies that everything was not always sweetness and light in early Christian communities. We can see early Christianity slowly absorbing so much of Greco-Roman culture that gender roles become more patriarchal and that men who do not conform to the gender norms of the time become more and more suspect. We also see a deep rejection of the embodied beauty of sexual intimacy as a joyful expression of committed love. The profound unitive gift of erotic expression between loving and mutually committed people as celebrated in the Song of Songs in the Old Testament fades slowly into the background. A divide opens between the "perfection" of the celibate monastics and the perceived second-class status of those not committed to that way. The early theological arguments against homoerotic relationships are also colored by absurd Greco-Roman mythical beliefs about animals such as hyenas and hares. Nevertheless, what we have is a positive picture of exemplary behavior, which must have outshone the bad behavior to such a degree that it became persuasive to those outside the movement. The aim here is to seek to underline the profound integrity of the exemplary behavior of early Christians and to be inspired to a Christ-like posture in our own moral discernment as we engage sexual and gender minorities.

Conclusion

In this chapter we have explored the exemplary picture of early Christianity as a movement that was characterized by love and charity. We examined the sparse historical material we have about the lives of early Christians who were in homoerotic relationships. We started to trace the trajectory of early anti-homoerotic rhetoric in "The Epistle of Barnabas" and its fanciful arguments rooted in odd Greco-Roman beliefs about the behavior of animals. Early Christianity was clearly not particularly focused on opposing homoerotic relationships. Rather, it focused on imitating the life of Christ, sharing the good news of forgiveness and the hope of the resurrection, bringing healing to body and soul, and doing extraordinary acts of kindness to their own community and pagan neighbors. We have explored how, under Greco-Roman influence, the division between body and soul or flesh and spirit started to influence Christianity into a more and more austere view of all forms of sexual pleasure. This was particularly evident in the fledgling monastic movement and reflected in the teaching of Clement of Alexandria. Anti-homoerotic rhetoric in this period was influenced by a rejection of all forms of sexual pleasure and even simple ways of offering bodily solace to one another. It was also rooted in Greco-Roman prejudice mixed with odd beliefs about animal behavior. A strong Greco-Roman bias about gender roles also started to influence early Christianity. Women were considered inferior, weak and ruled by passion and it was scandalous for a free Roman man to behave in ways that was considered "womanly." So, for example, early forms of women's leadership in Christian communities soon succumbed to the idea that males only could serve in the priestly class. As Christianity became the religion of the Roman Empire in the 4th century its position, reflected in the preaching of Chrysostom and the writing of Augustine, became strongly anti-homoerotic. So vehement was this rejection that both these founders of Eastern and Western Christianity advocated the death penalty for those in homoerotic relationships. Paradoxically, the necessity to preach against homoerotic practices suggest that some early Christian communities were tolerant of people in their midst who were in homoerotic relationships. Augustine's own possible bisexuality expressed in a deep love for a male friend during his youth attests to the common occurrence of homoerotic relationships in the wider Empire at that time.

We can be inspired by the exemplary behavior of early Christians. We can also trace a history of the development of anti-homoerotic teaching which is sparse during the first three centuries and becomes vehement during the fourth century when the church gains power. As we attend to this process we need to look more closely at these developments and their origins as well as the implications for the frightening torture and killing that would ensue in the medieval period. First, we need to uncover the influence and importance of the work of the Jewish scholar, Philo of Alexandria. Philo is the subject of the next chapter.

CHAPTER 6: THE RISE OF HOMOPHOBIA – PHILO AND CHRISTIAN MANLINESS

This chapter explores the textual and cultural sources of the development of vehement Christian anti-homoerotic sentiment as it comes to fruition in the 4th century. During the ferment of the first three centuries of Christian faith it slowly enculturated in the Greco-Roman world, moving from a First Century Judaism to a new hybrid of Jewish religious traditions mixed with Greco-Roman cultural beliefs and philosophical ideas. In this process, gender is reshaped by the influence of both traditions. The emergence of a new Christian conception of maleness provides the key to understanding later Christian rejection and persecution of men in same-sex relationships. This chapter will explore the crucial construction of manliness and unmanliness in the first four centuries and its implications for the treatment of people accused of sodomy.

As 4th century ideals of manliness and anti-homoerotic convictions emerge in Christianity, Philo of Alexandria, rather than Paul, plays the more decisive role. Philo's revision of the interpretation of the story of Sodom and Gomorrah became the source of homophobic teaching and brutal practice in the medieval church and in Christian convictions that continue to this day. As the story unfolds, we will see how powerfully the myth of the homoerotic sin of Sodom, created by Philo, would cast its spell over the varieties of Christian orientations that were to come in the next 2000 years. As Christianity ascended in the declining Roman Empire, the myth of Sodom, as exemplified in same-sex sexual intercourse, merged with the profound cultural bias within Roman culture against forms of sexuality that were considered unmanly, womanly and passive. Christianity absorbed that bias and built its moral theology on Roman conceptions of Patriarchy, manliness, and what was considered "natural." This trajectory of thought and bias significantly has shaped the future development of Western moral conceptions that lingers until today. Even though the idea of Sodom as exemplar of God's judgement on homoeroticism is no longer accepted in current Biblical research, visceral reaction against "sodomy" lingers both ecclesiastically and culturally in countries shaped by Christian teaching. To understand this trajectory in Western Christianity we need to consider the Jewish Scholar Philo of Alexandria, Pagan Roman, and developing Christian conceptions of manliness.[211] First, we turn to Philo's change of status from an important Jewish apologist in late Roman antiquity to a mythical honorary status as a "Christian Bishop."

The Christian Philo

Philo lived in Alexandria between 25 (BCE) and 50 (CE). He was a Jewish scholar who made primary use of the Greek translation of the Hebrew Bible known as the Septuagint. It appears that he had only a cursory knowledge of classical Hebrew. He tried to interpret the Greek version of the Hebrew Bible to the Greco-Roman world through allegory. He also courageously represented Alexandrian Jews before Emperor Gaius (Caligula) in Rome after tensions developed between the Jewish and Greek communities. Most of what we know about Philo comes through the writings of another early Jewish historian and apologist, namely Josephus (37-100). Philo had some influence in the rabbinic academies around the Mediterranean during his life-time. However, soon thereafter, his influence within Judaism faded. Philo's possible influence on the New Testament text remains in debate. So, for example, it has been argued that the way he developed the concept of the *logos* in Judaism influenced the early Christian conception of *logos* ("In the beginning was the Word (logos)" as we find it in John 1, and later Christian apologists). The academic debates on this presumed influence continues without clear resolution. More interestingly, it has also been argued that he might have had an influence on Paul's writings. Some scholars argue that Philo's influence was so pervasive that Paul's exposure to rabbinical formation and teaching before his conversion to Christianity would have included the study of Philo's writings. This matter also remains open for debate. For example, Paul does not pick up on Philo's argument that connects Sodom to homoerotic excess, which might suggest that Philo's influence, if any, was probably not direct.

By the fourth century Philo's writings became quite influential in Christian circles. David Runia, one of the most prominent Philo scholars of our time, devotes a whole chapter in his book on Philo in early Christian literature to what he calls *"Philo Christianus"*, the development of the Christian myth that Philo converted to Christianity and even served as bishop.[212] Even though these stories were not true, many fourth century Christian leaders referred to Philo's work and some may have believed the myth. Most of the documents that contain Philo's writings were preserved by the bishop Eusebius (260-340) who collected them in his library. Runia discusses in detail the history of transmission of Philoic texts and their sources.[213] That many copies of Philo's writings were being used and shared in Alexandria and Palestine is now clear. For example, a Christian copy of two texts were discovered in the Egyptian town of Coptos (today known as Qift) in a hidden alcove wrapped in fragments of the Gospel of John.[214] It is unclear and unlikely that Augustine was directly influenced by Philo's writings in his views on homoerotic relationships. If he did access Philo on this topic it was most likely in Latin translations of the Greek texts that were in circulation in the 4th century.[215] There is a whole literary industry devoted to collecting early manuscripts of Philo's work and reconstructing the best knowledge of the original texts.

Philo did not feature strongly in medieval rabbinical scholarship. Within Christianity his influence stretched right into the medieval period through his novel interpretations of Genesis 19, and it continues today in the historical outworking of the text through violent attitudes towards homoerotic relationships. For example, in Chapter 3 we noted Franklin Graham's Facebook post that associates "Sodom and Gomorrah" with transgender rights. The first credible turning point in the early modern study of his work and influence came with a dissertation produced by Johann A. Fabricius in 1693. He successfully challenged the reigning medieval belief in Philo as a kind of honorary church father.[216] Although there is much more to be said about Philo and his contribution to Christian theology, here we will focus on his attitude towards homoerotic relationships.

Philo and Homoerotic Relationships

Until the writings of Philo, in both Biblical and Christian sources, there was no reference to the idea that the story of Sodom and Gomorrah, and particularly Sodom was associated with violent same-sex rape. In fact, no Old Testament reference makes a direct connection between Sodom and sexual excess. This is also mostly true of the New Testament. In the 2nd and 3rd century BCE a series of texts known as the Pseudepigrapha books, became popular in Judaism. These include books such as *Enoch, The Assumption of Moses, Jubilees*, and *The Testament of the Twelve Patriarchs*[217]. Some of these books started to make a connection between heterosexual rape and Sodom.[218] Mostly, they associated the sins of Sodom with pride, arrogance, apostasy, and idolatry which builds on Old Testament references to Sodom as a place of exploitation and injustice.[219] Thus, Isaiah 1:9 places the sins of Sodom squarely in the area of socio-economic exploitation, oppression, and injustice. The Pseudepigraphical books add the idea of a lack of hospitality (*The Wisdom of Solomon*). When Jesus refers to Sodom it is in the context of a lack of hospitality, which is consistent with the views pre-Philo. Within the New Testament all references to Sodom relies on the Septuagint translation of the Old Testament.[220] There are 11 New Testament references to Sodom. Paul and the Book of Revelation follow the older Old Testament traditions on Sodom. The Gospels start to add insights on lack of hospitality in Sodom and Gomorrah.

The Pseudepigraphical influence towards a sexual connotation for Sodom starts to appear in the New Testament in the letters of Jude and 2 Peter. These two books are considered some of the latest writings in the New Testament corpus, and their status in the New Testament remained contested into the second half of the second century. 2 Peter seems to draw on Jude in its Sodomic references. Jude is the first place in the Bible where Sodom becomes associated with "fornication" and "going after strange flesh" (KJV translation). Neither of these references directly refer to homoerotic relationships. It is generally assumed the Jude verse 7 refers to Gen 6:2-4, where sexual relationships with "sons of God" is mentioned. However, closer examination of these texts suggests that these references actually rely on two Pseudepigraphical books, *The Assumption of Moses* and *The Book of Enoch.*[221] It is important to note for our exploration of interpretation history, that none of these references indicate homoerotic relationships, but rather heterosexual excess. In Judaism in general homoerotic relationships received sparse treatment until Philo.[222]

This is thus the situation when Philo comes on the scene in the first century as a contemporary of Jesus and Paul. There are three references to homoerotic relationships in what is preserved in Philo's writings. These appear in his books, *On Abraham, Special Laws II,* and *The Contemplative Life.*[223] It is clear from Philo's references that he is drawing on his experience in the city of Alexandria at the time.[224] In his Greco-Roman context homoerotic practices included three categories. First, was what the Greeks called "paiderasteia"- a kind of lovesickness for a teenage boy or young man.[225] Second, there were men who acted and sometimes dressed like women often described as "effeminate"- a practice that Greco-Romans ridiculed because of misogynistic conceptions of manliness. Third, were the "Galli," religious castrati or eunuchs who served in different forms of pagan worship which might involve sexual intercourse. Philo is clearly disgusted by these practices and starts to associate them with the sins of Sodom. It is therefore very important to stress that Philo rejected and critiqued homoerotic cultural practices *of his time* which he considered as excessive and culturally reprehensible.

Philo argued that the "law of Moses" is coterminous with "the law of nature."[226] In this he is following the Platonic school of philosophy which elevates "nature" as a universal norm for human behavior. Thus, for Philo, these practices that he observed around him were "against nature" in the sense that they did not fit with what was considered culturally exemplary behavior. It is helpful to consider the motivation for some of Philo's disgust against homoerotic relationships of his time. Most important is that Philo viewed the difference between female and male as a binary. Female for Philo represented the human body and its needs and desires which he considered, following Greek philosophers, the impassioned, weaker lower carnal part of a person.[227] It is easy to see how this misogynistic conception of women became conflated with men who behave too much like women and why this would disgust Philo. This conflation is even more dramatic if we recognize that Philo considered the male to be the higher "spiritual" part of the human person and the female weak and carnal. To defend Judaism within the Greco-Roman world of his time, Philo stressed the ideals of the "law of Moses" as harmonious with high-status Greco-Roman cultural ideals of reasonable non-erotic spiritual manliness. Philo also develops a theory of double creation to fit with the idea of the ideal that transcends the physical. The idea is that God first created the ideal exemplar – the rational-spiritual, and then its physical-carnal imperfect version that can be perceived by the senses.[228] For Philo the part of the human condition that reflects the image of God is reason without passion. The sexual dimension of the human being is part of the lower, corrupted state.[229] Philo as an expositor of Judaism in the Greco-Roman world, together with early Christianity, were increasingly swept along by the idea that the physical existence and the sexual reality of the human condition is a problem rather than a divinely blessed state. Philo's exegetical argument for his position on a Greco-Roman double creation is based in his reading of the Genesis creation stories and his exposition of the story of Sodom and Gomorrah based in its Greek-Septuagint translation.

When Philo examined the Mosaic Law, he consistently uses the Greek Septuagint version of the Old Testament rather than the classical Hebrew version. In a meticulous study, Biblical Scholar William Loader shows how this Greek text creates sexual innuendo that is not present in the classical Hebrew.[230] Philo therefore draws on these sexual innuendoes inherent in the Septuagint to read the story of Sodom and Gomorrah as a story of homoerotic sinfulness. He incorporates these innuendoes into his understanding of the prohibitions of Leviticus 18:22 and 20:13 as addressing what he perceives as disgusting homoerotic practices in his own cultural world of first century Alexandria. He maintains that the Levitical prohibitions constitute a law of nature which makes it the duty of the state and its citizens to execute anyone who practices homoerotic relationships. Through Philo these biblical texts gain new meaning and importance that in turn echoes on through history.

In his book *On Abraham* Philo describes the people of Sodom as adulterers with an unbridled sexual appetite. In *The Contemplative Life* he adds that *paiderasteia* is an undignified passion that deviates from nature and that it constitutes "sickly femininity" that corrupts males.[231] The influence of Philo's cultural context is evident in his disgust at men wearing female garments. Although influenced by biblical texts like Deut 22:5, the level of disgust easily merged with the Greco-Roman derision of males that take on female roles. A fuller quotation illuminates Philo's vehemence,

Much graver than [adultery] is another evil, which has ramped its way into the cities, namely pederasty. In former days the very mention of it was a great disgrace, but now it is a matter of boasting not only to the active but to the passive partners, who habituate themselves to endure the disease of effemination, let both body and soul run to waste, and leave no ember of their male sex-nature to smolder. Mark how conspicuously they braid and adorn the hair of their heads, and how they scrub and paint their faces with cosmetics and pigments and the like, and smother themselves with fragrant unguents . . . In fact, the transformation of the male nature to the female is practiced by them as an art and does not raise a blush. These persons are rightly judged worthy of death by those who obey the law [of Moses], which ordains that the man-woman who debases the sterling coin of nature should perish unavenged, suffered not to live for a day or even an hour, as a disgrace to himself, his house, his native land and the whole human race.[232]

In the Greco-Roman world of Philo's time, homoerotic behaviors that he encountered evoked a sense of ridicule, particularly for the "passive" partner in a relationship. When it came to street parades and religious functions, there was a sense of comedic indulgence for most Romans. What happens in Philo's argument is that this negative cultural attitude is shifted to a brutal demand for death. Not death through a proper legal process, but Philo demands that such people should be killed and not allowed to live a "day or even an hour." This vengeful disgust was a new phenomenon that would eventually take shape in the horrors of medieval torture and killing and the inquisition. It is telling that Philo would seem to incite mob violence against such "effeminate" men. The echoes of that spirit resound throughout history to this day in the lynching mobs of Uganda, Russia, Iran, and even hate crimes in North America.

Philo draws on the Greek version of the Old Testament and adds to the condemnations of Lev 18:22 and 20:13, the prohibition against men or women wearing each other's clothes (Deut 22:5) as well as the banning of eunuchs from the presence of God (Deut 23:1). His argument is only against the "effeminate" or "passive" partner in a homoerotic relationship. In this he is consistent in line with Greco-Roman cultural ideas of the time. However, because Philo understands Lev 18:22 and 20:13 as verses to support his perspective, he also has to explain why both partners in such a relationship should be put to death. Thus, Philo argues that male same sex relationships threaten the human race by working against procreation leading to the depopulation of the world. He uses the metaphor that such sexual relationships are like a farmer wasting seed on stony ground.[233] Consequently Philo moves far beyond Greco-Roman prejudice to deep disgust and extreme violence against all those engaged in such relationships. Philo does not comment on lesbian relationships. In fact, there is no mention of such relationships in the Old Testament. Although we cannot be sure, the likely reason for a silence on lesbian relationships in both Judaism and early Christianity is the patriarchal cultural context where such relationships among women would not threaten the hierarchy and power of patriarchy.

Before discussing the Greco-Roman concept of manliness and its impact on the development of anti-homoerotic sentiment, it is also important to notice some parallels between the Greco-Roman world of Philo's time, the excesses of the court of Emperor Gaius (Caligula), and Paul's letter to the Romans. As noted above, scholarship on the influence of Philo on Paul is inconclusive and will probably remain so. There are also important pieces of Philo's argument re: Sodom that are not present in Paul's writings. The major parallel between these two authors is their respective attempts to make Judaism and Christianity intelligible to a Greco-Roman audience during roughly the same general time-frame. Both were Roman citizens. Both were deeply rooted in the Rabbinic discourse around the Eastern Mediterranean, and both made extensive albeit not exclusive use of the Septuagint translation of the Old Testament. There are also strong strains of the influence of Greek philosophical ideas such as Stoicism and Platonism detectable in their writings that were simply "in the cultural air" of their times. Two elements in Paul's rhetorical argument in Romans 1 deserve mention. First, his use of the concept "nature." The meaning of the expression "against nature" (leave behind what is natural Rom 1:27), remains a matter of interpretive debate. There are very good reasons to conclude that Paul was influenced by the idea of a culturally defined "law of nature" as used by Philo in his attempt at defending Judaism in a Greco-Roman context.[234] Contemporary Christian anti-homoerotic arguments vigorously defend the idea that "nature" in Romans 1 refers to the creation narrative. However, the historical evidence as well as the use of similar terms in other contexts in the New Testament make that interpretation highly unlikely. Our discussion of manliness that will follow will build further on this insight. The other parallel between Philo and Paul is citing the consequence of death. In Romans this occurs in verse 32 claiming that "people who live in this way deserve death (Good News Bible)." This verse, amplified by the writings of Philo, would later become the primary rationale for the torture, abuse, and live burning of people in homoerotic relationships. It is sobering to note that verses 29 and 30 in Romans 1 precede this invocation of the death penalty. The vice list in these two verses specifically lists excessive destructive and hurtful behaviors which forms part of Paul's rhetoric on the pervasiveness of sin. It is also sobering to remember that Paul's rhetorical argument in Romans 2:1 turns the table on his readers who might be agreeing with his rhetorical condemnation. As noted earlier, the Good News Bible reads, "Do you, my friend, pass judgment on others? You have no excuse at all, whoever you are. For when you judge others and then do the same things which they do, you condemn yourself." Paul is not heading towards killing the various sinners he is describing; he is heading to his core refrain in Rom 3:23, "all have sinned and fall short of God's glory." Moreover, in Rom 5:12 he points to the move from death to life. I submit that the Apostle Paul, was going in a very different direction with the Gospel of life than Philo of Alexandria. It is therefore so much more disappointing that Philo's hunger for extreme violence would become the perspective that would win over a power focused Christendom from the fourth century onwards.

Philo's disgust was rooted in his cultural context that became merged with his contextual interpretation of Old Testament texts. His desire and agenda were to make Judaism acceptable in the philosophical Greco-Roman culture of his time influencing his strong binary and misogynistic conceptions of manliness considered culturally "natural." Philo also read the Hebrew Bible through the lens of the Septuagint Greek translation which adds sexual nuance in the story of Sodom and Gomorrah not present in the classical Hebrew version. Philo's most reprehensible but unintended contribution to the Christian church is his advocacy for violence, killing and even mob action against people in homoerotic relationships. He also added an emphasis on the lack of procreative purpose as a reason for the rejection of homoerotic relationships. In this he was influenced by stoic philosophy. He moved significantly beyond the traditions of earlier Judaism, exemplified in Song of Songs, and started to add a rejection of the enjoyment of sexual love of all forms under Greco-Roman influence. Even though there are some cultural parallels between Philo's writings and Paul's letter to the Romans, we must note that Paul's ultimate Gospel direction is an emphasis on life and grace which is opposite to Philo's emphasis on violent death for people in homoerotic relationships.

Unfortunately, as the Christian church enculturated in the Greco-Roman world it became increasingly captive to an anti-physical and anti-sexual enjoyment ethos. When Christianity became the official religion of the Empire by the fourth century it was Philo's arguments and not Paul's that lead the church towards brutal acts of torture and killing of people in homoerotic relationships. By reading the New Testament through the lens of Philo and patriarchal Roman Cultural prejudice the idea of the "the sin of sodomy" took root. Eventually this led to branding of individuals as "sodomites." Eventually, this "sodomitic" designation and judgment became the accepted moral position of the church of late antiquity and the medieval period. Before detailing the part of the story that discusses the teaching of the church on "sodomy" we first need to understand better how the Greco-Roman world of the first four centuries understood manliness and how this understanding relates to emerging Christian toxic manliness.

Manliness

In an earlier chapter we have noted some of the current research on violence against gay men in North America. The research shows that peer pressure and the need to prove manliness plays key roles in the inspiration of such violence.[235] This phenomenon is not a modern one; it has been part of the story of Western conceptions of manliness since the Roman Empire evolved into a Christian empire. The rejection, condemnation, and killing of some kinds of men was a way for the men of late antiquity and the medieval period to assert their own manliness. These perspectives and actions to project male dominance and power. They were also ways to assert manliness in the face of the gender insecurity of the accusers and abusers.[236] Although cultural conceptions of manliness today are different from that of late antiquity, this process of proving manliness still has traction and remains inscribed in different forms on male bodies. Earlier we explored how moral decisions and judgments are made on an intuitive basis and how internalized alienation and internalized homophobia contributes to the process of scapegoating of people, particularly men, in homoerotic relationships. These human processes were also likely at work in the Greco-Roman world as it transitioned to the adapted conceptions of manliness of the Christianity of the Empire. There is one caveat, however. Much of what we know about Greco-Roman conceptions of manliness reflect the views of the upper classes and the educated clergy. By necessity, the extant documents were written by people of a literate class who likely shared high social status. It is therefore prudent to consider that the picture of pagan Roman manliness and sexual mores is an ideal that was not necessarily shared or even followed by a large section of the population, including ordinary Roman Christians.

Between the first and fourth centuries the concept of manliness underwent a gradual reconstruction in the melting pot of Roman decline and the rise of Christian influence. In this process gender became reconstructed and mutually reshaped by Roman and Christian ideas. Christian apologists strove to make Christian faith relevant to their Roman context and Roman Christian leaders reshape gender to fit the new reality. Building on the work of Peter Brown, Virginia Burrus explores this process of the reconstruction of maleness and the disappearance of the woman through her reading of Patristic texts. In her highly acclaimed book, "*Begotten not Made: Conceiving Manhood in Late Antiquity*," she argues that the heart of this process lies in the doctrinal debates on the doctrine of the Trinity. The evacuation of the woman and the elevation of the male to the spiritual realm is symbolized in the rising importance of celibacy and the ascetic male bishop – men are begotten not made.[237] Björn Krondorfer describes Burrus' argument as explaining how manliness became "rooted in a transcendent, immutable order."[238] Burrus demonstrates how Roman manliness and a stoic misogynistic conception of the man as rational and spiritual and the woman as passionate and of a lower order becomes reframed in the sexual asceticism of the manly eunuch-bishop. In an important work described by reviewers as a corollary to Burrus' study, Mathew Kuefler focus' on the more material reality of the gender ambiguity of the eunuch during this period and the way the destabilizing gender role of the eunuch illuminates the social construction of manliness.[239] Because Kuefler is focused on the material outworking of these concepts of manliness in late-antiquity, I will draw particularly on his argument to demonstrate the implications for people in homoerotic relationships. We must also ask how these historical insights relate to our present situation. The historical gap between late antiquity and the 21st century is wide. Can any kind of conclusion be drawn in a reasonable way? On this I would like to defer to Virginia Burrus' wise comment,

…the very act of addressing the difference of the past always implicates the present…[240]

Christian conceptions of manliness and gender developed in a Greco-Roman world that was already shaped by misogyny. This misogyny informed Tertullian's conceptions of manliness and would lead to an emerging Christian conception of a new form of manliness and unmanliness.[241]

Earlier in this chapter we have encountered the way Philo of Alexandria applied misogynistic assumptions to his rejection of homoerotic relationships. The role of misogyny remains an important consideration in any evaluation of the evolution of Christian conceptions of manliness and unmanliness. The distinction between the virtue of Roman manliness and unmanliness served to support the patriarchal structure of the whole culture.[242] For a Roman man, his status as a military man proved his manliness. As the Empire crumbled, the ideal of the military way became increasingly challenged by military defeat and what was called *vita mollitiae* (the life of effeminacy) meaning: drinking; sexual excess; the enjoyment of luxury; and general self-indulgence.[243] It is telling to note the parallel between this cultural conception and Paul's use of the Greek equivalent to the Latin *mollitiae - malakos*, in 1 Cor. 6:9, and the erroneous and biased translation of that word as "homosexual" by 20th century translators.[244]

Masculinity was also underlined by the patriarchal system of the *patria postestas* (paternal power), and the rise of the first-born son to become *paterfamilias* (father of the household) with absolute power over the extended family, slaves, and the whole household. Although the absolute power of the father of the household declined over time, this institution with its matrimonial dimensions remained an important marker of masculinity. As men's military prowess and power over their families declined, the *vita philosophica* (the philosophical life), which emphasized sexual restraint (in the stoic tradition) became more and more influential in late antiquity.[245] There is also an evolution of the idea of *pudicitia* (sexual modesty/manliness) and *impudicitia* (sexual immodesty/unmanliness). For women modesty was understood as submitting to the control of their male guardians. In this evolution, men's modesty came more and more in line with women's modesty in the sense that older practices that included prostitution became less acceptable. The earlier practice of the sexual exploitation of household slaves both male and female also became frowned upon towards the early fourth century. The social censure against sexual homoerotic relationships was in the pagan Roman context about a concern for manliness. To be penetrated by another man was to "denigrate" the man towards weak and passionate "womanly" behavior.

In 342, the Christian Co-Emperors Constans and Constantius II issued a law that banned marriage between men, and by 390, this ban, in its Theodosian version included the death penalty with the reason given that such acts would denigrate men into women.[246] These laws, their meaning and provenance, have been a matter of ongoing debate. What kind of relationship was banned? Mathew Kuefler advances the theory that it was actually the marriage between a Roman man and a eunuch that was banned. No matter the exact meaning, these 4th century laws of the Christian Empire started to enforce the death penalty on homoerotic relationships so strongly urged by Philo, Chrysostom, and Augustine. How then did the manliness of late antiquity merge with Christian conceptions of manliness? It is to this question we now turn.

The enculturation of Christianity in the Greco-Roman world over the centuries created a reality that has shaped all subsequent enculturations particularly where it involved Western Christianity. It is therefore helpful to explore how Christian conceptions of masculinity in

Western culture was shaped by the Greco-Roman enculturation of the faith. One difference we need to note in early pre-Empire Christianity is its rejection of the masculine ideal of the military man (*vita militaris*). Early Christianity was opposed to war, saw involvement in it as sinful, and many Christians withdrew or were martyred for their refusal to participate in battle. After 312, when Christianity became legal, the Roman military world became increasingly Christianized. Emperor worship and sacrifices to pagan gods phased out, but the uneasy relationship between Christian faith and military action remained. Although Augustine is rightly associated with the emergence of "just war theory", it must not be forgotten that he, and many Christian leaders, remained largely critical of Christian military involvement as a kind of necessary evil. In essence the Roman virtue of a man as military man, and the Christian virtue of manliness as *patientia* (patience, or submissive endurance) came into tension. Particularly, during the first three centuries of Christian faith, *patientia* became a key marker of Christian manliness. Thus, in the 3rd century Tertullian describes *patientia* as "the height of virtue and manliness."[247] The third century bishop, Cyprian of Carthage wrote of *patientia*, "It makes men humble in prosperity, brave in adversity, meek in the face of injuries and insults."[248] Such Christian manliness came to expression through the brave way martyrdom was faced and stands in stark contrast to Roman militarism. In fact, as early Christians' manliness was being critiqued by pagan Roman neighbors, the Christians defended their patient courage and humility as a new kind of Christian soldierly bravery described as *miles Christi* (soldier of Christ).[249] In fact, the use of the word *sacramentum* for baptism as Christian initiation, is the same word that was used for Roman military initiation. There is thus a paradoxical process of demilitarization of manliness, and then the remilitarization of Christian manly virtue.

The brave but submissive Christian martyr then starts to mock the weak (*molles/malakos*) unmanliness of the captors. Manliness also becomes spiritualized as an interior battle against sin and even a spiritual cosmic battle against the devil.[250] Even though Christian men appeared to be submissive to God and even feminized as "brides of Christ", they asserted authority through the office of the bishop which became the sole domain of men. The "flight from the world" for the pursuit of spiritual devotion became a strong theme. As bishops gained power they became rivals and challengers of the authority of the Emperor. This resulted in a transformation of the conception of God that becomes an increasingly Roman-like manly-God representing the concept of *virtus* (Roman valor, manliness, excellence, courage and worth).[251] It is in male submission to God that men paradoxically gain the power to dominate others. A divine male authority is gained in the world through spiritual submission to God.

In matters of sexual and marital relations, early Christians up to the 4th century built on rather than rejected the pagan Roman trends described above. However, they started to emphasize the perfection of celibacy and virginity as ideals. The complete rejection of all sexual relations was never accepted as orthodox thus retaining the patriarchal and misogynistic elements of pagan late antiquity. The radical Christian re-definition of pagan military manliness and the gaining of clerical authority were the new elements brought to masculinity by Christianity in late antiquity. In sexual behavior and marriage customs and legal changes were small and very much in keeping with Roman custom.[252] Fourth century Christian morality was part of a steady cultural trend in pagan Roman culture that frowned upon the pursuit of male sexual promiscuity. Moreover, under the influence of Greek philosophy, the encratic (world denying monasticism) dualism between body and soul and flesh and spirit had taken full root within the Western Christianity of the fourth century. No one represents the emphasis on sexual denial more strongly than Jerome who translated the Bible into Latin (347-420).

Interestingly enough, rather than rely on the Bible, Christian moral teaching on sexuality relied on reason and Roman styles of rhetoric with references similar to Philo of Alexandria's framing of the "law of nature."[253] "Nature" here meant the normative conception of manliness in Roman culture. Christian bias against homoerotic relationships thus developed under the influence of Roman conceptions of manliness. Fourth century Christianity did not change much of pagan Roman conceptions of sexual behavior but transformed its significance and introduced a new kind of manliness defined by means of sexual renunciation. While Christians at this time of transition accepted Roman medical ideas of sexual desire, the rise of the idea that the Fall of humankind into sin was essentially a fall into sexual desire took root. The idea of "original sin" thus became "the original sin of sexual desire." In fact, for Augustine it becomes a fall into sexual desire and activity.[254] Thus, the idea gains ground that manliness is expressed in not marrying and thus sublimating sexual desire. Relational affection in the family was discouraged and the cultivation of male friendship as a support against giving in to sexual desire became important. The 4th century misogynistic bias is further demonstrated in the encouragement of male friendships with other males. So, for example, Augustine argues that Eve was not created for friendship but for sexual procreation. He considers her an unworthy partner for true friendship.[255] Eve, and by extension women, thus simply became a bodily vehicle for bearing children. The new Christian ideal for manliness that emerges in the fourth century carries with it a dimension of reasserting male power and dominance. Mathew Kuefler writes,

I suggested in chapter 1 that manliness and unmanliness were useful categories for Roman men because they helped further the larger task of buttressing male social privilege. By labeling as "effeminate" the men who did not live up to the ideals of masculine behavior and demoting them into the category of women, the men who were in control were able to perpetuate the myth that they dominated their society and its men and women because of their moral superiority. I want to suggest now that the same motivation made manliness and unmanliness equally useful categories for Christian men. We have already seen numerous instances in preceding chapters in which Christians asserted their moral superiority by claiming greater manliness. By extending the contrast between manliness and unmanliness to a parallel contrast between Christianity and paganism, Christian men could assert their holiness and manliness as Christian men over a sinful and pagan and effeminate society. Masculine privilege rewrote itself as Christian privilege.[256]

By the fourth century Christian understanding of gender had moved radically away from the sentiment expressed in Gal 3:28, "So there is no difference between Jews and Gentiles, between slaves and free people, between men and women; you are all one in union with Christ Jesus."[257] In the Christianity of the Roman Empire, male dominance, misogyny, and a gender and class prejudice and binary re-emerges. In this context no homoerotic relationships can be tolerated. Such relationships threaten the powers of manliness. Strong gender binary and male dominance became the way that the Christianity of the Roman Empire made itself at home in the culture. Nevertheless, counter traditions persisted. So for example, many legends of early Christian holy women that were forced to live and dress as men (known as the transvestite saints), in resistance to the misogyny of pagan culture, continued.[258] In one case, Ambrose of Milan even tells the story of a transvestite Christian man.[259] However, the fortunes of all people in the Empire, including Christians who engaged in homoerotic relationships had taken a turn for the worse. From this platform of anti-homoeroticism and misogyny a theology of profound disgust, violent suppression, torture and killing would emerge.

Conclusion

As we consider the amalgamation of Judaism, New Testament Christianity, and Greco-Roman culture, we observe several important patterns that influenced the church's response to homoerotic relationships. A general pagan cultural disgust against homoerotic relationships that challenged conceptions of manliness in the Roman tradition became apparent. This disgust might also have been influenced by various moments of well-known sexual excess among Roman Emperors. Philo of Alexandria attempted to defend Judaism in this cultural context by developing the myth of Sodom as homosexual rape which he associated with cultural practices of his time. He adds to the cultural bias the idea that such people deserve the death penalty and that this applies to both male partners.

Late Roman antiquity, under the threat of a declining Empire, also found traditional patriarchal conceptions of manliness under threat. The response was to draw on the Greek stoic tradition and a larger cultural dichotomy of a division between body and soul and flesh and spirit emerged that devalued bodily existence and the enjoyment of sexuality. By the fourth century Christianity increasingly absorbed these trends. Under the influence of Philo of Alexandria's arguments, they developed a focus on retribution and the killing of people in homoerotic relationships rather than following Paul's emphasis on grace for all. Christian manliness established a new patriarchy based in sexual renunciation, and patient suffering while reinforcing the dominant role of men under submission to God. Male clergy emerged as the new symbols of manliness and they would later defend their power by violently suppressing homoerotic relationships.

The significance of the story of this chapter for the theme of this book are found in the sources of moral judgments that emerge in fourth century Christianity which lends biblical texts a new Romanized dimension and sharp edge of judgment, condemnation and prosecution. The picture that emerges of Christianity in late antiquity is one demonstrating that moral decisions about sexuality and gender are based in Roman conceptions of manliness and the shifts in general culture. The outright condemnation of homoerotic relationships in the emergence of the new Roman Christian tradition does not flow from a careful reflection on the Gospel and the teaching of the Bible. Rather, it emerged out of a reading of the Bible shaped by the cultural pre-conceptions of patriarchy and misogyny. Far from being rooted in clear and consistent theological reflection on the spirit in which moral judgments are to be made this form of Christianity chooses to assert a new kind of patriarchal and church-state enforced power in Christian manliness. The next chapter will trace how these fourth century realities would shape the sacrament of confession and the pinnacle of theological homophobia reached by the 12th century. As sure as we can recognize the vast chasm of historical and cultural difference between then and now, so sure can we also see how it implicates our present.

CHAPTER 7: THEOLOGIZING HOMOPHOBIA – CONFESSIONAL MANUALS AND CHRISTIAN DISGUST

To tell the story of the practice of the confessional and its role in shaping a deeply homophobic culture in Western Christianity we return briefly to Augustine and his mentor Ambrose of Milan. I have previously noted that Augustinian theology served as a marker of the development of anti-homoerotic sentiment. This feature is not surprising. Augustine was the architect of Western Christianity as it unfolded in both Roman Catholic and Protestant forms. It is also important to note a caveat regarding Augustine's influence. Augustine was a complex figure and his opinions were not always consistent. Both Ambrose and Augustine were products of their times, and both represented the upper crust of Roman society in late antiquity. Both were converts to Christianity when the Empire and its power collapsed. It would be more accurate to say that Augustine's writing reflected the burgeoning anti-erotic bias in Christianity. His few comments on homoerotic relationships became influential in the medieval period. From Ambrose and Augustine, we return briefly to Jerome and the Latin translation of the Bible known as the Vulgate. Then we will trace the story to the critical moment when Pope Gregory the Great established his moral teaching rooted in the seven deadly sins. During his leadership, the medieval church developed the sacrament of confession along with the manuals of confession to assist priests in hearing confessions and to guide them in the penances appropriate for particular sins.

A casuistic discipline of confessional practice developed that enhanced the idea that the "sodomitic sin" was the worst sin imaginable. This sin also increasingly described as "the sin against nature," would evolve to have many different practices associated with it including masturbation and some forms of heterosexual intercourse. Incest and the rape of women became considered lesser forgivable sins in the medieval hierarchy of sins. By the 12th century this process of rehearsing and constructing the sins of Sodom, and particularly detailed descriptions of genital activity that constitutes this sin, would establish the basis for violent persecutions, torture and killing, all in the name of Jesus Christ. It would also establish a new preoccupation with the genitals and their function in homoerotic relationships; foci that continue to exert influence right into 21st century Christian debates.

Ambrose and Augustine

Ambrose of Milan (340-397) is important to this story because he exercised a great influence over the formation of the spirituality of Augustine. Ambrose was also familiar with the work of Philo of Alexandria. Runia notes that Ambrose is the church father that most consistently engaged Philo's work.[260] There is no clarity on how Augustine was influenced by Philo's ideas. It may have been simply through Abrose's familiarity with Philo, or, Augustine, who did not read Greek, may have read some of Philo's work in Latin translation. Ambrose's interpretation of Sodom departed from biblical traditions that focused on injustice and inhospitality. He understood the narrative Sodom to reference indulgence and lasciviousness.[261] Augustine (354-430) adopted the idea of Sodom as a symbol of general human sexual depravity. In his book *De civitate Dei*, Augustine described the sin of Sodom as the desire of men to partake in "debaucheries of men" when the citizens of Sodom seek to have sexual relations with the Angelic visitors staying with Lot.[262] In Augustine's opinion Lot offered his daughters because the rape of women was considered to be less serious than homosexual rape.[263] Augustine's bias against homoerotic relationships was consistent with his context of general anti-eroticism and misogyny with a fear of "the violent eruption of disordered sexual passion."[264] When this anti-erotic bias is joined with misogyny it evolved on its own course. We can see how clearly Augustine's view on homoerotic relationships was shaped by his misogyny. He commented, "the body of a man is as superior to that of a woman as the soul is to the body."[265] Thus, for a man to act like a woman in a sexual relationship was regarded as disgusting. This moral judgment reflects the views of Roman patriarchal culture and Philo of Alexandria. It further distances the 4th century development of Christian moral theology from the New Testament perspective. It also proved to become an important step in the relentless process towards judging homoerotic relationships as the most grievous of sins. In contrast, lesbian relationships only received passing comment from Augustine when he urged nuns to refrain from "shameless playing with each other."[266] Such relationships did not directly challenge the male-dominated misogynistic Christian culture of manliness that emerged by the fourth century.

The other dimension of Augustine's contribution to the growing anxiety in Christianity about sexuality is what he adds to the developing idea of original sin. Although Augustine cannot be considered the inventor of original sin, what he stressed was the idea that sin is essentially rooted in sexual desire and that is passed on from generation to generation through the fallen state of sexual intercourse. Consequently, Augustine rejected all forms of sexual activity within marriage except those which lead to procreation. Christian wives were instructed by him to send their husbands to prostitutes to satisfy other manly desires which he considered a pragmatic part of the male condition.[267] This model became a tradition in Christian moral teaching that was in stark contrast to Paul's teaching that sexual relations are a normal component of committed Christian relationships.[268] The model also created a sexual double standard for men and women. What is surprising about Augustine's arguments against homoeroticism is that he does not rely strongly on the New Testament references from Romans, Corinthians or Timothy that would be popular in debates today. It appears that for him the issue was more deeply rooted in Roman cultural logic than in New Testament moral teaching. Augustine also initiates the evolutionary trajectory of thought that homoeroticism is particularly heinous because it is ultimately an affront against God. In his *Confessions* he writes,

Even if all peoples should do [such acts], they would be liable to the same condemnation by divine law, for it has not made men to use one another in this way. Indeed, the social bond which should exist between God and us is violated when the nature of which he is the author is polluted by a perversion of sexual desire.[269]

For Augustine the Roman conception of "nature" as Roman cultural bias became merged with the focus on procreation as the only reason for sexual eroticism. Thus, Augustine considered this Roman cultural version of "nature" to be divinely authored. This Augustinian conviction still firmly held in anti-homoerotic arguments made within many Christian circles both Catholic and Protestant today. For Augustine, the sexual arousal of the male, even when unintentional, provided proof of the deep seated and indelible influence of sin towards rebellion against God.[270] As Christian manliness became associated with the renunciation of the sin of sexuality, and as the worst sexual sin imaginable was homoerotic relations, the stage was set for medieval moral theology.

Jerome

Jerome (347-420), the translator of the Latin Bible (the Vulgate), was a contemporary of Ambrose and Augustine. It is particularly through his translation of the Bible into Latin that his influence stretches into the contemporary world. In fact, the Vulgate translation became the accepted and authoritative translation of the Bible and the key way in which Christian theologians in the West engaged the Biblical text until the 16th century Reformation. Within Roman Catholicism the Vulgate was considered the authorized translation of the Bible into the 1960s.[271] For the few people who could read and had access to books through the medieval period, the Vulgate became their primary biblical source. Jerome was a great proponent of sexual renunciation, but his biggest influence on the development of medieval homophobia was his use of the Latin word *luxuria* to translate various Hebrew and Greek terms in the Bible. Jerome, as a superb biblical scholar, was well aware of the Old Testament and New Testament interpretations of the sins of Sodom and he echoes the Book of Ezekiel that described Sodom's sin as essentially rooted in pride. He interpreted and glossed this kind of pride as brazenly boasting of sins committed and argued that such a shameless attitude of boasting was born of a life of opulence which in Latin becomes *luxuria.*[272] Through Jerome's translation, the development of Christian manliness in late antiquity as the renunciation of sex subtly enters his Biblical translation by means of the use of the Latin word *luxuria*.

Drunkenness, gluttony and sexual excess became associated with the use of *luxuria* in the Vulgate. The Vulgate describes the activities of the prodigal son as *luxuria.* In Paul's vice list in Gal 5:19 *luxuria* follows fornication and uncleanness.[273] In 2 Peter *luxuria* is associated with blasphemy and the desires of the flesh and in Jude it refers to corrupted false teachers of the Word of God.[274] Two translation decisions by Jerome would also have an impact on the perception of homoerotic relationships. In an earlier chapter we briefly considered Paul's vice lists, particularly the Greek words *malakoi* and *arsenokaitai*. For *malakoi* Jerome chose the Latin *molles* which has a wide range of meanings including soft, pliant, feeble, weak, cowardly and untrustworthy.[275] In 1 Cor 6:9 Jerome translated *arsenokoitai(s)* with the Latin *masculorum concubitores* which literally means "those who lie with men." This phrase could mean prostitution or acting as a passive male sexual partner in the Roman culture of the time. With the onset of the Reformation, the translation of these terms assumed new dimensions with a strong homophobic character. The basis for this shift towards anti-homoerotic meaning lies in the development of medieval moral teaching. It was when Pope Gregory the Great (540-604) interpreted *luxuria* as one of the seven deadly sins that the stage became set for medieval moral theology's violent rejection of all homoerotic relationships.

Gregory the Great (540-604)

Pope Gregory the Great occupied a pivotal role in the development of Western Christian moral theology. The consequences of his focus stretched far beyond the actual content of his writing to the way in which his teaching on the seven deadly sins shaped the medieval world, the practice of confession, and Western culture in general. Gregory built his anti-homoerotic teachings upon the structures created by Philo, Chrysostom, and Augustine to associate the sin of Sodom primarily with sins of the flesh and by implication with homoerotic relations and rape.[276] Gregory was well-aware of the Old Testament and New Testament traditions of interpreting the sins of Sodom as pride and inhospitality. However, the force of the new Christian-Roman moral conception, particularly the general anti-erotic sentiment amongst influential Clergy like himself, swayed him towards a sense of revulsion against sexual relations in general. This shift became clear in comments he made in his book on the *Moral Teaching of Job*. It is helpful to quote Mark Jordan's conclusion in full on this pivotal moment in the formation of Christian moral teaching,

"At one point in explicating Job, Gregory wants to gloss the image of sulfur. He thinks at once of the destruction of Sodom. "That we should understand sulfur as signifying the stench of the flesh, the history of the holy Scriptures itself testifies, when it narrates that God rained down fire and sulfur on Sodom." Sodom is punished for "crimes of the flesh" (*scelera carnis*), for "perverse desires from the stench of the flesh" (*peruersa desideria ex fetore carnis*), for "what they did from unjust desire (*ex iniusto desiderio*). In his *Pastoral Rule*, Gregory makes the moral explicit: "To flee from burning Sodom is to refuse the illicit fires of the flesh."[277]

Gregory also wrote to address a situation where a priest is accused of idolatry and "the crime of the Sodomite." This letter of guidance would ultimately play a key role in the future of anti-homoerotic teaching as "the crime of the Sodomite" is, by the 10th century erroneously translated with the abstract phrasing "the crime of Sodomy."[278] Gregory did not create the term Sodomy, but his writing and its mistranslation in the 10th century, marks the further development of a full-fledged medieval teaching against homoerotic relationships conceived as an abstract state of being.

Gregory's most important contribution to the development of Western moral theology on sexuality can be found in his emphasis on the sin of *luxuria*. Mark Jordan explains that for Gregory this is the last, but most important sin to attend to amongst the seven deadly sins.[279] *Luxuria* for Gregory came to represent self-indulgence and self-gratification of both the "flesh" and heart. Most importantly for the subject here, Gregory associated *luxuria* with the genitals and with effeminacy and animality.[280] Gregory was so focused on sexual expression as sin that the loins themselves turned into the source of the whole of the sin of

96

luxuria. Mark Jordan correctly points out that for Gregory *luxuria* was a much wider concept very much like Augustine's idea of disordered desire. However, whenever Gregory discussed *luxuria,* he gravitated back to sexual sins suggesting a profound bias towards seeing sexual expression as the root of this sin located in the loins. The concept *luxuria* thus ascended from the pagan world of the late Roman Empire, which understood it as luxurious and self-centered living, into the Latin Bible of the Roman church where it ascended to the place where it represented sexual desire as sin. In hierarchy of sin, homoerotic relationships thus took the honorary place as the worst kind of sin, a sin that offends against both "nature" and God.

At this point in time "the Sodomitic life" (*vitium sodomiticum*) was not yet clearly defined as something exclusively homoerotic. Even by the 8th century Boniface (676-754) would then describe the crimes of the sodomite as incest, promiscuity in general, adultery, and impious unions with religious cloistered women.[281] At that time the meaning of sodomite is still mingled with heterosexual sexual transgressions.

Penitential Manuals

The process of shaping of the extreme rejection and persecution of people in homoerotic relationships had begun, and all the pieces were in place for the next stage of development. Nevertheless, there was not yet a clear consensus on the sodomitic sin and its meaning. The next stage in the development of revulsion at the sins of Sodom would be marked by the important emergence of medieval confessional practice.

Priests who had to hear confession were in need of practical guidance in hearing confession. What kind of questions were appropriate within the confessional? How do priests avoid asking wrong questions that might lead the faithful into sins they had not even previously imagined? What are the appropriate penances to be prescribed for particular transgressions?

From the 7th century onwards, penitential manuals (penitentials) became a staple of the medieval church.[282] These manuals contained a series of developing concepts associated with the sins of Sodom. These concepts included fornication in the Sodomitic manner (*sodomitico more*), and sins of the Sodomitic custom (*sodomitico ritu*). The obsession with genitals and their role in these sins, as outlined above, becomes apparent in graphic descriptions of "fornication in the rear" or "fornication between the legs."[283] Penitential manuals not only served to give guidance; they also served as disputational documents to settle controversies of the time. Of necessity, these manuals contained their own forms of rhetoric. In their enthusiasm, the authors of the manuals misquoted and conflated texts from older authorities to strengthen an anti-homoerotic case.

The practice of confession and penance evolved as the way the church dealt with the problem that baptism did not remove all sinful action from a believer's life. By regular confession and penance such matter were dealt with. Paradoxically, despite the essential anti-legalistic approach of the earlier forms of Christianity, the practice of confession and penance turned medieval Christianity into a legalistic religion. Inevitably, it also became a way for the medieval church and clergy to extend and exercise power over the people.

There is thus truth in the French Philosopher Michel Foucault's claim that the modern concept of sexuality was created by the church's practice of confession and further extended by the disciplines of psychiatry and psychology in the 20th century.[284] Some writers of penitentiary texts wrestled with the double edged sword of the potential that the practice that sought to bring relief of sin could lead the confessee into sin through the questions asked by the confessor.

In the section to follow I will rely further on Mark Jordan's ground-breaking text, *"The Invention of Sodomy in Christian Theology."* In the history of the development of anti-homoerotic penitentials, the 11th century manual by Peter Damian (1007-1073) called *The Book of Gomorrah,* he   established a particularly important and vehement form of rhetoric that would have far reaching consequences.

Peter Damian – The Book of Gomorrah

Peter Damian (1007-1072) drew on many sources but relied particularly on a penitential by Burchard of Worms (950-1025) for his material in *The Book of Gomorrah.* He added several important new dimensions to penitentials of that time. First, even though Peter Damian addressed the classic seven deadly sins, he exerted the bulk of his energy in writing on *luxuria* and particularly a detailed taxonomy of homoerotic sins. He placed *luxuria* last but, like Gregory the Great, he gave it the most importance. The effect is that homoerotic sins become singled out as the most important matter to be dealt with in the hearing of a confession. Peter Damian also continued the obsessional trend describing genital activity in detail. He adopted Burchard of Worms' taxonomy of genital activity but reversed it. In Burchard of Worms' version of confessional interrogation the penitent is asked about anal intercourse, intercourse between the legs, pleasuring another man, and masturbation.[285] Peter Damian reversed the order of questions to culminate with anal intercourse. In this process "the Sodomite" became more specifically defined in terms of specific genital activity. He also moved beyond Burchard, who took the idea of the death penalty for such sins metaphorically, to argue for literally putting people to death.[286]

Even though the rhetorical structure of *The Book of Gomorrah* implies the possibility of penance and change, the content seems to relay the idea that being a Sodomite is a kind of identity that cannot be changed.[287] As these ideas took root from Peter Damian on, it eventually led to a conviction that sodomy had to be dealt with by putting the "Sodomites" to death to save their souls. The implications of this growing conviction would reach into the 21st century when the death penalty for the "crime of sodomy" remains in effect in some countries. Finally, it is with Peter Damian that the idea of the Sodomite and the sodomitic sin became abstracted to the essentialized idea of "sodomy."   In fact, Peter Damian described the homoerotic expression of *luxuria* as a lethal disease that ruled the body with madness, poison and infection.[288] Mark Jordan points out that *The Book of Gomorrah* created an approach of entrapment for the one who comes to confess. On the one hand it seems to offer alluring images of healing, while in fact, Peter Damian seemed to fundamentally doubt the possibility of healing.[289] When the nineteenth and twentieth century psychiatric tradition invented the concept homosexuality and described it as a disease which is an inversion, it is not without influence from this medieval development of turning homoerotic attraction into a disgusting disease. To track the trajectory of growing homophobic violence we move next from the 11th century to 1215 and the decisions of the 4th Lateran Council in Rome.

The Fourth Lateran Council Onwards

The Fourth Lateran Council called for the appointment of preachers and more penitentiaries to assist bishops in their task to hear confession and to prescribe penance. The council also formalized the practice of regular confession in Canon 21 which required going to confession once a year. Paul of Hungary's widely used *Summa Penance* seems to have been a response to the Council around 1219. In his *Summa Penance,* Paul of Hungary was particularly concerned with "the sin against nature." He devotes forty percent of his book on this problem. His penitentiary relayed the medieval anxiety with all possible forms of incest. Thus "unnatural coupling" with your wife would constitute a sin against nature and it was considered worse than committing incest with your mother.[290] For him the "sin against nature" included lesbian sexual expression, and he came to define this sin for men as any spilling of semen outside the reproductive vagina of your wife.[291] He concluded that any intercourse outside of the procreative act properly executed in one's wife's vagina constituted the sin of "sodomy."[292]

Robert of Flamborough (probably 1135-1219) added to the discussion with a particular concern about invoking sin by posing questions that would suggest things to the penitent that they had not previously imagined. He instructed the use of a sensitive process for extracting information from the penitent. Interestingly enough, his central concern was not homoerotic sin but masturbation. The theme of masturbation accrued new importance in the 13th century. Robert of Sorbonne (1201-1274) argued that masturbation was a form of incest. He understood incest to mean having sexual relations with someone close to you. As you are closest to yourself masturbation constitutes the worst kind of incest.[293] In his conclusion on this period and particularly 13th century developments, Mark Jordan reflects on the growing trend towards not naming Sodomy in preaching or confessional practice. He concludes that the increasing reticence of the one hearing confession towards addressing this sin is an ironic testament to the power that the myth of Sodom started to wield over the clergy of the time.[294] It is perhaps a commentary on what would become, in the 19th century in the words of Lord Alfred Douglas, "the love that dare not speak its name." The growth of shame, inner disgust, a conviction of an unchangeable state of sodomy, a fixation on the judgment of fire and sulfur on Sodom, and a prescription for the death penalty to save the soul of the offender would soon lead to some of the most disturbing moments of religious violence in Christian tradition.

At this point in time a new creative interaction between the European medieval world and the superior science and medicine of the Islamic world took place. Islamic texts in science and medicine were translated into Latin and became available in Europe. Albert the Great (1200-1280) was one of the towering polymaths and theologians of this time. He integrated this new creative interaction and learning from Islamic science in his thinking on sin and penitential practice. He would, however, refuse to use these Islamic insights in his conclusions about homoerotic relationships. The consequences ultimately played-out in the torture and killing of people in great numbers in Rome, Venice, Florence and the Spanish Inquisition. In the early 14th century in France the Knights Templar would be wiped out on false charges of Sodomy by their debtor, King Philip IV, and their possessions would be confiscated by the Crown. In this process, a Roman obsession with Patriarchal misogynistic manliness and anti-erotic sentiment would shape Christian moral theology into a force that would become responsible for some of the most shocking acts of brutality and violence.

Albert the Great

The major sources for medical knowledge in the 13th century were texts translated from Arabic. One of the most influential was Avicenna's (Ibn-Sina)(980-1037) *Canon of Medicine* which originated in the Golden Age of Islam from 10th century Iran. Most of the texts translated into Latin dealt medically with sexual acts and sexual functioning and they refer to homoerotic relationships. The focus was on medical explanations for sexual functioning and dysfunction. In the matter of homoerotic relationships, the texts would note that such sexual interactions are against Islamic law, but it would then set this legal judgment aside to continue to dispassionately investigate what the medical causes might be for such behavior.[295] When it comes to *aluminate* – homoerotic relationships as described in an Arabic Islamic context – Avicenna considered it to be an ailment. Thus, he considered it a condition to be studied as a medical issue. He identified causes for this condition. Jordan summarizes these causes as an excess of desire or spermatic matter; and overpowering mental affliction; a degenerative custom linked to depravity; and the result of anatomical irregularity.[296]

It is illuminating that, in the Latin translation of *Canon of Medicine* used by medieval Christian scholars, the translator interposes a commentary that challenges Avicenna's claim that there was no cure for the condition that makes a man seek to be a passive partner in the homoerotic relationship. First it claimed that, that section of *Canon of Medicine* is "empty" and after the challenged section it adds that, that disputed section is "a wicked part of science."[297] The implications for this gloss of the Arabic text in 13th century Christianity are many. One example is that the disputed section of *Canon of Medicine* represents a position that labels homoerotic relationships as a medical condition. This trend would come to full bloom in the 19th century coining of the phrase "homosexual" and its importation into biblical translations during the 20th century. The 13th century Christian commentary reflects just how powerful the anti-homoerotic disgust and its religious power had become by the 13th century. It also shaped the way that homoerotic relationships will be treated differently from other sexual sins by Albert the Great.

When Albert considered the study of sexual deviance as perceived in the 13th century, he essentially followed the same kind of approach as the Islamic scholars in noting the legal strictures of Christian moral theology, while continuing to study and enquire about the possible medical dimensions and cures for such conditions. However, when it comes to *luxuria,* now very much perceived as a homoerotic assignation, he described it thus:

"*Luxuria* is an experience of pleasure according to the reproductive power that does not comply with law."[298] Homoerotic sexual relations thus became for Albert, "sin against grace, against reason, and against nature."[299] Albert's explanation of what makes the sin of *luxuria* different from other sins was that it is the "illicit use of the power to procreate."[300] Albert also moved the trend towards a preoccupation with sexual organs and positions a step further by theorizing that the use of organs, such as the placing of the penis in the vagina, is legitimate because it accomplishes its end. The same is true for sexual positions, because a woman's vulva is presented at the front of her body human copulation must occur from the front.[301] These conclusions continue to implicate anti-homoerotic discourse right into 20th century debates about sexual morality and Christian theology in the form of the sexual complementarity argument. In his commentary on Luke 17:28-29 Albert referred to the wicked sin of Sodom as the burning and flaming desire that is beyond what the natural order permits. Even though, reflective of the trend of his time, he was cautious not to name "Sodomy," but he presents it as an infectious disease.[302] As we trace the power trajectory of the rising violent homophobia, we have to move finally to Thomas of Aquinas who would become the architect of contemporary Roman Catholic teaching on homoerotic relationships.

Thomas of Aquinas (1225-1247)

In his sensitive treatment of Thomas Aquinas' approach to homoerotic relationships, Mark Jordan argues that the larger structure of Thomas' moral theology should caution readers into judging his position too harshly. In fact, Thomas focused more on virtue than on vice and his treatment of the sin of *luxuria* is arguably not a central part of his argument in his *Summa Theologica*. On the other hand, as Jordan points out, it is the use of Thomas' theology by those who followed as a kind of casuistic canon law that led to so much physical harm done to human beings in the name of theology. In fact, by the time of the Council of Trent, Thomas' *Summa Theologica* was elevated to the level of official Roman Catholic teaching.

For Aquinas, the sin of *luxuria* is rooted in an excess of venereal pleasure.[303] Thomas follows Emperor Gratian's (359-383) list of vices which includes fornication, adultery, incest, deflowering, and abduction. However, he added a sixth category, "the vice against nature." It is this vice which contains his teaching against Sodomy. In some ways Thomas' teaching simply reflects the developing trends outlined earlier in this chapter. There is the placement of category of *luxuria* essentially in the area of venereal pleasure. He echoed the long tradition that sees the only appropriate place for sexual activity as that which is procreative. Thomas understood sodomy as a sin against nature in the light of the long tradition originating with Philo and Greek philosophy. He also reflected the growing trend not to be specific or graphic in his description of sexual activity. Jordan also points out that Aquinas made two intentional misappropriations in his argument. First, he read Augustine's statement on the judgment of Sodom through his 13th century lens that turns this event of judgment into a judgment on homoerotic sin.[304] Secondly, uncharacteristically, he chose to misappropriate Aristotle's distinction between bestiality, which was against nature, and homoerotic relationships which Aristotle considered to be against "good custom." He conflated these two Aristotelian categories equating homoerotic relationships, including lesbianism, with bestiality and thus against nature and ultimately as sins against God.[305] Thomas went as far as to claim that these sins against nature were worse than other carnal sins that affect other human beings, such as rape, exactly because they are sins against nature.[306] So strong was Thomas's visceral disgust against homoerotic relationships that he inserted the Latin word *turpis* (wicked) twice in his rendering of Aristotle's book *Politics* when it refers to sexual acts between men.[307]

Conclusion

As sympathetic as we ought to be to all the authors and thinkers, we have encountered for being children of their time and for being employed later in ways not originally intended, we should also take seriously the profound human cost of ideas that take a path towards violence and the killing of other human beings. In effect, this is what happened to Thomas' teaching as it started to exercise its influence into the 14th century. The next section of this book will be concerned with the real-world material outworking of these ideas in late medieval and Renaissance Europe. By the time Thomas' *Summa Theologica* was penned, a profound visceral reaction was deeply rooted in the patriarchal medieval culture of the time, particularly in the clerical world. Of course, there were clergy that acted differently, more pastorally, and sometimes immorally by the standards of that time, but, the consensus of the time was one squarely and violently opposed to homoerotic relationships. This violent opposition to homoerotic relationships was now ensconced in penitentiaries, and in the major theological works of the time. The emphasis on anatomically correct, frontally engaged sexual relations within marriage with only procreation in mind was solidly established. Any other form of sexual, genital expression and any deviance from the standards of patriarchal maleness was not tolerated. At the same time there was a certain laxness for male sexual desire with the tacit ecclesial support for heterosexual brothels and prostitution. Such practices of prostitution were sanctioned by Augustine and Aquinas as necessary evils. It was thought, notwithstanding the official teaching of the church, that men will be men and if they must fornicate an appropriate outlet must be provided for these lesser carnal sins. When it came to men, and sometimes women in homoerotic relationships indulgent tolerance was not practiced.

These doctrinal developments during the medieval period are very important as we seek to discern a Christian moral response to sexual and gender minority people today. We need to note the ramping up of prejudice to the point of representing the modern concept of homophobia. We can also see how this "sin against nature" had taken a path far beyond its ancient meaning and intention. "Nature" and God's act of creation became closely associated and the idea developed that nature is a model for moral behavior. A significant part of the arguments that supported this development was not based in reality. The extreme disgust with this "sin against nature" combined with the rising power of local authorities and new laws inspired by church teaching, became the basis for one of the saddest chapters in Christian history.

CHAPTER 8: THE LAW AND CORRUPTION – THE EXPLOITATION OF DISGUST

God, detesting the sin of sodomy...brought down his wrath upon the cities of Sodom and Gomorrah and soon thereafter flooded and destroyed the whole world for such horrible sins; [hence] our most wise ancestors sought with all their laws and experts to liberate our city from such a dangerous divine judgment.[308]   (1458 - The Council of Ten, Venice)

This confident declaration of the fabulously wealthy Council of Ten in the city of Venice in the mid 15th century reflects the growing power of religious homophobia in medieval Europe.   By this time, the association of homoerotic relationships with Sodom and its destruction is considered self-evident.   All those who wish to protect their economic assets needed to heed and be mindful not to transgress this prohibition because harbouring such sinfulness against nature and God might lead to God's punishment by either flood or fire. Those engaged in homoerotic relationships feared being hunted down and punished by burning or drowning on behalf of God.   The alternative might lead to the loss of economic prosperity or as they then thought, could trigger plague or famine to a city. If such disasters did strike, the way to deal with them was to find and punish the "sodomites" responsible for bringing down God's judgment on the city.   So concerned were the Council of Ten in 1458 with this great danger to their prosperity that they removed the task of hunting down and prosecution of "sodomy" from Venice's infamous Night Police and took it on as their own responsibility.   Thus, the fruits of a homophobic theology had ripened; it bore no relation to the New Testament fruit of the Spirit or the way of Jesus of Nazareth.

Having explored the trajectory of Christian teaching from the early church through to the high point of Christian rejection and extreme condemnation of people in homoerotic relationships in the 13th century, we turn now to the application of these growing convictions in Roman and medieval law.   The alliance between church teaching and the law would grow like a slow burning fuse from banishment and the seizure of property to brutal executions by the 13th century. When such radical punishments have church approval and the force of civil law, they set up temptations for further exploitation and corruption.   This is exactly what happened.   This chapter examines Western legal developments and considers three major moments when corruption in the name of morality became particularly evident.   Together they tell a cautionary tale of the corruption of Christian morality in the name of "the sin against nature."

The Law

In most ancient near eastern legal models, homoerotic relationships only came under legal scrutiny in cases of incest, rape or a false accusation for being the passive partner in a sexual encounter.   When false, such accusations were considered slander.[309]   Even though there have been some arguments that ancient Israel was concerned with Canaanite worship practices that included male temple prostitution, the evidence for such practices is weak.

Within western tradition, particularly in the Greek and later the Roman traditions of law, the major concern was with the passive male partner in a homoerotic relationship. It was a law concerned with citizens and their behaviour, and it did not apply to slaves. But the first clear Roman statute that censured homoerotic relationships was issued by Emperor Constantine as Christianity rose to the position of religion of the Empire. However, Constantine's law is mild and uses traditional Roman legal arguments about Roman virtue and unmanliness; it also censures the "passive" partner in a sexual relationship. Consistent with the slow process of theological development described in the previous chapter, the first overt biblical reference in law to the story of Sodom comes with the laws of the Christian Emperor Justinian (527-565) wherein it refers to the crimes of Sodom "for which whole cities are destroyed." These laws known as the *Corpus Juris Civilis* became the foundation for the prosecution and killing of people in homoerotic relationships during the medieval period and grew to a frenzy by the 15th and 16th centuries[310].

In the early medieval period Justinian's law was lost and the so called "Barbarian" legal systems that medieval jurists drew on did not have a tradition of censuring homoerotic relationships. However, church law, known as Canon Law, became the legal locus of the anti-homoerotic bias. In the previous chapter we followed the trajectory of Christian theological thinking from the early medieval period through to the 13th century. Canon law developed in concert with these penitentiary traditions and mirrored the growing conviction that homoerotic relationships constitute the terrible crime and sin that is against nature and against God. The conviction grew that this particular crime and sin was considered on par with the evil of witches and heretics.[311] However, despite laws on the death penalty that can be traced to 966,[312] the increased use of capital punishment only came into full sway in the 13th century under the rising influence of the teachings of Thomas of Aquinas that supported the idea that homoerotic relationships are a grievous sin against nature.[313] The sodomitic sin came to be considered equal in gravity to murder and a crime contrary to reason, nature, and the will of God.[314] In our reflection on Christian moral discernment and the doing of material harm, it is important to note here the confluence of a rising theological homophobia and harsh penalties under civil law.

In 1100, Justinian's *Corpus Juris Civilis* was rediscovered initiating a flourishing of medieval legal scholarship particularly at the University of Bologna. Despite the distinction between civil and canon law, most graduates received a dual doctorate in both civil and canon law.[315] This burgeoning legal tradition revived and expanded Justinian's code against the sodomitic sin. Scholars at the time were aware of changing and developing traditions. Thus, the famous medieval legal scholar Accursius (1182-1263) noted that there was no law against "sodomy" until 342.[316] As a result of these legal and theological developments, anxiety about homoerotic relationships started to rise. The 3rd Lateran Council (1179) declared that clerics caught in the sodomitic sin should be defrocked and cloistered and that lay people be excommunicated. By 1215, the 4th Lateran Council appealed for civil help in fighting heretics and those who commit the sodomitic sin. It was also declared that only Bishops had the authority to grant absolution for this sin. From 1220 onwards, the Papal Inquisition took charge of the prosecution of those accused of the sodomitic sin. During this period, with the rise of counter religious movements in Northern Italy, Southern France and Bulgaria, the heresies of the Cathars also known as the Bougres, and the Bogomils (Bougres) of Hungary became associated with homoerotic relationships. It is here that the legal term "buggery" (from "Bougres") originated, and that term came into common use in the British Empire through Henry VIII.

Although the Holy Roman Emperor Frederick II (1194-1250) resisted including "the sodomitic sin" in his civil legal code, other jurisdiction such as that of Alfonso X of Castile, St Louis of Anjou and Edward I of England all moved towards requiring capital punishment for the sodomitic sin.[317] There is some evidence that the ecclesiastical Council of London promulgated a law against sodomy in 1102 and the legal document known as *Fleta* from the late 13th century England makes mention of the burning of people for the sodomitic sin.[318] The rising spirit of mob violence and religious homophobia was reflected in 1233 with the enlistment of lay orders in Bologna to prosecute people accused of homoerotic relationships. Another example was the city of Perugia offering bounties for informers and the punishment of burning of the accused with their property.[319] In 1457 Pope Nicholas II initiated action against homoerotic relationships through the Papal Inquisition. In Valencia in 1519 there was mob violence and the burning of 4 victims, and the Papal Inquisition in Portugal sanctioned burning or banishment to the Galleys in 1562. In 1569 Philip II introduced the death penalty in Sicily.[320] These increasingly belligerent and violent legal reactions parallel the theological developments arising out of the 13th century.

The Temptation of Property

A growing tradition took root in 14th century Europe of combining harsh forms of capital punishment with the confiscation of all property of a convicted "sodomite" by the Crown. Previously, in 1260, St Louis of Anjou decreed that the sodomitic sin should be punished by mutilation, castration and the confiscation of property.[321] Even though the Germanic civil law traditions did not address homoerotic relationships, as the ecclesiastical influence grew, the first laws in the Holy Roman Empire introducing the death penalty occur in 1532, with the appearance of the *Constitutio Criminalis Carolina* enacting the death penalty against sodomy which is described as "unchastity against nature."[322] In 1533, Henry VIII introduced the English law against buggery which prescribed the penalty as death by hanging and sanctioned the confiscation of all property by the Crown.[323] We will see later how this growing trend was employed by Philip IV of France in his dispute with the Templars and by Isabella I of Castile and her husband Ferdinand II of Aragon. We will also see the temptation to confiscate property for the Crown that might have influenced Henry VIII's law against "buggery."

The overt use of charges of "sodomy" or "buggery" to confiscate property had its earlier genesis in the medieval battles between the Ghibellines and the Guelphs. These movements that battled between the monarchic and Papal powers, used charges of the sodomitic sin to prosecute each other and to confiscate each-other's property.[324] As the 16th century unfolded, and the struggles of the Reformation raged in Europe, charges of Sodomy became some of the most powerful tools to discredit and prosecute one another as enemies. In this way, as theological and religious homophobia became more commonplace, it assumed an unholy alliance with avarice and other political and religious motivations. Accusing and laying charges against people for what is considered the most grievous crime against nature and ultimately against God, wielding a power that becomes irresistible to those in search of more power. In the following two chapters we will look at the painful and violent consequences for people in Renaissance Catholicism and Protestantism. In this chapter, we will focus briefly on the economic exploitation of laws against Sodomy by highlighting three examples of the use of these laws to serve political and economic ends.

Philip IV of France and the Templars

Philip IV (1268-1314) inherited a bankrupt kingdom. He was both ambitious and ruthless. His war against Edward I of England and Flanders would further bankrupt him, forcing him to take loans from the Lombard bankers, Jewish merchants and the Knight's Templar. With this massive indebtedness hanging over his Crown, he devised plans to rid himself from the burden of debt. His first step, in 1306, was to expel the Jews and to confiscate all their property for the Crown. He took similar action against the Lombard bankers and also seized property from some wealthy abbots. His actions against the church raised the ire of Pope Boniface VIII, and the conflict between Philip and the Pope led to the famous Papal bull *Unam Sanctam* which claimed Papal supremacy. As the conflict increased, Boniface narrowly escaped arrest and then died. This led to the election of a French archbishop as Pope Clement V. Thus started the famous period of the Pope living in Avignon under Philip's protection and control. The ensuing economic crisis caused such riots in Paris that Philip had to hide in the Paris Temple of the Knight's Templar. However, as Philip's last major creditor, the situation did not bode well for the Templars.

The Knight's Templars, a military order established in 1119 to support the Crusades, became very influential throughout medieval Europe and in the feudal state of Jerusalem established in Palestine. Their fortunes rose and fell with the different Crusades and was further complicated by their rivalry with the other major military order of the time, the Knight's Hospitaller. Their major feature became the way they acted as one of the most important bankers of Europe, circumventing canon law against usury in creative ways. The result was that they became bankers and major creditors to the wealthy and powerful in medieval Europe. The Paris Temple became the major commercial hub of this activity and despite their personal vows of poverty, chastity, and obedience, the Templars attained great wealth. There was also much speculation about their "secret rule" – a prescribed Templar ritual - and secret midnight meetings. The "rule" and rumours about their midnight meetings gave Philip an opening to get his hands on their wealth.

In the Fall of 1307, by issuing secret orders throughout his realm, Philip's agents arrested the Templars in his kingdom.[325] Based on rumours that the Templar rituals involved homoerotic practices and orders to commit sodomy, Philip had the Grand Inquisitor of France, William of Paris, proceed with charges against the Templars, including Jacques de Molay the Grand Master. This challenge was considered legal because theological opinion at the time considered sodomy a form of heresy and apostasy. Periods of brutal torture ensued

106

extracting various levels of confession from the Templars. In Paris, 36 Templars died as a result of the torture.[326] The confessions extracted from Templars ranged from "admitting" to spitting on the crucifix and denying Christ and committing various forms of sodomitic acts. Even de Molay buckled under the torture and confessed to apostasy. Papal resistance against these actions were weak as the Avignon Pope was dependent on royal support. Louis Crompton reports,

The articles of interrogation also implied that the knights condoned and even enjoined sodomy within the brotherhood. The formal accusations included these charges: "Item, that in the reception of the brothers of the said Order or at about that time, sometimes the receptor and sometimes the received were kissed on the mouth, on the navel, or on the bare stomach, and on the buttocks or the base of the spine . . . Item, [that they were kissed] sometimes on the penis . . . Item, that they told the brothers whom they received that they could have carnal relations together . . . [and] that they did this, or many of them did.[327]

The tortures to which the Templars were subjected to extract confessions of such acts included roasting the feet until the bones fell from their sockets.[328] Testimony in the bishop's courts reported stretching on the rack, dropping people from the ceiling, and hanging weights from genitals and other body parts.[329] It is telling that in other jurisdictions such as England and Germany where Templars were also arrested, but where torture was not used, very few confessions were extracted.

Given the theological homophobia of the time and the legal developments outlined above, it is easy to see how these charges and their extraction under pain of torture would serve as an excellent public relations campaign for the king covering his own religious, economic and political motives. At the time, the Knights Templar were highly regarded as defenders of the faith and fearless warriors on behalf of Christendom. They were also immensely powerful through their control of economic resources and religious independence. It required radical charges to publicly discredit them. The theological consensus and the rising anxiety of the time associated sodomy with blasphemy, heresy and witchcraft. These kinds of accusations were also an integral part of the inquisitorial propaganda of the time.

In 1310 Pope Clement V finally moved to try the remaining arrested Templars. When they were transferred to Papal jurisdiction de Molay and many others started to retract their confessions. Philip, seeing his case collapse, ordered the archbishop of Sens to transport 54 Knights to a field outside Paris where they were burned without a proper trial.[330]

For Philip, the ultimate issue was getting control over the assets of the Order. In 1312, Clement V convened the Council of Vienne to deal with the Order. It was clear that the majority of the investigating commission of the Council did not believe that there was sufficient proof of heresy among the Templars. Philip mustered his troops outside the city. The Pope hastily forbade debate and condemned the Order and shut it down. Jacques de Molay in his final trial retracted all his confessions, but Philip, acting swiftly, had him burned that very evening before the religious court could respond.[331] It is worth citing Louis Crompton's commentary on this chapter in history,

The fate of the Templars shows how effective an instrument the fear of sodomy and heresy, so frequently linked, could be in the hands of a Machiavellian ruler. Philip, however, lived to enjoy his gains only a few months. Dante, at work on the composition of his "Purgatorio" during the Templars' persecution, denounced Philip (in Canto 20) as a new "Pontius Pilate" whose "cruelty and avarice" had despoiled the Temple.[332]

Historians continue to debate Philip's motivation and the complexity of the religious and political world of the time. There is increasing consensus that part of the struggle between Philip and the Templars was motivated by a desire to make the Capetian monarchy into the mystic foundation of a Papal theocracy.[333] Such aspirations required ruthless action. Economic power and theological homophobia, together with its legal counterpart in civil government, granted Philip the power to act. It is of course true that this kind of violence, torture, lies and abuse was not unique in the medieval and religious world of the time. It is equally true that it bears no resemblance to the life, ministry, and example of Jesus of Nazareth. Under the guise of moral outrage and long-standing theological arguments, a profound immorality functioned in the heart of the Christian church.

The Economic and Power Dimensions of the Spanish Inquisition

The next chapter will reveal some of the abhorrent practices of the Spanish Inquisition which gained full force under the reign of Ferdinand and Isabella of Castile. Here we will only note some of the economic and political dimensions of charges of sodomy in that time and context. In the Spanish context the legal code known as the *Siete Partidas* (1265) established a particularly cruel punishment for sodomy. It claimed that sodomy could be blamed as the cause of natural disasters and as a sign of God's displeasure with the culprits. Alphonse X required castration with death by hanging upside down three days later as the punishment for such crimes. Ferdinand and Isabella favoured death by live burning, a punishment ensconced in an edict issued in 1497. Such punishment went with the Crown having full power over confiscating the possessions of those accused. In the midst of an atmosphere of mob anger, easy accusation, and confessions obtained by torture, charges of sodomy became a powerful political tool for Ferdinand and Isabella. It also served Isabella's carefully cultivated image of a pious woman fighting for the truth of God.

One of the key political programs that Isabella and Ferdinand engaged in was to unite their kingdoms under the Catholic faith. As part of this political and religious effort they obtained permission from the Pope to prosecute sodomites through the Spanish Inquisition.[334] The use of their growing political and religious power led to a kind of religious totalitarian regime that instilled fear in the population. In fact, the constant use of informants and the practices of torture of the Inquisition followed by large public celebrations of the death penalty that instilled a thirst for blood and fear in the population became a mark of their reign. The *auto da fe* were baroque-like public celebrations with large numbers of *familiars* - specially uniformed laymen – who animated the events. The inquisitorial tribunal of Valencia had 1638 such *familiars* registered. They served as informers, spies, and police.[335] One side benefit of such a coercive power in the name of the Church was the benefit of the confiscation of property.[336] One of the most notable examples of such abuse of power is the arrest and killing of Don Sancho de la Caballería, the grandson of a Jewish convert to Christianity who was unsuccessfully accused of heresy. When this charge failed, the charge was changed to sodomy to enable his execution and seizure of his property.[337] As the kingdoms of Castile and Aragon moved into the 16th century, sodomy had become the convenient scapegoat of the time. The die was now cast for state sanctioned economic and political exploitation rooted in profound Christian homophobia. Across the channel in England this drama would play out in the avarice of Henry VIII as he set his sights on the valuable and profitable monastic lands of England.

Henry VIII

Martin Luther's 95 Theses in 1517 launched the full-fledged version of the Protestant Reformation which had been brewing for some time. In England these ideas created a growing anti-clerical discontent. For Henry VIII (1491-1547) this discontent was a convenient development in his conflict with Pope Clement VII over the requested annulment of his marriage. Henry faced the personal and political reality of his desire to annul his marriage and to find a legitimate successor to the throne along with the problem of his economic bankruptcy. In 1533 parliament passed the law against buggery. This law made "buggery" a felony "without the benefit of clergy." This stipulation became important. It meant that clergy, and those with sufficient Latin and Biblical skill, could escape the death sentence for murder but not for "buggery." This law against "buggery" in England came to be understood as meaning any form of anal intercourse.[338] It excluded lesbian sexual intercourse. This exclusion made it different from many of the continental laws that came into effect. Byrne Fone also notes that the 1533 law moves "buggary" from a sin to a secular vice. The implication is that trials are now held by the secular authority rather than the church, and that repenting of the "vice" described as "buggary" is no longer possible.[339]

The economic benefit of Henry's law to the crown would become clear in the actions that followed. In 1534 parliament passed an act that made Henry the head of the English church. In 1535, Thomas Cromwell, Henry's chief minister, sent agents to monasteries in England to determine assets, uncover superstition, and reveal sexual misconduct. In sympathy to the economic need of the crown, the agents produced documents called the *Compenda*. These documents, read in the Parliament House, made accusations of sexual misconduct and superstition against the monastic orders which outraged the hearers. Chief among these claims were charges against many monks for being sodomites. The term "sodomy" included anal intercourse, but also accusations of bestiality, and masturbation. The charges proved an effective public relations exercise for Henry's cause with parliament. In 1538, the important shrine to Thomas Beckett was destroyed in Canterbury, and Henry was excommunicated by the Pope. By 1542, the monasteries were dissolved and their assets confiscated by the Crown completing Henry's program to fill his coffers. A letter dated in 1543 survives in which Henry counsels the Scottish regent to follow a similar path that he claimed would lead to the "great profit and honour" of the nobles in Scotland.[340] There is no evidence that the law against "buggery" was used in the prosecution of the monks. However, the accusations and their implications in the culture of religious homophobia of the time did the work adequately. What we do know is that Henry used the 1533 law effectively against one of his enemies. Lord Hungerford, associated with the Northern rebellion, was charged with treason and buggery which led to his beheading in 1534.[341]

I will describe in a further chapter as the Protestant Reformation took shape in Europe, charges of "sodomy" from both sides of the divide became one of the primary weapons of attack in the public relations war. In England, which now had a church that had turned Protestant due to its rupture from Rome, "sodomy" also became a favourite accusation leveled at the Roman church and its followers. One good example is John Bale's Protestant morality play with the title, *"The Three Laws of Nature, Moses, and Christ, Corrupted by the Sodomites, the Pharisees, and Papists"* (c. 1536). When Mary succeeded Henry in 1553, she restored Catholicism and abolished the law of 1533 – perhaps because of its use against Catholics during Henry's reign. However, after an accusation against a Spanish Protestant clergyman, Cassiodoro de Reina, who was probably falsely accused of sodomy during the reign of Elizabeth I, the law was reinstituted.[342]

As the kingdoms of the British Isles moved into unification and the British Colonial Empire came into being, the law against buggery was exported to British colonial properties by means of penal codes throughout the empire. In 1861 in the United Kingdom, the death penalty was changed to life imprisonment. This law remained in force in England until 1967 when homosexuality was decriminalized. Unfortunately, throughout the former colonies, anti-homoerotic laws remained in effect in some cases up to the present time. In homophobic states like Uganda, the law against homosexuality is now considered part of the African heritage rather than the British colonial import it actually is. The widespread presence of anti-sodomy laws now mostly cancelled in Western democracies find their genesis in this complex and questionable history.

Conclusion

In this chapter we have traced the development of anti-sodomy legal traditions in Western culture. These laws, due to their European origins, were also exported, during the colonial period to colonial possessions around the world where they are sometimes still being used with

destructive consequences in countries like Uganda. We have seen how relatively mild legal treatments strengthened to extremely punitive laws through the medieval period. With the increasingly virulent homophobia in theological thinking evolving out of the confessional guides through to the great theological works of authors such as Thomas of Aquinas, sodomy grew to become the principal and most grievous sin of Christianity. It came to be considered worse than incest and on par with murder and heresy, but worse because it is against nature and God. Both canon and civil law worked in concert to establish the harsh penalty of torture and death as a general standard throughout Europe. With the rise of powerful kingdoms such as that of Philip IV of France, Frederick and Isabella of Castile, and Henry VIII of England, the application of sodomy law took on a new and nefarious purpose. It came to be an excellent tool for extending the monarch's power and filling the coffers of the crown. In the case of Philip IV, besides gaining the wealth of the Templars, it also served the purpose of exerting the power of his throne over the Pope. In the case of Frederick and Isabella, the unifying power of public prosecution, the blood sports of the *auto da fe* and the resultant fear and oppression the Spanish Inquisition imposed, served the unification of their kingdom and the removal of opposition. In the case of Henry VIII, it helped him establish his independence from Papal control and the seizure of monastic properties and assets for a bankrupt crown.

This story should give us pause. How does the Christian faith with its roots in the stories of the life, ministry, death and resurrection of Jesus fit with such abhorrent behaviour? How could the gospel of grace lead to a "gospel" of torture, avarice, and political expediency? How could the tradition of him who taught to judge not, so that you not be judged, become a race to torture and burn living, breathing human beings? Christian teaching, canon law, and religious confession would lead to severe consequences for many people who were in homoerotic relationships. Biblical texts and theological teaching increasingly took on intensified and condensed oppressive meaning and power. Perhaps the implications of this dimensions of European history also has implications for various forms of homophobia in other faith communities through the spread of colonialism? To be responsible, faithful and accountable before God in our moral discernment we must tell the story of human suffering and profound harm in more detail. This next chapter will tell the story of such suffering people with reference to Venice, Florence and the Spanish Inquisition.

CHAPTER 9: THE BRUTAL FRUITS OF THEOLOGY – RENAISSANCE TORTURE AND EXECUTION

Eleven Portuguese and Spaniards have been captured. They had assembled in a church near Saint John Lateran where they had performed some ceremonies of a horrible wickedness which sullied the sacred name of matrimony, marrying each other and being joined together as husband and wife. Twenty-seven or more, it is said, were discovered altogether on other occasions, but at this time they were not able to capture more than this eleven, who were given to the fire as they deserved.[343]   (Antonio Tiepolo, Venetian Ambassador to Rome, 1578)

These burnings occurred under the auspices of Pope Gregory VIII. They would be followed by the despicable and violent acts of his successor, Sixtus V (1585-1590). In their magisterial eleven volume series on civilization, Will and Ariel Durant note both the barbarous cruelty and the puritanical efficiency of Pope Sixtus V. He inaugurated his reign with a massive purge during which no mercy was shown for bandit, adulterer or sodomite. The Durant's wrote,

Soon the countryside was dotted with corpses swaying in the wind, and the wits of Rome calculated that more severed heads were nailed to the Sant' Angelo Bridge than there were melons in the market stalls.[344]

A priest and his boy victim were burned for sodomy forthwith. There was a significant subculture of resistance against prosecution of homoerotic relationships during the Renaissance. The above story of the Venetian Ambassador is supported by Montaigne's comment in his diary (sometime between 1580 and 1581) upon visiting Rome where he records a similar story of same-sex marriage ceremonies being conducted.[345]

The publication of John Boswell's provocative book, *Same Sex Unions in Premodern Europe,*[346] triggered a lively debate on the meaning of the liturgies known as *adelphopoiesis* – literally meaning brother-making - where men were joined to men and women to women in a holy liturgy. Boswell argued that the content of the liturgies and their placement in documents containing marriage liturgies made them very similar to holy matrimony in early medieval Christianity. Many historians have critiqued both his translations and the conclusions he has drawn. Though some of these counter arguments could themselves be shaped by an anti-homoerotic bias, they do point to the incomplete picture we have of these phenomena. However, in the cases cited by Tiepolo and Montaigne, there seems to be evidence that people in the late 16th century Europe did treat such ceremonies as a kind of marriage which was considered by the authorities as abhorrent and illegal despite willing participants and officiating priests. It is therefore likely that these rites celebrated marriage-like committed relationships of a sexual nature. They also suggest that there was, in some parts of the church, a certain level of religious acceptance of these rites. Some scholars have argued that homoerotic practices during the Renaissance were almost exclusively forms of exploitative adult on child encounters. Although young poor boys prostituting themselves was a sad reality, recent research has uncovered a different picture about deeper and more lasting homoerotic relationships similar to what we encounter in Western societies today among sexual minorities. The rites described by Tiepolo and Montaigne suggests long term committed same-sex relationships. The research of Rafael Carasco and Luiz Mott and the records of Dom Pedro León, who recorded the confessions of condemned sodomites during the Spanish Inquisition, paint a complex picture that included faithful loving same-sex relationships.[347] There were then as there are now people who sought to be in loving and committed relationships with members of the same sex. Also, in some geographical locations there was a fair degree of acceptance and tolerance of such relationships.

By contrast, periods of brutal suppression reached their zenith during the Renaissance. The intention here is not to defend practices such as sexual exploitation of minors, nor so to vilify individual actions of persecutors or to claim that prosecutions and merciless burnings were going on all the time. The contrary is more likely although records are incomplete or not yet fully examined. In 1990, the Italian scholar Giovanni Dall'Orto noted that the severe punishments meted out often created a great reticence among the population to report suspected homoerotic transgressions.[348] It appears that ordinary people had more grace in their hearts than the religious and state authorities. The intention in this chapter is to recount the shocking level of brutality to which both Christian and civic authorities would go to punish homoerotic relationships and encounters. Given the harm done by both religious and civic authorities, inspired by theological ideas, we should be deeply concerned by the ongoing Christian complicity in non-affirming teaching and practices that causes psychological harm, encourages civic discrimination, and even supports severe penalties in some jurisdictions. The first part of this chapter will describe the mindset and practices within the cities of Florence and Venice. This focus is due to the availability of written records that have made possible reliable research of the treatment of people in homoerotic relationships. Thereafter, we will return to the Inquisition and particularly the brutal actions of the Spanish Inquisition.

The Florentine Affliction

With the growth of economic development, the city of Florence slowly shed its feudal system during the 11th and 12th centuries. From 1434 onwards, the Medici family dominated the governance of the city and its wider territories. By 1569, Pope Pius V cemented the power of the Medici family by declaring them grand dukes of Tuscany. The city was known in the early Renaissance for its indulgent attitude towards homoerotic relationships. So wide-spread was the city reputation that the German verb "florenzen" became the equivalent of "sodomizing."[349] Neither the civil nor religious authorities shared this attitude. Reflective of the theological developments discussed earlier, the Florentine legal code, from 1325 onwards, mandated the death penalty for sodomy. However, this penalty was rarely applied with the authorities preferring, castration, corporal punishment and fines. Florence instituted a special night police, the *ufficiali di notti*, whose task was to track and convict sodomites. Although the great preacher of Siena, St Bernadino, preached a passionate series of sermons against sodomy, it did not seem to have a lasting impact on the population. Florence kept good records and in recent times the research of Michael Rocke has uncovered copious information about the treatment of people in homoerotic relationships. It appears that the city mostly applied mild sanctions in the form of fines. Rocke found that ten percent of Florentine boys were charged with sodomy between 1478-1483.[350] Some of Florence's greatest artist such as Leonardo da Vinci, Sandro Boticelli, and Benvenuto Cellini were all subject to accusation of committing sodomy.[351] Between 1432 and 1502, the city records of Florence recorded more than 2500 convictions for sodomy. Between 1478 and 1502 there are accusation records against more than 12,500 men and boys.[352]

What is relevant to our examination here is the relationship between civic law and practice and theological motivations. Louis Crompton notes that in 1365 the records document that the prosecution of sodomy is necessary because it is a wicked crime that will bring God's wrath on the city. In 1418 it was noted that sodomy would cause terrifying judgment, and in 1458 it noted that sodomy was an abomination and an offense against God.[353]

What were the human consequences? One example describes the fate of Giovanni di Giovanni, a fifteen year old boy who was paraded through the streets, publicly castrated and then branded in the anus.[354] St Bernadino's sermons in Sienna give a unique picture of how the attitudes of Christian leaders became immune to human kindness and grace of the gospel. Crompton writes,

To edify his congregation, Bernardino described the burning of a sodomite in Venice. "I saw a man tied to a column on high; and a barrel of pitch and brushwood and fire, and a wretch who made it all burn, and I saw many people standing round about to watch." Bernardino compared the spectators to the "blessed spirits of paradise [who] blissfully glory in witnessing the justice of God" punishing sinners in hell. So religious faith in this age anesthetized any sensitivity to human suffering.[355]

The preaching and actions of the Dominican Girolamo Savanarola (1452-1498) also deserves special mention. Savanarola's own violent and gruesome end, which included condemnation by the church and public execution by burning, reflects the kind of punishment he wished to inflict on others. In his preaching, Savanarola focused on denouncing the Medicis and their rule, a call for reform of the papacy, and the eradication of sodomy. When Piero de Medici fled in 1494, Savanarola established a republic and instituted new severe anti-sodomy laws advocating for the stoning and burning of sodomites. The uncooperative population effectively resisted this move by simply not accusing neighbors, thus drying up sodomy convictions.[356] Very frustrated by this shift, Savanarola kept urging public burnings in his sermons. Savanarola's fortunes and popularity waxed and waned over time, and convictions for sodomy slowed down dramatically after his excommunication. At a dramatically poignant moment in Savanarola's execution, a man grabbed the fire from the executioners and lit the pyre himself and shouted that, "the one who wanted to burn him was himself being put to the flames."[357] Perhaps this statement is reminiscent of the words of Jesus recorded by both the Gospels of Luke and Mark that urges the disciples not to judge so that they may also not be judged?[358]

114

The Republic was taken back by the Medici family, and, after lightning struck the Cathedral dome in Florence, Cosimo de Medici introduced a severe anti-sodomy law in response. It was under this law that Benvenuto Cellini was later arrested.[359] Finally, in 1795, Fendinandino III of the House of Hapsburg-Loraine abolished the death penalty for sodomy in Florence. Even though the prosecutions and public sentiment did not match some of the extreme actions in other Renaissance locations, the painful suffering of those accused and sentenced, is a function of theological homophobia. Even as Florence seemed to be more indulgent than other jurisdictions, its extensive and ongoing campaign against homoerotic relationships represented a long-term systematic program of suppression.

The Pyres of Death in Venice

From 697 onwards Venice rose in economic importance and functioned as a republic. In 1197 it became an oligarchy with strong merchant control exercised over commerce to ensure economic success. The city's rise to economic power was particularly aided by its evolution into a principal port city on the Adriatic during the crusades. The city was conquered by Napoleon in 1797 at a time when its commercial importance was in decline. In 1866 the city became part of the Kingdom of Italy.[360] Venice is particularly important in that it has preserved much of its city records including court proceedings and sentences. These have become the objects of research over the last twenty years. They contain details that present a disturbing picture of the treatment of people in homoerotic relationships. Whereas sanctions were milder, more extensive and systematic in Florence, prosecutions in Venice distinguished themselves as brutally savage.[361]

In 14th century Venice sodomy fell under the authority of the *Segnori di notti* the "Lords of the Night" who investigated petty crimes. The first known execution for sodomy occurred in 1342, correspondent with the development of the extreme theological homophobia of the 14th century Christendom. To ascertain confessions, the *Segnori* was given the right to apply extreme torture. Crompton reports that this empowerment was followed by records of 13 cases of public live burning over the next 60 years. From 1446 onwards, victims were decapitated and then burned.[362] In the previous chapter we noted the merging of economic, political and theological reasoning. In Venice, the concern with assuring its commercial success led the city in a process towards harsh and inhumane punishment.

Executions were done on the *Piazetta* between the columns of justice. Louis Crompton graphically describes these brutal punishments:

This "Little Square" is the open space before the Doge's Palace that connects Saint Mark's Square with the Grand Canal, the civic and ceremonial heart of Venice in the Middle Ages and the Renaissance, today a focus for casual tourism. The medieval Columns of Justice, dramatically visible from the lagoon, stand where they stood six hundred years ago, one surmounted by the winged lion of Saint Mark, the other by Saint Theodore and his crocodile. In all likelihood more homosexuals died on this spot than anywhere else in Europe before Hitler.[363]

In 1354, Rolandino Ronchaia, a man whom today might be understood as transgender, was executed on this spot by live burning. The trial records from that time are dehumanizing in character as if it were only concerned with determining which genital entered which orifice to establish if the crime of sodomy took place. However, from time to time, the human story of the victims permeates the homophobia and legalistic language. For example, records from 1357 tell of a four-year love affair between Nicoleto Marmagma, a gondola operator, and Giovanni Braganza his employee. When apprehended and charged, Nicoleto, in his love for Giovanni, bravely tried to argue that he forced Giovanni into the relationship. Rather than go free without Nicoleto, Giovanni confessed that he was a willing partner and both were burned alive.[364]

In 1407 a scandalous case arose that implicated thirty-three Venetian citizens. Particularly disturbing was that fifteen were noblemen and one of them was from one of the most prominent and influential Venetian families, the Contarini. Claro Contarini was found guilty and publicly burned. After this event, the Council of Ten discussed in the previous chapter decided to take over control of the prosecution of sodomy from the *Senori di Notti*. Up to that point, the Council was only concerned with treason and counterfeiting. Sodomy was added to its responsibilities because it was considered to be a threat to the security of the city and its commerce by potentially evoking the judgment of God. In 1418 the Council took full control of the prosecution of sodomy as the Council judged that the *Senori* did not torture people vigorously enough to obtain confessions.[365] The purpose was to eradicate completely the vice of sodomy and to make it a crime of which people would not even speak. Crompton notes that Venice at this time was considered a city of renowned sexual opportunities. Heterosexual prostitution was actively encouraged and institutionally supported under the theological rationale of Augustine and Thomas of Aquinas.[366] The frequent public executions of sodomites became a kind of public insurance policy for the city's economic prosperity. This Venetian orientation serves as a good example of the scapegoating process identified by Rene Girard discussed in Chapter 3.

In this chapter we are concerned with the real-world consequences of theological homophobia. Both Guido Ruggiero[367] and Patricia Labalme[368] have conducted detailed studies of the victims of sodomitic prosecutions in Venice. They found that a representative cross section of Venetian society was caught in the net of prosecutions with a majority coming from the profession of barber. Like with the Spanish Inquisition, the Council of Ten sought to create an atmosphere of fear with rewards for informers and instructions to their agents to, "comb the city day and night with their associates and secret spies . . . searching for sodomites, for boys who were *patientes*, for companions of unequal age, surveying all shops, schools, porticos, taverns, brothels, and the homes of pastry chefs and prostitutes."[369] It is particularly distressing to see how the attitude toward children changed under this form of religious and economic fervor. From 1424 onwards, the Council, which previously considered boys – known as *patientes*- as victims of sexual exploitation – they now decreed jail sentences of 3 months and twelve to twenty lashes for boys between 10 and 14 years of age. Those over 14 were considered adults. The human cost to these teen boys is demonstrated in a recorded case where a boy of 16 was so tortured that his genitals were mutilated and his arm had to be amputated.[370] Although clergy were considered beyond the reach of the Council of Ten, there are isolated cases of clergy being condemned to death in Venice. They were not burned alive. Rather, they were suspended in a cage on Saint Mark's Square until they starved to death.[371] A final example of the extreme inhumanity comes from 1552 when a man was dragged from a church, tied to a horse's tail, dragged to the Rialto bridge where his hands were cut off. Then he was decapitated and publicly burned.[372]

Such violent and brutal treatment, although exacted in this case by the civil authority, derived its legal legitimacy from the growing theological homophobia represented in Christianity with roots in the homophobia of Philo of Alexandria, picked up by Augustine, with its culmination in the work of Peter Damian and Thomas of Aquinas. The introduction of torture and the death penalty only came to be broadly accepted after the development of 13th century ideas of Damian and Aquinas. The suffering and pain, the bloodthirst and the ruthless torture, all testify to a theological tradition that should be deeply suspect to any followers of Jesus Christ. Besides the examples from the cities of Florence and Venice, we also need to return to the Inquisition and its actual consequences for people in homoerotic relationships.

The Inquisition

Students of the Christian Inquisition and its actions usually divide it into three stages. The first is considered the Episcopal stage which is generally associated with the period beginning with the legitimization of Christianity in the Roman Empire in 312. The second is described as the Papal stage beginning in 1232 under the reign of Pope Gregory IX. The third is described as the Royal stage most closely associated with the Spanish Inquisition which lasted from 1478-1834.

The Episcopal Inquisition was in the hands of bishops, and this earlier Christianity, despite its rising power within the Empire, preferred to deal with heresy by means of excommunication but generally opposed to physical sanctions.[373] Of course this did not mean that all matters of heresy were dealt with without violence as some of the conflicts between Arians and Orthodox Christians attest. As Christianity became more entangled with the Empire, heresy came to be associated with an offense against imperial dignity and consequences for being convicted could lead to the confiscation of property and banishment or a death sentence. As the medieval period began, the general tenor remained that faith is to be secured by persuasion and not force. This approach came under severe strain as millennial anxiety rose and the violent military crusades became a way of dealing with increasing violence in feudal Europe by directing the banditry outward. The Cathar (Albigensian) movement in France and Northern Italy, and the Bogomil movement in the Bulgarian Empire created a new anxiety on church home ground. This anxiety led to the extremely violent crusades instituted by Pope Innocent III against the Cathars between 1208 and 1229. These crusades made use of indiscriminate extermination of the whole population in the Languedoc Region whether Cathar or Catholic. Accusations that Cathars encouraged the sodomitic sin were made mainly because Cathars were against all forms of procreation, and some considered same sex sexual expression as less evil than procreative forms of sexuality. The association between sodomy and heresy became stronger due to the battles with the Cathars and the Bogomil. In fact, the idea developed that there is a "heresy of the spirit" – heretical beliefs - and a "heresy of the body" – homoerotic behavior. As noted in the previous chapter, this nomenclature became identified by the "buggery" derived from "bulgar" or "bogomil" and in German the use of the word *ketzer* (*ketter* in Dutch) for heretic which came from "Cathar."[374] It now became possible to be a *ketzer* of the flesh if one engaged in homoerotic behavior.

A gradual shift from Episcopal Inquisition to Papal Inquisition took place during this period. Pope Gregory IX (1227-1241) is normally associated with the stage known as the Papal Inquisition. When Emperor Frederick II tried to find and burn heretics, Gregory sought to regain church control by moving such investigations under Papal control and moving the implementation of the Inquisition away from the episcopate to the Dominican and Franciscan lay orders. In its early stages this Papal approach favored strong admonishment of the unfaithful with a culmination of sanctions in harsh imprisonment.

From then on, as the 13th century unfolded, punishment and methods of the inquisition became increasingly harsh. In 1252, Innocent IV authorized torture, the confiscation of property and handing over of the accused to civil authorities for burning at the stake.[375] It is telling that this move towards torture is one that goes directly against the larger Christian tradition of that time. For example, the Roman Emperor Gratian (359-383) forbade torture to Christians in his *Decretum*.[376] It thus required the famous Papal bull *at extirpanda* to introduce torture into Christian practice. At this time church canon law tended to be slightly more lenient than feudal law.[377] Thus a process began where church and state cooperated in violence. The cooperation with the civil authority allowed the church to claim that it was not violating the commandment not to kill. At the same time the church encouraged the civil authorities to do the killing. Prisoners were handed over to the civil authority in a process called "relaxing prisoners" to the civil authorities. It is this process of "relaxing," and the growing cooperation between the authorities of church in state in meting out cruel punishment, that casts deep shadows over the moral behavior of Christian theologians and church authorities. Despite what might be considered a general cultural harshness in punishment during the feudal era, it is clear that a vestige of Christian memory remained of the tradition of grace and non-violence. Nevertheless, the church circumvented its own gospel to achieve ends of power and control.

The move towards Royal control over the Inquisition of the church is generally associated with the reign of Ferdinand II (1452-1516) of Aragon and his wife Isabella I (1451-1504) of Castile. They make up the famous *Reyes Católicos* (Catholic Monarchs) of Spain. In the previous chapter we noted the legal developments and their implications for power and control that went with the rise of the Spanish Inquisition. Here we will briefly note these developments and then we will focus on some of the stories that show the human consequences of the reign of terror brought by this close cooperation between church and state. Between 1524 and 1530, Pope Clement VII authorized a state-run Inquisition in

Aragon, Saragossa, Valencia and Barcelona.[378] By 1560 the *Suprema,* a kind of supreme council for the Inquisition in the kingdom, was created in Madrid. Increased central control was exercised from there, establishing the all-pervasive system of informers and *familiars* that would create a reign of terror enforced by the large celebrations of public shaming and execution known as the *auto da fe.* The authorization and the encouragement of torture included the use of the pulleys, water torture and the rack.[379] Sodomy became officially designated as a crime *mixte forti* which meant that it fell under both church and state authority thus allowing the harsh civil penalties to be applied liberally.[380] Thus far the story appears somewhat dispassionate. But what did this mean for real human beings?

The stories of most victims of the increasingly homophobic theology and culture of the 13th century will never be known. Louis Crompton mentions a few general examples of the human cost.[381] In 1277 King Rudolph I, founder of the Hapsburg dynasty, is recorded burning Lord Haspisperch for sodomy. In 1292, the burning of Jan de Wettre, a knife maker in Ghent, is recorded. In 1290 an unnamed "Moore" is recorded burned for "lying with others" in the kingdom of Navarre. In 1345, two Jews, Juce Abolfaça and Simuel Nahamán, are burned near Pamplona for committing the sodomitical sin. Crompton notes that some of what occurred in Pamplona can be deduced from records of payment. The trumpet player who trumpeted the victims to the pyre received an honorarium and so did those who administered the fire.

As the Spanish crown gained power and control under Ferdinand and Isabella, the punishment for homoerotic relationships became increasingly frequent and harsh. One of the most vivid descriptions we have of the human cost precedes their reign dating from the time of Alfonso X (1221-1284) of Castile. The renowned early-modern historian William Monter notes that in 1495 a German traveler, Hieronymus Münzer, recorded an eye witness account of executions in both Almeria and Madrid. He reported seeing the six naked corpses hanging upside down with their genitals cut off and hung around their necks in Almeria. He wrote that they were Italians. Later, however, Münzer also reported a similar scene, this time with Castilians suffering the same plight in Madrid.[382] Monter notes that the level of proof for charges of sodomy were particularly lax. The prosecution did not have to prove "a completed and consummated act", but simply, "acts which were very proximate and close to its conclusion."[383] It takes very little imagination to place ourselves in the shoes of these victims. Accused in an atmosphere of homophobia, presumed guilty, the lure of economic gain for the crown due to the confiscation of property, and torture to extract confessions and then the sentence …castration, and bleeding to death.

One of the foremost researchers in the area of the Spanish Inquisition is Rafaël Castellar, presently teaching at the Université Paul-Valéry in Montpellier. He documents a curious but critical moment in the development of theological homophobia in Spain. Under the inquisitorial code developed by the Inquisitor General of Aragon, Nicholas Eymeric (1316-1399), the Pope held final power of life and death of Christians as vicar of Christ. As Christ is not on record of condemning homoerotic relationships, it was doubtful if the Pope could exercise such final power in sodomy cases. It was also not clear if Papal power of death extended to non-believers such as Muslims and Jews when it comes to enforcing canon law. However, in 1494 an anonymous functionary in the Inquisition in Valencia solved this problem by citing an alleged text by Augustine and Jerome that told of the legend that all engaged in homoerotic relationships were exterminated by a great light at the moment of Christ's birth.[384] This legend, that originated with a commentary by Hugh of St Cher around 1230, exercised tremendous influence in creating theological homophobia right into the 18th century.[385] Thus 13th century theological homophobia, by the 15th century, had turned Christ by virtue of the great light of his birth into a mass murderer.

We will see in the next chapter, due to recent research by the historian Nicholas Terpstra, that Europe in the 16th century can be characterized as being in a state of flux marked by great numbers of religious refugees. These great movements of people included not only those in the Protestant Reformation, but also Jews and Moors. Religious xenophobia went hand in hand with homophobia. Nothing shows this rising combination of xeno-and-homophobia as clearly as Pope Clement VII's statement that accompanied his approval for the Spanish Inquisition to prosecute sodomites:

We have learned, not without distress to our soul, that in the Kingdoms of Aragon and Valencia and in the Principality of Catalonia—as the world continually goes to the worse, alas—among some children of the infidels [Moors] the horrendous and detestable crime of sodomy has begun to spread and that if these debased kinds of men are not isolated they can drag down the faithful into this corruption.[386]

Conclusion

As we consider these few examples out of a sea of known cases of great suffering caused by the homophobic theology of the sin of sodomy and its flesh and blood implications during the Renaissance, I argue that it behooves those of us who are Christians to consider carefully what fruits were brought forth by this way? The tide of homophobic theology in the 13th century led inevitably to a wave of merciless and ruthless violence. It led to the instigation of torture in the name of Christ. It led to xenophobic attitudes and regimes of intimidation and fear. Most of all, over it hangs the black cloud of murderous and torturous killing of human beings created in the image of God. We can only ask how could this come to be? How can the Gospel of grace be warped into this shape? Surely there was another way? One might hope that the Protestant Reformation would chart a different path. However, nothing could be further from reality. Protestants, it turns out, joined the theological homophobia with great alacrity accusing burning, and drowning their Roman Catholic opponents, their Muslim slaves, and even their own children as young as 14 years old. It is to the witness of these suffering bodies that we now turn.

CHAPTER 10: A SAVAGE REFORMATION - DROWNING TEENAGE CHILDREN IN BARRELS OF WATER

(Dr) …Fioravanti and his fans knew that the most thorough way to purge threats from any body was by expulsion. A doctor's care of the body might involve amputating a limb or purging bad humours by drawing blood or stimulating vomiting, urination, or bowel movements. So too, it could take radical action to purge the Corpus Christianum of what made it sick. This extreme action would become more familiar and more common over time. Europeans would start by expelling those who were religiously alien – the Jews and Muslims – but as they became familiar with the tactic they would move progressively towards expelling other Christians who differed from them over points of doctrine. Alongside forced expulsions were the many who fled on their own, either a step ahead of authorities, or once they had survived a bruising examination or trial. But like Fioravanti's cure or bloodletting, severe purgations could seriously weaken the very bodies they meant to save.[387]   (Nicholas Terpstra commenting on the rise of the paradigm of purgation in 16th Century Europe)

There are many lenses through which we could examine the 16th century Reformation in Europe. Such lenses include socio-economic and political analyses, or a theological lens through which we see everything in terms of theological disputes. Recently, Nicholas Terpstra, from the University of Toronto, has suggested an additional lens; seeing Reformation Europe through the perspective of large movements of refugees as different jurisdictions tried to purge their communities. The principle metaphor of the lens thus becomes the body and its healing through purging, amputation, or in extreme cases, the killing of a small number of people "for the good of many." This metaphor helps cast light on such phenomena as the Inquisition its actions, and its Protestant counterparts symbolized by the execution of Michael Servetus in Geneva and the systematic forced drowning of Anabaptists and killing of Roman Catholics by Protestants. The results, as Terpstra points out, was large numbers of people fleeing for their lives and, of course also the fanning of the flames of war. The rise of the medical metaphors of purging and amputation as well as extermination in no small measure derive from the great famine and black death of the 14th century. It is helpful to think of this perspective as we examine the theological homophobia and resultant actions of Protestant Christians in the 16th century onwards. These became combined with the conviction that not acting violently and decisively against someone branded as a heretic were thought to dishonor the glory of God. Despite many theological differences, both formal Catholic and Protestant traditions still acted within this larger medicalized paradigm of the social body.

Terpstra refers to Alexandra Walsham's apt description of the attitude of theological leaders at this time as "charitable hatred."[388] Purging, amputating, and killing human beings for the greater good in the name of Christ and the Gospel only makes sense when understood as actions of love for the greater good of the whole community, conceived as a corporate body. The understanding of such despicable acts of violence committed on human bodies in the name of morality only makes sense if one believes in this overarching metaphor of purgative healing. And, significantly for the theme of this book, vestiges of this understanding remain within Christian communities. These are expressed by such ideas as "tough love," and the condemnation and the shunning of sexual and gender minority people "for their own good." Because such people are branded people as those who "disobey the will of God," they are to be welcomed but not affirmed in their full humanity. Additionally, this attitude also contributes to the ongoing agitation against the provision of equal treatment before civil law including opposition to marriage equality. In the minds of those in charge during the Reformation period, their motivation was considered to be true to a high level of Christian morality. Leaders worked together under the assumption that they had an obligation to preserve the community both inside the church and within the civic order.[389] As they defined good and pure behavior, they also assumed the challenge of discerning how to deal with the inevitable delinquents of society.[390] Prominent leaders in the Reformation such as John Calvin argued that heresy had to be punished by death in order to preserve God's glory.[391] Research has shown that much of what took place under the guise of religion during the Reformation was not really based in theological conviction. Nevertheless, almost without exception theological arguments were employed to justify violent and degrading actions.[392] It is sobering to remember that theological ideas have real human consequences.

This phenomenon of a kind of cynical exploitation of Christian theology was first identified by Max Weber. Terpstra summarizes it in this way,

Max Weber argued, the instigators and beneficiaries of this purgative violence were to be found further up the social ladder among political and religious authorities and literary elites who were more cynical and strategic. Scapegoating and prosecuting a common social enemy paid benefits to those religious authorities who could name the threats and to those political authorities who could prosecute them. This was authorized violence that built the apparatus of the state.[393]

From the stories collected in the previous two chapters, we can surmise that much truth inheres in these claims. Still, we must remember that people in the 16th century did not examine their motives in the same way as we might do today. Nevertheless, such violent actions, reaching a frenzied zenith between the 15th and 18th centuries, set the stage for the 20th century phenomena of Hitler and Stalin and other terrible genocides. Christian faith, despite losing its grip on the power of the state, cannot be exempted from moral complicity both by setting the historical example and by continuing behaviors still rooted in these attitudes in contemporary churches. People in homoerotic relationships fared no better under Protestant jurisdictions than Catholic as targets of "charitable hatred." Here we will examine a few cases to demonstrate this point. First, we turn to the Protestant city of Geneva.

The Reformed City of Geneva[394]

Nowhere did the Reformation triumph so definitively as in French-speaking Geneva. Under Calvin's leadership, the Genevans established a theocracy that subjected every aspect of life to a stern code inspired by the Old Testament. During the proceeding century, we know of six sodomy trials in the city. In the 125 years following Calvin's triumph there were sixty—thirty ending in burnings, beheadings, drownings, and hangings. If we consider the small size of the city—Geneva had only about 12,000 inhabitants when Calvin took office—the actual rate of executions far surpassed that of the Inquisition in contemporary Spain.[395]

Protestants often delight in pointing to the excesses of the Inquisition. However, history reveals a terrible a story about the record of Reformed Christians throughout Europe. Even though the Reformation preached a Gospel of grace for all who are sinners, its actions belied its teaching. It is sobering, as the historian William Monter notes, that even though executions for sodomy in Calvinist Geneva did not rank as high in numbers as murder and witchcraft, it was enforced with a high degree of strictness.[396] Some of their victims involved three Turkish slaves captured in a battle with the Duke of Savoy in 1590.[397] These slaves were burned alive. A spate of executions occurred in 1610. In this case a Genevan official Pierre Canal was arrested for treason and sodomy. Protestant Geneva used the torture and execution instrument of the wheel. Victims were tied to a large wagon wheel and systematically beaten with a club or iron cudgel until their limbs would break and give way through the spokes of the wheel. Eventually, slowly and very painfully they would die. Canal was first broken on the wheel and then his body was burned for sodomy. He had named accomplices and several trials, and more executions followed.

Geneva was a refugee city, giving refuge to many religious refugees from France, Italy, Germany and the Lowlands. Geneva saw an influx of 25,000 foreign refugees between the years 1550 and 1560. The many executions for sodomy almost uniquely involved such refugees.[398] In Geneva, the "Consistory" (Church Council, Council of Elders) functioned as a kind of inquisition or "moral tribunal" that would hand culprits over to the civil authority to execute sentences. Schoolboys were often involved in sodomy trials with relative frequency between 1555 and 1672.[399] Punishment for boys under 20 usually involved severe beatings. Monter notes that the most striking feature of the brutal sodomy sentences in Geneva is the correlation between rising religious zeal and convictions for sodomy.[400] There also appears to be a correlation between the leadership of Calvin's successor, Theodore Beza, and an increased number of sodomy prosecutions.[401] Beza was accused of sodomy by his Catholic critics based on love poems that, as a young man, he wrote for another young man.[402] Perhaps Beza felt compelled to demonstrate his moral uprightness and manliness?

The second case of a post-Reformation execution in Geneva occurred with the hanging of a young Frenchman accused of sodomy in 1550. Three legal opinions were sought by the Genevan court from refugee jurists. Two of the legal opinions drew strongly on the theological themes that developed in 13th century Europe. One jurist advised that this sin is one of the most appalling and forbidden demonstrated in God's flaming destruction of five cities. This crime, even though in this case no acts were consummated but only intended, the jurist concluded, deserved severe punishment.[403] The second legal opinion cited 1 Cor 10:16, Gen 19 and Ex 20:1[404] as rationale for execution. The third legal opinion suggested further torture of the accused to ascertain that he has not committed other acts of sodomy. A final case in Geneva deserves further attention. In 1568, a woman was convicted and sentenced to be drowned for the crime of lesbianism. This case is peculiar because the prosecutions of lesbian relationships were rare. The Genevan jurist Colladen opined that the sin of lesbianism is equal to sodomy and that, "Such a detestable unnatural case deserves the punishment of death by fire..."[405] Here Colladen echoes the concept of the "sin against nature" which played such an important part in building the 13th century version of theological homophobia. Monter notes that executions for witchcraft and sodomy decline around 1650 in Geneva. The last execution for witchcraft occurred in 1652 and for sodomy in 1662.[406] The decline in these executions go hand in hand with the decline in religious fervor and the power of the Consistory in Geneva. We note that in this Protestant jurisdiction the medieval association between heresy, witchcraft and sodomy, embraced by the Reformers, contributed to the harsh, theologically motivated punishments meted out. We also note that the unbiblical association between Sodom and homoeroticism was uncritically accepted in the context of a homophobic theology.

The Burning and Drowning in the Protestant Lowlands and the Netherlands

As Protestant-Catholic battles evolved in the Lowlands (the Netherlands and Belgium of today), sodomy became one of the principle charges used by new Protestant authorities. Protestants specifically targeted monasteries, accusing Monks and Nuns of homoerotic relationships. Thus, the French researcher Maurice Lever records that in 1578 several Franciscan brothers were burnt in the city of Bruges, and, in Ghent, where the new Protestant Council of Eighteen came into power, eight Franciscans and six Augustinians were burnt at the stake.[407] Surprisingly, during the 18th century, some of the most heinous acts of terror and killing occurred for the sin of sodomy in the free Dutch Republic. It remains a story that should invite all Christians from the Reformed and Presbyterian families of faith to hang our heads in shame.

By all accounts, the 18th century Dutch Republic was unusually tolerant, creating a home and refuge for Huguenots, Jews, English Puritans and Catholics alike. The city of Amsterdam even hosted a Muslim Mosque – a phenomenon unheard of anywhere else in Christian Europe.[408] The last burning for witchcraft occurred in 1595. Louis Crompton describes the events that occurred from 1730 onwards as the "most deadly persecution of homosexuals known to us before Hitler..."[409] A frenzy of Protestant Christian hysteria followed the arrest of two men on charges of sodomy in the city of Utrecht. One of them, a 22-year-old ex-soldier, Zacharias Wilsma, implicated a network of 140 men. Many arrests and trials followed. A number of those implicated fled the Republic. The extreme public and legal actions taken against sodomy must be contrasted with the relatively tolerant tenor of the Republic. Behind this reaction, as with of old in the great trading port of Venice, lay a sense of deep vulnerability of the Republic and its sensational economic success. The Republic thrived due to the work of the Dutch East India Company. By 1730, its dominance and economic power was on a slow decline. Fears were suddenly raised about the security of the state because of the theological conviction that God's judgment would come down on the Republic if it did not act swiftly and with brutal execution against the sodomites. These concerns were further amplified by floods that occurred in the vulnerable areas close to the ocean during 1728. Then, in 1731, dykes collapsed due to woodworm, but public opinion and Reformed clergy attributed this to the "sodomites."[410]

On July 21, 1730 posters were displayed in prominent public places providing the justification for the mass arrests that occurred,

Be it known herewith to everyone that we have perceived, to our most heartfelt grief, that in addition to other transgressions of God's most sacred laws, whereby his just wrath towards our dear Fatherland has been inflamed time and again, some terrible atrocities have been committed for some time past in our dear states of Holland and West Friesland, offending Nature herself, and that many of our subjects have turned so far away from any fear of God as audaciously to commit crimes which should never be heard of, on account of which God Almighty had in earlier times overturned, destroyed, and laid waste Sodom and Gomorrah.[411]

Combined with the reference to Sodom and Gomorrah, the subsequent collapse of the dykes in 1731, was deemed to be judgment from God because of medieval association of Noah's flood with judgment against sodomy. History yet again demonstrates that theological ideas can lead to brutal and harmful consequences. Sermons were published that claimed the disasters as judgment upon the lax attitude towards sodomites. In 1730, Leonard Beels published an influential book with the title *Sodom's Sin and Punishment.* It blamed the Sodomites for such diverse disasters as the collapse of the spire of Utrecht Cathedral in 1674, an earthquake in 1692, and the flooding of the town of Stavoren in 1657.[412] Crompton chillingly records the civil mood in some prominent art from this period. In the famous engraving *Justice Triumphant,* St Paul is quoted from Romans 1, and behind men in a "sodomite club" is a backdrop of fire raining down on Sodom and Gomorrah.[413] Another engraving records a set of scenes which Crompton describes thus,

Grimmer and more explicit in its realism is a series of scenes in an engraving entitled *Timely Punishment Decreed for the Abominations of the Most Godless and Damnable Sinners.* In the first scene two men quit an elegant salon, hand in hand; then they are shown fleeing their homes, leaving wives and children behind. Arrested in the street, they next appear in prison lamenting their fates. The last and most elaborate scene shows a huge crowd in the city square in Amsterdam, where five men dangle from a gallows, two are garroted on posts, and another pair drown in barrels. At the side, bodies of dead men burn on a grill, while in the foreground a skeleton holds a scroll showing ships taking corpses to be thrown into the sea.[414]

What did this theological anxiety and homophobia mean for accused people? The reality was shockingly close to the artistic depictions. The scope of arrests and prosecutions were tremendous. Crompton reports that 250 trials took place. One hundred accused who fled were convicted in absentia. 75 brutal executions were conducted.[415] What did these consequences of theological homophobia look like? I take the record of executions as recorded by Louis Crompton directly from his text. As brief as these reports are, so profound is the pain and suffering they relay.

(In) Amsterdam:

• Pieter Marteyn Janes Sohn and Johannes Keep, decorator, strangled and burned, June 24, 1730

• Maurits van Eeden, house servant, and Cornelius Boes, eighteen, Keep's servant, each immersed alive in a barrel of water and drowned, June 24, 1730

• Laurens Hospuijn, chief of detectives in the Navy, strangled and thrown into the water with a 100-pound weight, September 16, 1730

Another thirteen perished in The Hague:

• Jan Backer, middleman for hiring of house servants, and Jan Schut, hanged and burned, June 12, 1730

• Frans Verheyden; Cornelis Wassermaar, milkman; Pieter Styn, embroiderer of coats; Dirk van Royen, and Herman Mouillont, servant, hanged and afterward thrown into the sea at Scheveningen with 50-pound weights, June 12, 1730

• Pieter van der Hal, grain carrier; Adriaen Kuyleman, glove launderer; David Munstlager, agent; and Willem la Feber, tavern keeper, hanged and thrown into the sea at Scheveningen with 100-pound weights, July 21, 1730

• Antonie Byweegen, fishmonger, hanged, then burned to ashes, July 21, 1730

• Jan van der Lelie, hanged and thrown into the sea, September 24, 1731[416]

Thus we have the fruits of 1400 years of evolving Christian theological homophobia now executed by Reformed Protestant Christian authorities under the encouragement of clergy.

Even though the prosecutions and persecution lasted about a year, these do not capture the full story of the excesses of this time. The most disturbing events in the history of Protestant theological homophobia are arguably those that took place in the small Dutch Village of Faan in the province of Groningen. In this case we can associate this form of theological homophobia with child-abuse. A Reformed Minister in the area, Henricus Carel van Buyler, published a book against sodomy in 1731.[417] Even though Faan was really a small agricultural village and not connected in any way with the prosecutions going on elsewhere, the ordeal started with a blind boy of 13 making an accusation against another boy who was also 13. Stern interrogation rendered accusations against seventeen other youths aged between 17 and 20.[418] The local magistrate and friend of Buyler, Rudolph de Mepsche, was the chief instigator in prosecutions and torture. Now accusations took on a life of their own and started to involve political differences in the community. Those arrested, both men and boys, were subjected to brutal torture leading to some confessions. Eventually 21 men and boys were convicted of whom 19 were sentenced to death.[419] The records show that of the executed, nine boys were in their teens with one as young as 14 and another 15.[420] Several more men were still in jail awaiting trial, but one died because of torture and the provincial authority intervened and Mepsche was eventually discredited for his behavior.

In the rest of the Republic in the ensuing years, more arrests and executions occurred sporadically. Attitudes changed slowly to become more tolerant. This example from history is instructive as we consider the way Christians make moral decisions and judgments. Perhaps, most poignantly, we need to remember, confess, mourn, and repent from the beliefs and actions that put teenage boys to death. We must remember the boys of Faan and eighteen-year-old Cornelius Boes of Amsterdam held under water in a barrel until he drowned... The next example we will look at will come from the 19th century in Britain.

Clergy Agitation and the Rise of Regency Executions in England

Homoerotic relationships did not do well in the realm of law in the United Kingdom of the 18th century. Despite the impact of the enlightenment and more relaxed laws in jurisdictions like France, Britain was still caught in profound cultural homophobia. In 1698, Jeremy Collier, an Anglican priest, published an essay that argued that sodomites should be "exterminated from the earth."[421] In 1709, Ned Ward, in his satirical book on London Clubs, would describe those involved in homoerotic relationships as "misogynists" a term that would stick and become part of public outrage in the early 19th century.[422] This was followed by a book by John Disney (1710) in which he argued that the punishment of sodomy was important "because this sin draws down the Judgments of God upon the Nation where tis suffered in a very particular manner."[423] A ballad of the time moves these claims to branding such people as "women haters." In 1750 Lord Chesterfield wrote that the death penalty was not enough and that sodomites should be dismembered while alive, their entrails cut out and thrown in the fire before killing them by burning. He finishes by calling sodomy a "treason against the majesty of Heaven."[424] During that time, Edward Gibbon, in his famous history of the Decline and Fall of Roman Empire writes,

I touch with reluctance, and dispatch with impatience, a more odious vice [than adultery] of which modesty rejects the name and nature abominates the idea. The primitive Romans were infected by the example of the Etruscans and Greeks.[425]

We must note that Gibbon represents the transition from religious to medical ways of thinking about homoerotic relationships. He mentions both the theological "against nature" dimension and then uses the medical language of infection. The 19th century would become the century during which homoerotic relationships were moved from the realm of religious morality to that of psychiatric disorder. In the mid-18th century William Blackstone takes a similar homophobic position when he writes that sodomy is a crime "of so dark a nature that the accusation if false deserves a punishment inferior only to the crime itself."[426]

The famous and now celebrated legal reformer of the time, Jeremy Bentham, held much more enlightened views of homoerotic relationships. The cultural atmosphere was so unreceptive that he did not dare publish these views during his lifetime.[427] Notable is Bentham's argument that the use of such language as "abomination" and "perversion" prejudices all discussion.[428] In this Bentham anticipates the idea of homophobia. The painful legacy of the exported homophobia of the British Empire still stamps Christian attitudes in former colonies. At the end of this chapter we will note that the British penal code even inspired the Nazis.

The general rise of a homophobic culture in England was fed by sensational journalism and the establishment of *The Society for the Reformation of Manners* in 1691 onwards. This society recruited clergy and lay people to act as informers against neighbors and the stamping out of sodomy was one of its aims. The Society issued a pamphlet by an anonymous Anglican clergyman with the title, *The Sodomite's Shame and Doom.* Ominously, the pamphlet warns "your names and places of abode are known."[429] And the effort netted sodomites and raids on the "Molly Houses" of the time. "Sodomites" were executed at a steady pace through the 18th century. Even though *The Society for the Reformation of Manners* fell into disrepute and was disbanded in the 18th century, the homophobic culture it represented and created remained virulent into the early 19th century. In England the religious homophobia took on the form of disgust at effeminacy, perhaps in some ways like the concerns about "unmanliness" in the Roman Empire? This is in part due to the King James Translation of the Bible which used the word effeminate to translate the Greek word *malakos* in 1 Cor. 6:9. The epithets of misogynists, women haters, unnaturals, abomination, perversion and effeminate became the stuff of 18th and 19th century theological and cultural homophobia. The pillory was used to punish "attempted sodomy," and public hatred was so grave that people often died or lost limbs and organs due to sanctioned public violence directed to those defenseless in the pillory.[430] Byrne Fone provides a moving description of one event of frightening mob violence against those in the pillory for "attempted sodomy" that dates from 1810. In that case the presence of those pilloried literally caused a traffic jam for the frenzied mob.[431]

The human consequences for being accused of homoerotic relationships in 18th and early 19th century England were thus extremely grave. Details of news reports and executions during the 18th century are meticulously documented by Rictor Norton.[432] And, during the regency period (1811-1820) when the Prince of Wales was in charge, brutal pillorying of sodomites in central London drew enormous crowds. Between 1806 and 1835 over sixty men were publicly hanged in England and another 20 executed by the navy.[433] Eventually the appetite for public violence and torture abated. In 1861 England abolished the death penalty for sodomy and replaced it with life imprisonment, still extreme and unusual punishment, and in 1967 "homosexuality" was decriminalized.[434]

While the British Empire was at the height of its strength, it exported both a homophobic law and a profoundly homophobic Christian theology to all its territories. That homophobia is still present in the world through the continued use of these laws in some jurisdiction and homophobic behavior in churches. There is a final comment that is required before we move on to the construction of a Christian moral response in our time. We cannot move from the witness of suffering in history without noting the role and complicity of Christian churches in the Nazi extermination of thousands of "homosexuals" in the concentration camps as well as being "sentenced" to be sent to certain death on the Northern Front. Moreover, with the allied liberation of the Nazi concentration camps, those accused of homosexuality were not liberated but re-imprisoned by the allied and political authorities. This cruel fate was in no small way due to the influence of Christian homophobia.

Nazi Homophobia and Christian Homophobia

In his influential lecture, Johann Neumann, professor of sociology and of law and religion at Tübingen University, documents how the German churches, both Protestant and Catholic were complicit with the Nazi suppression of "Jews, Gypsies, homosexuals, Socialists, Bolsheviks and "Liberal decadents[435]." The fate of people fitting into all these categories, especially the Jews and Gypsies were horrendous. It is only since the 1980's that the story of homosexual victims has become better known. The number of victims is very hard to determine. The United States Holocaust Memorial Museum records that over 100,000 homosexuals were arrested by the Nazi Regime. Between 5000 and 15000 were sent to the concentration camps and branded with the infamous pink triangle.[436] It is a tribute to the moral fortitude of Jewish reflection on the Shoah that this dark part of the Nazi story is documented at the Holocaust museum.

Because the Nazi's were also interested in "reparative therapy" for homosexuals, they conducted medical experiments on homosexual inmates. The results included mutilation, illness and in some cases death.[437] No one knows how many homosexual inmates died in the concentration camps but estimates range around 60% of those interned. That would place the number of victims between 3000 and 9000. Many more perished in other ways, particularly through harsh treatment in the military. The Nazi jurist, Rudolf Kläre, argued that the "Teutonic Legal Tradition" which in his mind represented the German, British and US law, that severely punished homosexuality, was superior to what he called the decadent Latin tradition which had a more relaxed law.[438] He became the influential figure in the Nazi move to increase penalties for homosexuality, and his views were partly informed by Christian theological thinking. Yet again we see that theological ideas have real, painful, and radical consequences for flesh and blood people. Theological homophobia is often described as a harmless Christian perspective and conviction. History demonstrates that it is by no means a harmless theology. It still does real harm.

In 1995, the translation of Günter Grau's extensive study of the plight of sexual minorities in Nazi Germany was published.[439] Grau's work meticulously documents information on the treatment, legal developments, philosophical assumptions, and terrible plight of sexual minorities in Nazi Germany. The complicity of a large consensus of Christian churches in this profound material harm done during the Nazi period and after the Second World War remains one of the darkest blights on the Christian faith and its churches.

Conclusion

In this final chapter on the history of ideas and actions of Christian institutions in relation to people in homoerotic relationships, we have uncovered examples of brutal actions in Protestantism. These actions were supported by Protestant churches theology and clergy. Often, as in the Dutch Republic and England, the motivation was claimed to be for the moral good of society. History witnesses how that combination of Christian faith and civic government executed profound harm on vulnerable people. For many Protestant theologians, it seemed self-evident that to be soft on what was considered the most heinous sin, the sin with a name that cannot be spoken, the sin that is against nature and offends the glory of God, would be sinful in itself. In great self-confidence, this line of thinking moved to the brutal torture and killing of those accused of homoerotic acts. Thus, Protestant faith developed an appetite for the "charitable hatred" of sexual and gender minorities. Contemporary ideas of "loving the sinner but not the sin," "welcoming but not affirming" and so called "tough love" are all variations on that "charitable hatred." Whether such "charity" involved drowning teenage boys in barrels of water, or "breaking" people on the wheel, or whether it involves the destructive religious bullying that leads to profoundly elevated suicide rates among sexual and gender minority youth, it is all part of that same spirit. Its consequences for people are severe and harmful. It is my hope that the dark and bitter fruits of this labor in the name of Jesus of Nazareth will lead Christian communities today to confession of our sinful complicity, repentance and penance. The next chapter will explore the rise of the Gay Rights Movement and its antecedents, the synthesis that developed between psychiatric homophobia and Protestant Christian heterosexist approaches to sexual and gender minorities, and the need to for Christian jurisdiction to take responsibility form harm and turn away from harmful behavior.

Section 3: Towards A Gracious Christian Response

CHAPTER 11: TOWARDS A CHRISTIAN RESPONSE

We have approached other peoples in their primitive tribal relationships and mercilessly involved them in our world's economic and political game, without taking into account the immeasurable damage we were doing to their hearts. For this reason, the missionary enterprise is actually doing penance when it enters this deeply wounded world in humility and love. Mission is thus the penance of the church, which is ashamed before God and man.[440](Johannes Bavinck, 1960)

As the previous chapter described, the stories of Protestant hatred and harm, including Nazi persecution and allied complicity in persecuting sexual and gender minorities preface dramatic changes that happened in the public perception in both North America and Europe. This perception was also aided by post World War II insights into the role of Christian faith in establishing harmful and exploitative practices through colonialism and triumphalist attitudes as witnessed in the citation from Johannes Bavinck above. To construct a Christian response to the history of homophobia and harm it is important to recount the slow process of developing rights for sexual and gender minority people. It is of critical importance for Christians to think deeply about the way hateful homophobic attitudes in the cultural world that surrounded it was influenced by the long history of Christianity itself. There is a circularity in the process of mutual influence towards homophobic attitudes. On the one hand, the Christian construction of "sodomy" and the legal and theological developments that ensue shape a homophobic culture. On the other hand, this homophobically shaped culture in turn influences Christian attitudes. As we recognize the role of Christian theological teaching and support for harmful and hateful behavior towards sexual and gender minorities, we would do well to identify how those influences still linger and shape an ongoing cultural bias. A brief look at the more recent history and the struggle of sexual and gender minorities for acceptance becomes an important factor as we consider how to mitigate harm.

From Sodomy to Homosexuality

In the late 19th and early 20th centuries a small but brave number of people started speaking up for equal rights and decriminalization of same sex relationships. Earliest among these in the context of the United Kingdom was the philosopher and legal theorist Jeremy Bentham (1748-1832). Unfortunately his ideas on sodomy were considered so unacceptable that they were not published until 1978.[441] Other advocates included the German sexologist Karl Heinrich Ulrichs (1825-1895), making the legal case for equal rights, the writings of John Addington Symonds (1840-1893) and Edward Carpenter (1844-1929) in the United Kingdom, and the advocacy of Edward Prime Stevenson (Pseudonym Xavier Mayne) (1858-1942) and Jennie June (given name Earl Lind)(1874-d?) from the United States.[442] The term "homosexual" was first used by the Hungarian-Austrian journalist Karl-Maria Kertbeny in a letter to Ulrichs in 1868.[443] Many of the arguments advanced in their time and context appear imperfect from a contemporary perspective, much of it infused with misogynistic ideas and stereotypes representative of the time. Yet these, advocates slowly blazed a trail away from the abhorrence of sexual diversity towards finding language for an equal place in society. Jennie June's work in particular attempted to find ways of understanding and supporting transgender reality by using such language as androgyne and hermaphrodite as well as "faery" as a way to put words to experience.

Over the 19th century, the focus in mainstream society shifted from the "sin of sodomy" to the psychiatric medicalization of sexual and gender minority experience as pathologies. In this, the emergence of the psychiatric profession played a key role through the influence of Freud and the particularly harmful and homophobic contribution of Alfred Adler in his essay, "The Homosexual Problem."[444] Of note, it would be hard to imagine the medical pathologizing of sexual and gender minorities without the centuries of bias developed in a Christian-shaped culture. Even though there is a shift from the "terrible sin of sodomy" to the "perverse disease" of homosexuality, this did not necessarily improve things for sexual and gender minorities. Throughout the British Empire and in its colonies and former territories, as well as the United States, homosexuality remained criminalized with severe penalties.

Progress towards acceptance and decriminalization of homosexuality moved slowly through the first half of the twentieth century. Awareness of gender bias and the role of patriarchy developed over time. The women's suffrage movement played a role in highlighting gender bias. Additionally, some evidence suggests that the two world wars facilitated a new awareness of sexual diversity. As a large number of soldiers, both male and female, were placed in situations where they related mainly to others of the same sex, the discovery of sexual experience with one another occurred.[445] Most of this reality is evidenced by the vehement and homophobic medicalized and criminalized institutional response within the military.[446] Between the wars there were flourishing sexually diverse sub-cultures in Europe as well as in some parts of the United States. There were two attempts at building advocacy groups in the late 19th and first half of the 20th century. One was Jennie June's "Cercle of Hermaphrodites" (1895) and the other was the "Society for Human Rights" initiated in Chicago in 1925. The latter was quickly shut down by the Police.[447] However, it was during and after World War II that so called "Homophile" societies arose to advocate for rights and to join together for mutual support and social interaction. The earliest group, *"Cultuur en Onstpanningscentrum"* was formed in the Netherlands in 1946. In North America these societies were a response to a dark chapter in the history of homophobia in the United States represented in the McCarthy era.

In the 1940's two important medical reports were published that moved towards normalizing male homosexual experiences. One was George Henry's *"Sex Variants: A Study of Homosexual Patterns"* 1941, and the second was the famous report by Alfred C. Kinsey, *"Sexual Behavior in the Human Male"* (1948). Kinsey's report claimed that 37% of US males had some same-sex experience and pointed to the fluidity of sexual orientation and experience. This was followed by Kinsey's *"Sexual Behavior in the Human Female"* (1953).[448] The reports caused a strong backlash.[449] *Time* and *Newsweek*, as well as *The New*

York Times played a key role in the negative response.[450]   Soon, homophobic outrage developed combined with anti-communist sentiment in the work of Senator McCarthy and his purported gay lover and assistant, Roy Cohn.[451] The impact on the US civil service was profound.   Homosexuality became associated with Communist leanings and a witch-hunt was launched.   The end result was that 8000 civil servants lost their jobs, 600 of whom were formally charged with homosexuality.[452]

Kinsey's report did not escape notice in mainline Protestant circles.   While Kinsey understood the prevalence of homosexual experiences among American males as a biological variance in the natural world, pastoral counsellors and ministers saw it as a call to action to prevent and treat the disease of homosexuality and to promote heterosexual sexual behavior.[453]

Responding to Psychiatric Prejudice

It is no surprise that the McCarthy era evoked a counter movement among sexual and gender minorities.   Although literature started to depict sexual minority experience with more nuance, challenging the crude stereotypes of the "pansy" or the "sexual predator," most depiction still forecast a tragic end to same-sex experiences with a preponderance of suicidal and violent endings.   The work of James Baldwin, and his essay, *"Preservation of Innocence: Studies for a New Morality"* (1949) identified the sources of homophobia quite accurately.   However, even Baldwin's famous and moving novel *"Giovanni's Room"* ends in tragedy.   Together with Baldwin, the work of Christopher Isherwood, Gore Vidal and John Horne Burns and the poetry of W.H. Auden started to depict sexual diversity in new ways. An politically activist response was also forthcoming.   In 1951, in response to the extreme prejudice and violence that gay men faced, Harry Hay founded the "Mattachine Society."   In the same year, Edward Sagarin published "The Homosexual in America" under the pseudonym Donald Webster Cory.[454]   Sagarin, who eventually became a sociology professor, argued that homosexual people were a persecuted minority that deserved civil rights.   In 1955, in San Francisco, four lesbian couples formed the "Daughters of Billits" society and started to publish their newsletter "The Ladder."[455]   These events and discourses placed gay rights in the context of human rights and urged public political action.   The stage was set for the turbulent sixties and the sexual revolution.

The Sexual Revolution

Throughout the 1950's scientists worked on developing and refining the birth control pill. In 1957, after successful trials the Federal Drug Agency provided limited approval and by 1960, the birth control pill was approved for marketing in the United States.   Surprisingly, it is hard to imagine the dramatic changes in sexual behavior and perceptions of sexuality without this biological innovation.   Although it is too early to fully assess the meaning and causes of the social change in North America and Europe due to the 1960's, it is safe to say that the new movement towards free sexual expression impacted to some degree on the fortunes of sexual and gender minorities.

Parallel to this, though not unrelated, is the emergence of the Feminist movement as the translation of Simone de Beauvoir's book *"The Second Sex"* became popular and raised the consciousness of women about the patriarchal system and the way it impacts on them. The Feminist movement and the Gay Rights movement that evolved out of the 1960's remained in an uneasy relationship but shared much in common as it sought equal rights on issues of gender and sexual orientation. Feminism contained a significant Lesbian movement which included Lesbian separatism and political lesbianism as choices. Some Feminist theorists were critical of the male gay rights movement and labeled it as part of the "phallocracy" and "male supremacy."[456] Nevertheless, the historical account explored earlier demonstrates how closely homophobia, and particularly religious homophobia, is integrated into traditions of patriarchal misogyny suggesting some important shared concerns.

The Christian religion in Canada, the United States and Europe was profoundly impacted by the cultural change that resulted from the 1960's. The Canadian sociologist Neil Nevitte characterized this period as a decline of deference to authority.[457] Such a decline in authority included politicians, police and religious leaders. Though we are still too close to this period of time for a fulsome assessment, sociologists such as Calum Brown and Hugh McLeod as well as the Roman Catholic philosopher Charles Taylor have offered some stimulating theoretical assessments of the change in religious sentiment in Europe and North America.[458] Most recently, Stuart Macdonald and Brian Clarke published an exhaustive study on changes in church participation according to census and denominational data in Canada that identifies some of the changes in the fortunes of Christian religion in Canada.[459] There is a growing consensus that the changes in the Christian religious landscape, the decline of religious adherence, and the increase in the number of people identifying as having no religion in North America, are linked to the social changes that occurred in the 1960's and early 1970's.

As part of the spirit of the time that sought to challenge middle-class sensibility and morality, some of the gay-focused literature of the 1960's described excessive practices of sadism and orgiastic gay encounters such as the work of William Burroughs and the poetry of Allen Ginsberg as well as others.[460] In turn, from the perspective of public perception, Byrne Fone reports that a survey of popular writings about sexual and gender minorities of the 1960's and 1970's use such words as "vermin," "perverts," "inferior," "cowards," "unconstrained," "socially worthless," "dangerous,"… etc. to describe homosexual people.[461] Despite the rabid homophobia represented by most literary and visual representation of sexual and gender minorities, slow shifts in opinion emerged. However, much of this shift was based in a therapeutic view of sexual and gender minority experience that saw it as a deviance from the ideal heterosexual norm.

As the perception of sexual morality and sexual orientation, as well as gender and identity, shifted in Western societies, Christian theologians and denominations started to respond. Although some denominations had moved to the ordination of women before the Second World War, it is really only with the rise of the Feminist movement that attitudes towards women in leadership started to change. In my own denomination, the Presbyterian Church in Canada, the decision to ordain women was taken in 1966. At the same time, in 1969 this denomination also advocated for the decriminalization of homosexuality and the relaxation of divorce laws.[462] Although these changes did not mean that the denomination approved of homosexuality or divorce, they argued that the principle of equity and justice should be applied. In the case of divorce it concluded that family and couple relationships are too complex to deal with it in terms of simplistic rules and laws. The rationale for the decriminalization of "homosexuality" was based on the developing view of this "condition" as a psychiatric condition to be treated. Nevertheless, many mainline Christian denominations started advocating for some form of equality and justice despite their theological positions that did not necessarily approve of either homosexuality or the break-down in marriage relationships. The development of a more affirming attitude towards the role of women in religious leadership demonstrates the circularity that occurs between cultural change and religious change. Even though the Feminist impulse cannot be seen as religiously driven, key biblical concepts like Paul's statement in Galatians 3:28, that male and female, slave and free are all one in Christ, resonated with a new sense that gender equality and mutuality had to be respected.

In parallel to the recognition of women's rights, changes in the legal position of sexual and gender minorities occurred. In the United Kingdom homosexuality was decriminalized in 1967, in Canada in 1969, in the United States, in some States since 1961, and nationwide since 2003.[463] In tandem with the process of decriminalization is the rise of strong gay rights movements in the United States, Canada, and the United Kingdom and to a lesser degree in other territories around the world. Many of the countries that still criminalize same-sex relationships are former British colonies that retained the deep ingrained British homophobia of the colonial period.

From Homophile Advocacy to Gay Liberation

Due to the global importance and cultural influence of the United States, its gay rights movement played a pivotal role in inspiring similar movements around the world. Within the gay community, a key symbolic moment in that movement was the eruption of the Stonewall Riots on June 27, 1969.[464] One reporter's ironic comment about the Stonewall riots, "limp wrists were forgotten," testifies to just how strong the stereotypical bias still was in media and culture.[465] It took fifty years, but on June 6, 2019 the NYPD apologized for their actions at Stonewall.[466] The events at Stonewall also inspired similar action in other places including the Bath House Raids incident in Toronto in 1981.[467] Historians rightly point out that Stonewall is more symbolic than an actual historic cause, since it was preceded by various events in other parts of the United States. Most important among these events was the New Year's Dance incident in San Francisco where local clergy became effective advocates for sexual and gender minorities in the face of police misbehavior which evolved out of the formation of *The Council of Religion and the Homosexual*.[468]

As the AIDS crisis emerged with an impact on the North American Gay community, the activism of Stonewall was resurrected, and, through the effective actions, demonstrations and civil disobedience of "Act Up." The result was that the US Government as well as pharmaceutical companies were moved to work more diligently on finding effective treatment for AIDS sufferers.

With AIDS and its unfortunate public identification as a "Gay Disease," homophobia, including religious homophobia increased. An interesting report in the Los Angeles Times dated June 12, 1986 discussed how religious views varied about AIDS at the time. On the one hand, it reported Charles Stanley from the Southern Baptist convention who claimed, "...AIDS is God indicating his displeasure and his attitude toward that form of life style, which we in this country are about to accept." On the other hand, it documented other more caring and thoughtful religious views. The report also noted with some irony how a religious leader commented on the idea that AIDS is a judgment sent from God,

"If God punishes people through sickness," quipped Episcopal Bishop Paul Moore of New York, "Don't you think those who perpetuate nuclear war . . . would at least get herpes?[469]

The movement that resulted from the AIDS crisis is powerfully described in the award-winning documentary *"How to Survive a Plague,"* is currently available on Netflix and also captured in a book with the same title.[470]

In addition to responding to homophobia and resistance to dealing with the AIDS crisis, sexual and gender minority activists have focused on attaining marriage equality for sexual and gender minority people. The Netherlands was the first country to grant marriage equality in 2001, followed by Belgium and various local jurisdictions in Canada. Canada approved marriage equality nationally in 2005, and South Africa became the first African country with marriage equality in 2006. After a landmark case, Obergefell v. Hodges, before the US Supreme Court, the United States approved marriage equality nationwide on June 26, 2015. With the Supreme Court ruling, a principal of civil equality for sexual and gender minority people was legally established in the United States.

Conservative and Liberal Protestants Embrace Their Versions of the Sexual Revolution

What is the role of Christian institutions in this changing landscape of sexual and gender minority rights? Are those within Christianity who seek a fresh approach of welcome and affirmation of sexual and gender minorities simply selling out to the "Gay agenda" in the surrounding culture as their detractors claim? Recent research on the role of Christian institutions in relation to the Gay rights movement over the twentieth century rendered surprising results.

The late nineteenth and early twentieth century process that pathologized sodomy as a disease and the shift towards using the language of "homosexual" arose out of a mutual influence between culturally present religious homophobia and the development of the psychiatric profession. When Richard von Krafft-Ebing (1840-1902) conceived of same-sex desire as the psychiatrically characterized perversion of *paresthesia,* he did not do so in a vacuum.[471] His prejudice was shaped by powerful cultural forces that were influenced by the Christian religion. In turn, when mid twentieth century Bible translators decided to use the term "homosexual," with the gathered pejorative therapeutic freight it now carried, they did not do so in a vacuum. They drew on a protracted process of therapizing theology.

The first Bible translation to use "homosexual" was the *Revised Standard Version* in 1946, other Bible translations such as the *New American Standard Version, International Standard Version* and the *Good News Bible* and later the *New International Version* followed suit. Heather R. White in her detailed study of the use of the word homosexual in Christian theological language, demonstrates how the cultural bias of the mid twentieth century shaped the convictions of the Bible translators.[472] So profound was the homophobia in Christian circles during the first half of the twentieth century that saying nothing about it was safer than speaking about it. White writes,

Although many Bible reference tools mention that damnable "sin of Sodom" the muddled and circular commentary on this "loathsome vice" offered little that clarified its nature.[473]

She notes that it was not fundamentalist Christian groups who forged the new simplistic connection made between ancient Greek words in the Bible and the modern invention of the category "homosexuality" but liberal Protestants who enthusiastically embraced the medicalization of morality. Of the new translations made, the 1978 *New International Version* stands out as the text that "homosexualized" the Bible.[474] White argues that tis gloss of ancient biblical terms with the word "homosexual," meant that the social movement towards the acceptance and normalization of sexual and gender minorities was placed in a stark contrast to what was considered self-evident biblical statements. There is, therefore, a move from "abomination" to "disease." However, this development does not represent a simple shift towards secularization. Rather, a whole new religious and cultural synthesis emerged out of a previously described complex set of changing ideas about same sex behaviors and relationships and the new emerging discipline of psychiatry. Heather White's provocative thesis does not deny what I argue - a long history of harmful Christian initiated homophobia - but rather that a peculiar new therapeutic dimension was added in North America and the Western world. A simplistic biblicism arose that equated the new and now accepted therapeutic term "homosexuality" with the history of a series of complex ideas to do with sexual behavior and perceived enemies of faith which manifest in diverse ways over time. The condemnation of "homosexuality" as something opposed by the Bible and as a disease that had to be healed had its origins in the liberal Protestant quest for a therapeutic faith merged with the therapeutic sciences. In fact, the pastoral counselling discipline is implicated in this development as White meticulously documents.[475]

A key development in Christian thinking about "sodomy" and "homosexuality" is Derrick Sherwin Bailey's *Homosexuality and the Western Christian Tradition.*[476] Bailey, as a Christian advocate for the decriminalization of "sodomy," testified before the committee that produced the *Wolfenden Report* that led to the decriminalization of the homosexuality in the United Kingdom. Although Bailey failed to recognize the profound harm that Church persecution had done to people accused of sodomy, he provided the first historical description and recognized the nuances of difference between the modern concept of "homosexuality" and ancient biblical terms as well as doctrinal and canon law developments over time. Bailey also squarely rejected the association of the story of Sodom in Genesis with the idea of "homosexuality." Bailey also followed the evolving theological integration of psychiatry and pastoral care by accepting homosexuality as a disease. Not surprisingly, probably due to the homophobic spirit of the time, Bailey's nuanced discussion of biblical material did not make it into the *Interpreter's Bible Dictionary* published in 1962. The entry which "updated" sodomy to "homosexuality" simply cited Bailey as proof that "the Bible is against homosexuality."[477] Mid twentieth century Christian responses to the creation of the "homosexual" became clothed in "compassionate openness" that presumed that a therapeutic response will bring "healing" which would appear in the movement away from same-sex attraction to "healthy heterosexuality."

As gay authors like Sagarin started to challenge the therapeutic and religious roots of the new psychiatric condition called homosexuality, a certain level of animosity developed between gay activism and religion, particularly the Christian religion.[478] Yet, Heather White shows that there was also the very real presence of the so called "stained glass closet" within Christian circles. A predominantly middle-class white male movement evolved that sought religious acceptance, albeit solidly in the closet.[479] While homophile journals such as *One* and *Mattachine Review* often contained a secular critique of Christianity particularly the church as institution, it also hosted a fair number of articles focused on biblical material and theological arguments including affirming contributions by clergy.[480]

Heather White demonstrates how mainline Protestants and Evangelicals in North America shared the new modernist view of homosexuality as a disease. Mainline Protestants tended to emphasize acceptance as a way towards "healing" that would lead the "homosexual" towards "healthy heterosexuality." The Evangelical stream of Protestantism regarded setting rules such as strict forms of celibacy and conversion of "homosexuals" towards heterosexuality by means of therapeutic techniques known as "conversion" or "reparative" therapy.[481]

As the religious culture wars developed through the 1980's, much of the Protestant Christian movement became strongly marked by the conviction that still saw the category of the "homosexual" as a form of deviance from God's divine plan.[482] Heather White is correct in arguing that the categories had shifted and that the modernist concept "homosexual," now fully embraced by different forms of Christianity and ensconced in new Bible translations, is substantially different from various practices described as "sodomy" in earlier Christian traditions. She is also correct in demonstrating how mainline Protestants, Evangelicals and even more conservative Christian Fundamentalists, embraced a new therapeutic view of sex. This new acceptance of wholesome and joyful sexual expression within religious boundaries was not the problem, but rather the heterosexist bias that it carried. The results of this bias turned out to be profoundly harmful to sexual and gender minority people within these Christian religious traditions. The harm became so acute and so demonstrably obvious that the Evangelical organization Exodus, which focused on "conversion therapy" for sexual and gender minorities, was eventually forced to close and apologize.[483] It is this harm that requires a spirited moral and ethical response from Christian communities today.

Towards Christian Penance

By this time, it should be clear that various forms of Christian action, teaching, and legal influence through history, have done and continue to do painful harm to sexual and gender minorities. I have argued that Christian ethical and moral discernment of healthy sexual relationships does not only include reflection on what is appropriate and life-giving erotic practice. It also includes reflection on how the Christian community's historical approach and treatment of people of sexual and gender minorities harmed them. At this point in history, having considered the painful history of abusive and harmful Christian behavior, and, having considered the complex history of how texts and teaching led to that harm, it is time to offer a Christian response.

It is encouraging to note that some Christian jurisdictions have changed their practice away from a drive to therapize sexual and gender minorities towards heterosexuality. These jurisdictions now practice an approach of welcome, affirmation and embrace. In Canada, the largest Protestant denomination, the United Church of Canada, approved the ordination of openly gay and lesbian clergy in 1988 and advocated for marriage equality. In 2014 the Presbyterian Church USA, one of the larger mainline Protestant denominations in the United States, approved marriage equality and the ordination of sexual and gender minority people. Various Protestant denominations in North America and Europe have moved to the ordination of sexual and gender minorities and towards various ways of recognizing and affirming same-sex relationships either in marriage or in church covenants.[484] Many affirming Christian denominations include a diversity of perspectives and allow non-affirming pastors and members to disagree and not participate in marriage equality and the ordination of sexual and gender minority people. This increased openness creates situations where denominations might be officially supportive but allow for discriminatory and sometimes harmful practices among some of its clergy and members.

As Christians, what ought to be a responsible perspective when we discover that others were harmed and are being harmed? Consistent in the witness of the Gospels about the preaching of Jesus of Nazareth is his call to turn to God's reign. Traditional Christian language calls this repentance. This reign is demonstrated in the life-giving, boundary-challenging ministry of Jesus that sought to bring well-being to the poorest and most marginalized people of his time.[485]

From that time Jesus began to preach his message: "Turn away from your sins, because the Kingdom of heaven is near!" (Mat 4:17 GNB)

In contrast to the anti-sexual minority texts of terror so often cited by some Christians, this call to repentance reflects the deepest structure of the message of Jesus unpacked, repeated, and reflected in the way the New Testament remembers Jesus of Nazareth. In short, such a turning to God's reign is not based in a series of proof-texts; it is representative of the "warp and woof" of the gospel message itself.[486] I propose that any consideration of moral discernment in relation to sexual and gender minority people needs to start in and with this basic gospel posture of repentance that turns to God's reign of justice and love.

As suggested by the citation from Johannes Bavinck at the beginning of this chapter, much of Christian faith retained its élan of colonial domination and triumphalism as it entered the twentieth century. As with the earlier history of the Gay Rights Movement, the Christian faith has also faced many changes over the twentieth century. At first, its posture was one of unbridled confidence in its superiority over other religions and its power to convert others to its cause. No event represents this moment of Christian triumphalism more dramatically than the Protestant Ecumenical Missionary Conference held in Edinburgh 1910. John Mott, one of the key organizers of the conference, published his influential book, *"The Evangelization of the World in this Generation"* in 1900. At this time many Western Christians from Europe and North America had a confidence in the superiority of their faith and the superiority of their Western culture. These assumptions were influenced by a modernist culture shaped by confidence in science and technology. This confidence was supported by the conviction that the successful spread of Christianity in its association with the Western colonial movement was providential. Not all Christians shared this optimism. Yet, triumphant optimism reigned from the centers of power in Western Protestant Christianity.

At the World Missionary Conference, Edinburgh 1910, there was little representation from the peoples that made up the objects of this Western missionary project. When some of these colonial representatives challenged this confident self-perception and inherent racism in the Western Christian movement, they were met with resistance.[487] In North America, exploitative and harmful attitudes of superiority led to the "Christianizing" and "civilizing" project of the "Native Residential Schools" in Canada, and various programs of cultural and physical genocide across the continent. In Canada, over the last twenty years, the churches and the government are slowly recognizing their moral failure via a path of apology, repentance and the seeking of reconciliation.

The World Missionary Conference in 1910 came to represent the end of this triumphalist spirit as Western Christianity was confronted with its complicity in the violent brutality of World War I. Western Christian Institutions had to come to terms with the reality that most Christian churches did not challenge the warmongering of national leaders. When war came, they saw it as their patriotic duty to support war against other nations who also identified as Christian. The superiority of Western culture and Christian Faith became exposed as an arrogant myth. Even as the Nazi party rose to power in Germany and Hitler started to round up Jews, Gypsies, "Liberals" and Homosexuals, most of the German churches supported his actions by either silence or voices of support, such as that of the "German Christian Movement." The counter movement of the "Confessing Church" in Germany was small. In Canada and the United States, when a ship, MS St. Louis, with Jewish Refugees came to seek asylum, the Canadian and United States Governments turned them away.[488] During that period of decision, the Canadian Prime Minister, Mackenzie King, noted in his diary that the principal of one of the prominent theological colleges in Toronto wrote him in a strongly anti-Semitic spirit.

David Bosch describes in some detail how the loss of triumphal self-confidence was evidenced in the ensuing ecumenical missionary conferences in the 20[489]th century. Slowly but surely, Christians and Christian churches became conscious of their complicity in brutality and hatred, and gradually, a sense of repentance developed in many communities. Nothing did more for this sense of repentance than the shocking discovery of the true dimensions of the holocaust during World War II. Some Christians on the Allied side were brave enough to face up to Allied brutalities inflicted on prisoners of war in the aftermath of World War II. Even as Bavinck's statement above signaled, a turn towards self-examination in repentance amongst many Christians, few Christian Churches faced up to their brutal history with sexual and gender minority people. In fact, after the Concentration camps in Northern Europe were liberated, the emaciated surviving homosexual inmates were re-imprisoned. No mercy or grace was shown. Christian voices did not defend them. Recognition of the indignities they suffered have been slow in coming, not least because of the long history of Christian and state complicity in oppressing people in homoerotic relationships.

Nevertheless, some forms of Christianity did enter a period of deep self-examination following World War I. David Bosch notes the early appearance of Paul Schütz's book "*Zwischen Nil und Kaukasus*" (Between the Nile and the Caucasus) (1927). This book consisted of a devastating critique of Lutheran mission efforts in the Middle East which Schütz traced to the attitude of the church itself.[490] In 1932, Karl Barth's lecture at the Brandenburg Mission Conference picked up similar themes. In that lecture he was prophetically bold in his critique of the Nazi party. The core of his message was a call for an unceasing repentant and humble and self-examining attitude in the proclamation of the Gospel.[491] The German missionaries who listened to his call and critique were not impressed. Previous to this post WWI awareness, 19th century missionaries in several contexts already started to challenge the entanglement of Christianity and the colonial powers, particularly within the British Empire. One such example is the work of the London Missionary Society in South Africa and, particularly, the work of Dr. T.J van der Kemp.[492] Also, evidence from the pre-conference questionnaires received for the Edinburgh 1910 conference shows that missionaries in the field were aware and concerned about the way Christian faith and colonial and state powers were entangled.[493] However, no recognition of the abuse of sexual and gender minority people was forthcoming.

The primary response to the self-examination that developed in 20th century theological reflection was an emphasis on engaging the world humbly and repentantly, rather than triumphally. Bavinck captures this shift well in his moving challenge, "…the missionary enterprise… is doing penance when it enters this deeply wounded world in humility and love." We need to broaden the concept "missionary enterprise" here to the whole Christian church as it engages its world and context. In the 1932 lecture referenced above, Karl Barth argues that we all are "Heiden[494]" (unbelievers/heathen), that those within the church are simply "Heiden" who have heard of and received grace and we churched "Heiden" need to stand in humble solidarity with the "Heiden" outside the church.[495] Thus, Barth echoed Paul's argument in the opening chapters of the Letter to the Romans where he noted that self-righteous judging Christians are themselves also judged. David Bosch would build this emphasis on a humble repentant witness of the church in the world into a theology of world engagement as represented in "bold humility."[496]

Confession – The Moral Engagement of sexual and gender minority people in Bold Humility

As we consider a process of moral discernment, as we consider how we bring intuitive and social biases to our arguments, and as we consider the painful history of terror, abuse and suffering inflicted on people in homoerotic relationships, we have no choice but to start with repentant confession. As done with many wrongs in the past, let us acknowledge and take responsibility for how the Christian tradition and Institutions and the cultures it shaped are implicated in doing harm to sexual and gender minorities. In the first three centuries of the Christian faith, there was not yet a long record of abuse, torture, murder and condemnation of people in homoerotic relationships. Today we face a long history of violence and harm, as well as some jurisdictions where direct and indirect Christian influences have created punitive legal persecution and discrimination. I propose here that we embrace Bavinck's admonishment for penitential loving humility as the proper starting point and posture in relation to sexual and gender minority people. Such penitential love and humility would require honest and forthright confession of profound wrongs committed by Christian churches of all traditions. Doing so requires facing up to the way, though perhaps sometimes unintended, in which many Christian churches in their teaching and preaching still contribute to an atmosphere of disgust, humiliation, and harm toward sexual minorities. Only by beginning here may we recover something of the moral high ground that seemed to have been present in the love and helpfulness in the best part of the early Christian movement. Where medieval Christianity developed a confessional practice of abuse, we are invited by the gospel to develop a confessional practice of humble confession of the wrongs inflicted in the past and the harm still being done by Christian churches. As many Christian Institutions have started following paths of reconciliation in the light of former support of anti-Judaism, slavery, racism, and discrimination against women, so the examination of the history of homophobia invites a similar response. In this spirit of repentance, Christian communities can become confessees rather than hearers of confession, to unbind the suffering of sexual and gender minorities.

Levels of Confession

Over the last thirty years a process of truth and reconciliation has become common in places where deep and violent wrongs have been committed. Such public truth and reconciliation commissions, as held in South Africa, Chile, and in Canada, have their roots in the core understanding of the Christian gospel that emphasizes honest truth telling and repentance and the hopeful possibility of moving forward in a new and reconciling spirit. In Canada the churches implicated in the Native Residential School abuses were invited to face up to their complicity in child-abuse and various forms of cultural genocide in relation to aboriginal peoples.[497] Bavinck's statement echoes that kind of process. Churches developed official statements of apology which were presented to leaders and survivors within aboriginal communities.

Truth telling, and confession have an individual dimension and always require the taking of individual responsibility. They also have a public dimension where the truth of suffering is publicly acknowledged and where a public commitment is made to stop such practices. From a Christian perspective it is not so much a process of inducing feelings of guilt, as it is about spurring action towards change and healing. Therefore, in relation to sexual and gender minorities, it is important that institutional Christian communities take steps to publicly acknowledge culpability and to commit to the cessation of activities that cause harm. Acknowledging the wrongs of the past is relatively easy, it is harder to face up to changing present behaviors and attitudes that cause harm. The story told in this volume makes an appeal upon followers of Jesus Christ to consider our own culpability in the wrongs of the past and the harm still being done. A public confession or apology is the beginning.

Repentance

Confessing the truth and making apology is the first and critical step. However, such a step is meaningless without Christian repentance. The word repentance can often be spiritualized into some kind of pious inner process or glossed in terms of guilt feelings. However, both in the Hebrew tradition, with the use of the word *teshuva*, and in the Christian Greek tradition, with the use of the word *metanoia*, "repentance" means turning and then walking in a different direction from the past. The turn is towards a whole new way of doing, being, relating and thinking. This new way is represented in the call to join in the reign of God. Within the Christian tradition, the content of that reign in demonstrated in the stories handed down and reflected upon in the four Gospels of the New Testament. Such a decisive turn requires a profound change of heart, attitude, and eventually action. The story told so far of the suffering inflicted by our Christian tradition and history requires us to turn and walk in a different and new direction. Much of the current debate within Christian communities is still centered on defending the status quo, parsing biblical texts, and then presuming the right to pronounce judgment over sexual and gender minorities. As religious communities, we have scarcely begun to examine ourselves, our own complicity in harm, and our own contribution to the destruction of the opportunity for sexual and gender minorities to live full and flourishing lives.

Mat 22:36 - 40 "Teacher," he asked, "which is the greatest commandment in the Law?" Jesus answered, " 'Love the Lord your God with all your heart, with all your soul, and with all your mind.' This is the greatest and the most important commandment. The second most important commandment is like it: 'Love your neighbor as you love yourself.' The whole Law of Moses and the teachings of the prophets depend on these two commandments." (GNB)(See also: Mat 7:12; Jn 1:17; Rm 13:9; 1 John 4:7-12)

144

Matthew 22:40 is a pivotal statement as the best memory in early Christianity of the way Jesus engaged and lived out biblical texts. It provides a beautiful picture of the function of the Scriptures and the core character of God's reign. In the original language, the phrase "depend on" in the translation cited above is actually "hang from." It paints the picture of the "Law" suspended and dependent on the concrete living out of love for God and neighbor. When Jesus did things that seemed to contradict that law, he did so always in the interest of the well-being of the rejected, the weakest, the powerless, and the neediest in the world of his time. As many Christians have taken up the challenge to turn away from anti-Semitism, slavery, racism, and gender bias, so God's reign invites a turning away from harming sexual and gender minorities. But what would such repentance look like, and how does it fit with a process of moral discernment concerning the boundaries of Christian sexual practices?

If we were to extend the many parables and stories in the Gospels that demonstrate God's reign of justice and love to sexual gender minority people today, we would be challenged to see in such neighbors, those beaten up and vulnerable lying next to the road, as in the story of the Good Samaritan. We would turn to welcome those considered an "abomination" and not welcome in the temple, like Jesus invited the unacceptable into the temple after challenging exploitative practices. We would see those intimidated into silence, and those who are the "Lazarus'" next to the unconcerned "Rich Man" metaphorically, as indicative of Christian communities that continue to harm in the name of faith. Repentance begins by viewing sexual and gender minority people through this gospel lens. It also involves hearing and listening intently to stories of suicide, rejection, family hatred, congregational abuse, and grief. Such perspective and listening invites us to empathy, love, and reconciliation. When we see and listen, we can discern and judge; and only when we have seen, listened, and discerned with profound repentant humility, can we act.

Repentance, therefore, requires us not to start Christian self-examination with the texts of terror, with all their problematic history and misinterpretation. Rather, we begin by considering the stories of God's reign in the Gospel accounts of Jesus Christ. Repentance requires humility rather than the assertion of political power in our communities to block equal civil rights. We can advocate for the kind of equality that Christians expect for themselves and even for their enemies. Repentance requires the creation of safe space in Christian communities for sexual and gender minority people where they will not be vilified, simplistically judged, or branded, threatened with ecclesial prosecution, and treated unequally. Repentance requires a change in "us" – those who preach non-affirming judgment - and not in "them" – sexual and gender minority people. Repentance requires the removal of the us-and-them divide which privileges power over those who are being harmed. Only after our humble confession, apology, and repentance can we move towards a process in community to ask how we understand the boundaries of Christian erotic sexual practice.

Those Implicated in Harm

In my experience of advocacy, I have encountered people with a "traditional" point of view who claim that they are being harmed by extending equality and justice to sexual and gender minorities. Allowing gracious room for people with different perspectives and inner struggles with change is important. However, claims of being harmed by ceasing harm to others represent a moral fallacy described in philosophical logic as "an argument to compassion" (argumentum ad misericordiam). To understand this fallacy, consider a parallel example. A slave owner claims that he is being harmed by setting his slaves free. It is true that the slave owner will suffer loss. That loss, however, is not an excuse for the ongoing moral and ethical harm inflicted on his slaves. In fact, the claim of being hurt by treating others fairly relays a lack of repentant insight. Repentance requires that we reject the legacy of doing harm and embrace the concept of mutual respect, acceptance, and love of humanity.

Conclusion

Our attempt at the moral discernment regarding the place and role of sexual and gender minority people in Christian churches today can only begin after the process of confession, apology, and repentance is engaged with integrity. In such a context we can then invite each other to move forward as we discern the erotic sexual moral logic of the Scriptures together. The final chapter will engage that conversation.

CHAPTER 12: THE BETTER WAY – DISCERNING A CHRISTIAN MORAL LOGIC IN RELATION TO LGBTQI+ PEOPLE

The sentries patrolling the city saw me. I asked them, "Have you found my lover?" As soon as I left them, I found him. I held him and wouldn't let him go until I took him to my mother's house, to the room where I was born. (Song of Songs 3:3-4)

The Judaistic tradition out of which the Christian Faith arose did not consider erotic love evil or sinful. As the book Song of Songs attests, it celebrated such passionate love. The love, comfort, and affirmation brought by deeply committed lovers was and is a matter of celebration. Sexual desire in itself and the erotic fulfilment of that desire was considered part of the good human condition. Our earlier exploration of history shows how the influence of misogynistic conceptions of women as the "erotically passionate" ones as opposed to the "rational male" started to shape early Christianity in the Roman Empire. Erotic passion, the Stoics believed, led to irrational passion and was thus unmanly. Roman conceptions of manliness were built on this ideal of the rational dispassionate male. Early Christianity, in its attempts to fit with higher Roman culture, moved away from its rootedness in good sexuality to a point where the sexual union of a couple was only considered permissible where it was about reproduction. In fact, the highest form of Christian manliness became associated with world withdrawal and celibacy. The reduction in early Christianity of sexual expression to reproductive acts only, and then grudgingly so, has profoundly impoverished Christian sexual moral logic. It has also contributed to an ongoing atmosphere of shame around all forms of sexuality and sensuality that has been harmful.[498] The theological trajectory of the "sin of sodomy" and its branding as the most grievous sin against nature, was largely built on this process that warped away from the positive spiritual side of the erotic union of human bodies.

As the story has been told so far, it unfolds the development of a strong anti-erotic sentiment in Christian tradition. This tradition, and its negative consequences for human relationships, does not only impact on sexual and gender minorities, it damages all Christian erotic relationships. It is not my intention to offer here a complete sexual ethic or an exhaustive discussion of sexual morality in the Christian context. Rather, I seek here to unravel some of the harmful bondage from a long history of textual readings and resultant practices that have bent Christian erotic practice away from contributing to the flourishing human community. The harmful anti-erotic strain of Christian tradition goes against the grain of the vision of God's reign and the beautiful poems of creation and the celebration of embodied love in the Hebrew Scriptures. Although much of what follows should simply make sense for all erotic relationships, the intention is to unbind the dark oppressive power of the spell that late-antiquity and medieval prejudice cast over sexual and gender minorities.

Changes to this procreative reductionism in Christian erotic practice emerged during the Reformation. At first, scandalized by perceived and real sexual promiscuity among the clergy, Protestant Reformers rejected mandatory celibacy and frowned on any form of celibacy as an invitation to lapse into adultery. Even though celibate monastic orders remained in some parts of Protestantism, celibacy was not something the Reformers encouraged. Marriage thus became a hedge and protection against falling into sexual sin. Paul's instruction to the Corinthians, "...it is better to marry than to burn with passion..."[499] became the ruling principle of erotic moral teaching. Reformation erotic moral logic remained largely negative. The idea of bad flesh and good spirit of the Greek philosophers still lingered. The idea that sexual desire is of necessity a "lust of the flesh" still exercised a strong influence. The Greco-Roman idea of Christian manliness thus still held some sway. Particularly because the 16th century Reformation was essentially an Augustinian movement and Augustine's biases still exercised great influence.[500]

The emergence of the English Puritan conception of marriage as the joining of spiritual soul-mates reintroduced a strain of positive sexual desire that became part of the Protestant theological tradition. This shift was not really the intention of the Puritans as they were suspicious of sensuality! Gustafson notes that a debate between Anglicans and Puritans arose on the meaning of marriage. Anglicans argued that marriage and its sexual dimensions is only about reproduction and societal order and they cited Gen. 1:28 as their Scriptural authority. Puritans countered that marriage is also about the "bond of affection" between marriage partners and they cited Gen. 2:18 as their authority.[501] Our contemporary theological conceptions in Protestantism, that see no wrong in the erotic union of husband and wife despite a lack of potential reproductive outcome, bears out this momentous change initiated by that debate. In many ways our present positive Christian eroticism returns to a more Judaistic conception of erotic love as captured in Song of Songs.

Very few Protestant communities would consider it inappropriate for a couple to have erotic sexual relations after having a vasectomy or after a hysterectomy. Yet, a vasectomy turns a man into a eunuch as understood in the Greco-Roman world. According to Deut 23:1, such men, due to the imperfection of their genitalia, are not fit to approach God in the Temple. One of our current problems in coming to terms with the sexual ethics of the Torah is our projection of later Christian conceptions back onto the law. It is important to remember that, in the context of the time the Torah was written, it was not primarily concerned with sexual desire but rather with the maintenance of a kinship-based system of justice. Within the limitations of that cultural structure it proposes boundaries that protected vulnerable women, the poor, the orphaned, the widowed and children. Often, Christians today read texts like Leviticus 18:22 and 20:13, through a lens of Greco-Roman conceptions of sexual desire and lust rather than through the lens of the protection of kinship and family justice.

In addition to such cultural, and theological realities that shape our understanding of erotic sexual boundaries, our contemporary insight serves to strengthen the concept of love, mutual comfort and healing generated through loving erotic union. Gustafson describes the importance of erotic sexual life this way: "There are meanings and feelings involved which are significant for our senses of well-being, individually and in relation to each other."[502] Positive, loving, erotic and physical expressions of love provide comfort, well-being and healing. They contribute to building a sense of wellness and are dimensions of the "help and comfort" that most marriage liturgies celebrate. In no small way, we have learned the importance of physical touch and physical cherishment from the research on babies who were deprived of human touch and the shocking harmful outcome of deprivation from human touch.[503] Moreover, we know today that skin to skin contact has a strong biological component releasing important hormones in the body. For adults, erotic love expressed with another person is one key way in which we can maintain both psychological and physical health.

Today, as a result of these insights, the Christian understanding of good appropriate sexual relationships acknowledges that such erotic relationships can never simply be reduced to the procreative-biological.[504] There is a profound spiritual dimension to a contemporary Christian understanding of erotic love, and we know now that this dimension is intimately entangled in the biological processes of our human bodies. The Christian traditions that considers erotic desire and arousal as essentially sinful and as against God's creative intent, is to misread the Scriptural tradition even if it is based in the wise theology of Augustine of Hippo. There is a tendency by those who reject same-sex erotic relationships to reduce sexual intimacy to genital mechanics. Such reductions represent a poverty in the theological understanding of the meaning of erotic love and the healing power of mutual loving cherishment. Our earlier historical accounts demonstrated how the preoccupation with sexual organs and how they "fit" arise out of medieval anxiety about "natural sex."

Present Christian traditions, in the light of recovering a more material Hebrew view of sex, has room for understanding erotic sexual desire as something that is not inherently bad or sinful. Rather, it is a gift to help us flourish. Even though the Puritans were suspicious of anything sensual, they were not wrong in emphasizing the importance of the "bond of affection."[505] Giving oneself unreservedly to a partner in cherishing erotic love strengthens the bonds of affection, comforts and strengthens one's partner and even contributes to both mental and physical well-being. In fact, in this act of love there is an opportunity to give oneself completely to the other, to become vulnerable before the beloved, and ultimately before God. A profound spiritual and gospel dimensions is embedded in such acts of erotic self-giving. Losing oneself in relation to the beloved provides opportunity to flourish, join and give, in a unitive way. Human flourishing results.

Of course, as a strong biological drive, erotic desire can become excessive and harmful. As much as a deep and profound loving erotic relationship can build health and self-esteem, so it can become harmful and a source of alienation, depression and abuse. When sexual love, in its giving and receiving, is used as a selfish tool of control and exploitation, it can become alienating, psychologically destructive, and may lead to depression and severe mental distress. The erotic always has inherent destructive sinful potential. Given what we know today about the healing dimension of sexual intimacy, counselling a legalistic rule of celibacy or a sublimation of the unitive role of sex in loving committed relationships is potentially harmful.

When Theology Does Harm

"Eleven years later, I still sometimes get nauseous when touching another man," writes a male victim recovering from Christian ex-gay "therapy."[506] The harm described here is not theoretical, there is now a great chorus of Christian witnesses of the inner rupture and spiritual abuse that "traditional" Christian teaching on same sex relationships inflicts. What is harmful, and how does it harm? There can be little doubt, after exploring the history of ideas about sex and gender in Western Christianity and the history of the abhorrent practices of live burning, torture, and child abuse, that some Christian activity has been and remains physically harmful. However, many Christians still argue that they can be welcoming of sexual and gender minority people, critical of past practices of harm, while not supporting same-sex erotic relationships. In fact, they argue that, the position of "welcoming but not affirming" is a loving and life-giving response.

One of the most concerted attempts at presenting this argument is in the best-selling evangelical author Preston Sprinkle's book, "People to be Loved: Why Homosexuality is not Just an Issue." Sprinkle tries to be fair and accountable in his discussion of Scripture and challenges non-affirming Christians when they become judgmental and rejecting towards homosexual people. He demonstrates a fair sense of the biblical debates, although he missed the work of Rabbi Jacob Milgrom on Leviticus. Ultimately Sprinkle still concludes that Christians should hold a warm welcoming but not affirming position towards same-sex erotic relationships. Is his approach non-harmful towards sexual and gender minority people?

Let us examine the possible prescriptions he offers. Sprinkle discusses "reparative therapy" – therapeutic approaches that seek to change sexual orientation - and reports the negative evaluation cast on that practice but then expresses doubt. One of the weaknesses in Sprinkle's book is that he makes use of anecdotal "evidence," He acknowledges that a friend of his who is a psychologist claims to have a fairly high success rate with "reparative therapy" (50%), he also acknowledges that this is not sufficient evidence.[507] Despite this shaky evidence, he continues to imply that reparative therapy might be an option for some people who experience same-sex erotic attraction. It is telling that Sprinkle quotes his psychologist friend as saying "Look, I know what all the websites say. But I can only tell you what I have seen…"[508] This quotation represents a lack of an evidenced based professional approach. I, too, use anecdotal examples in this book. Some anecdotes come from my own pastoral experience and others from the moving memoir of Garrard Conley and others. Nevertheless, these anecdotes are supported by reputable and peer-reviewed publications on harm. Sprinkle's argument tries to equate his anecdotes with such authoritative sources as the full clinical review of the American Psychological Association (APA). Such a logic is fundamentally flawed. Large volumes of reviewed psychological evidence are reviewed by the APA, and this evidence establishes that any lasting change in sexual orientation is highly unlikely and that "reparative therapy" is highly likely to cause harm.[509] Despite all the claims made by Sprinkle for compassion, his inattention to evidence based research is telling. What becomes clear is that he feels obliged to come up with a non-affirming position to retain his credibility within the Evangelical wing of American Christianity.

Sprinkle also claims that another prescription for people experiencing same-sex erotic attraction could be "mixed orientation marriage." He acknowledges that many attempts at so called "mixed orientation" marriage fail. However, he argues many heterosexual marriages also fail. He writes anecdotally about two gay friends who have fulfilling mixed orientation marriages. There is no reason to doubt Mr. Sprinkle's anecdotes. However, one has to point out that these anecdotes and the discussion in his book fail to consider the complexity of sexual orientation, its dynamic nature and the different levels or orientation experienced in people's lives. Some people may be at a less extreme point on a dynamic continuum of sexual orientation and might be closer to a bi-sexual orientation and therefore more able to live and even find fulfillment in a heterosexual relationship when they meet the right partner. The potential harm of mixed orientation marriage could be profoundly different from that of a failed heterosexual marriage. That harm has to do with the experience of shame and guilt that accompanies the non-affirming Christian teaching. There are profound ethical questions raised in relation to the heterosexual partner that becomes part of such a relationship. What harm and experience of rejection might a heterosexual partner in a mixed orientation marriage have to confront? What happens when things go wrong and the homosexual orientated partner is unable to fulfill the expectations of the marriage? As a pastor, I experienced exactly this problem with a gay parishioner who committed suicide after he was manipulated into a mixed orientation marriage by a former pastor. He tried but secretly kept failing to keep his marriage vows. The shame and guilt became overwhelming. The impact on his wife and two step-children was absolutely devastating.

The research on the mental health impact for people who are in non-affirming religious communities cited earlier provides another strong indicator that the prescription of a mixed orientation marriage brings great potential harm to both individuals and to children involved.[510] This harm, as described in chapter 3 includes a much higher risk of depression, substance abuse, self-harm, and suicide. Do the possible exceptions to this harm justify the teaching and attitude that still encourages such practices?

Finally, Sprinkle suggests that the final option for Christians who experience same-sex erotic attraction is celibacy. Sprinkle notes many of the arguments against a prescription of celibacy. He does not seem to see celibacy as a prescription but rather as a choice or calling. He provides anecdotal stories from gay people who have found the choice for celibacy a fulfilling way to live. Of course, if a person reaches a personal conviction to live a celibate life, that is fulfilling despite its challenges, there can be no reason to criticize this. People through the ages both heterosexual and homosexual have made this choice. What may do potential harm is a religious *prescription* of celibacy. Within Protestantism, celibacy as a requirement was rejected during the reformation period. Matthew Vines writes eloquently about this rejection and provides an extensive critique of the idea.[511]

Sprinkle also writes about his understanding about the difference between love and sex. His argument is that one can love without sex and have sex without love. Although this distinction is simplistic, there is a level on which it is accurate. The problem with this standard non-affirming response is that it applies a standard and prohibition to sexual minority people that it does not apply to heterosexual people. It is also an argument frequently made by heterosexual people as a prescription for sexual and gender minorities. If you are a sexual or gender minority you should be happy to love without a deep satisfying and mutually edifying and healing erotic expression. If you happen to be heterosexual that rule does not apply. If one would ask Mr. Sprinkle, after he fell in love with his wife, would he have been satisfied not to love and comfort her fully in a loving relationship that included erotic love, he might think differently about this.

From the perspective of psychology and psychiatry it is also important to note that the "welcoming but not affirming" argument in Christianity places people in a double bind. As noted in Chapter 3, a double bind is when two conflicting contradictory messages from the same source is imposed in a therapeutic or power relationship. Such a bind creates profound emotional distress and psychological harm. In this case the message becomes "your sexual orientation is not bad or wrong, but your tender love and desire for someone of the same sex is sinful and evil." This, as psychologists pointed out, is a particularly warped form of coercion because the desire associated with the love experienced does not do harm to the beloved. The result is that this form of moral manipulation leads to a constant sense of guilt and shame fundamentally related to the high incidence of suicidal ideation and other forms of mental agony and substance abuse. What harm does it do if two people of the same sex find themselves in a deeply loving and mutually satisfying erotic relationship? What harm does it do to forbid such people from loving one another fully?

The so called "welcoming but non-affirming" Christian position brings a large degree of potential harm to sexual and gender minority people. Not only is this established in social research, but many people, will bear witness to struggles with shame, depression, substance abuse, and suicidal ideation caused by this teaching. Given the argument on history, moral discernment and the Bible presented in this book, I argue here that a non-affirming theological position is not morally supportable. We know that we are doing harm to sexual and gender minorities and doing such harm is not a moral option for Christians.

What are the options for sincere and caring Christians who, after considering all biblical and historical arguments, still come to a non-affirming conclusion? I believe there is one possible ethical position for such Christians, that is not a compromise. This position could potentially minimize harm. It is to consider Christian erotic same sex relationships as a pastoral accommodation in the face of a broken world subject to God's healing grace. This is not my own position, but I could see some Christians hold this view with deep compassionate love that minimizes harm. Below, I will unpack this argument more fully

152

and argue why a "pastoral accommodation" approach may present a potentially faithful and non-harmful position.

Building a Scriptural Moral Logic

What then is the argument of this book, and how should we proceed? What is required to stop doing harm? Does this book propose a fallacy as one of my critical readers suggested? That reader understood the argument as, Christians did bad things to sexual and gender minority people so now we should repent and unreservedly welcome and affirm all such people in our communities. That reader pointed out correctly that we would then apply the same logic to murderers and their treatment in the past! However, that is not my argument. Here is a summary of the argument so far:

1. Christians have done great harm and are still doing harm to sexual and gender minorities.
2. There is no basis in Christian Scripture and tradition for doing harm to others. In fact, we are called to seek justice for and the flourishing of all. When it comes to erotic relationships, we need to practice moral discernment in the light of the gospel and the whole of the Scriptural witness rather than the classic anti-homoerotic texts of terror.
3. The doing of harm in Christian history is rooted in the reading and interpretation of a few isolated biblical texts that have been thinned, condensed and profoundly influenced by cultural context and social conditions that are questionable. It is also rooted in the development off many different traditions and periods of time that constructed ideas of sin against nature and the development of a biblically unsustainable argument against something called sodomy. The reading of these texts fails to consider the content of the texts themselves as well as a wider biblical moral and ethical logic as developed among ethicists that focus on "care," and "just love" as expressions of Jesus' call to turn to the reign of God.
4. The history of harm can be clearly and demonstrably linked to the historical contexts and processes of the past that have long departed from the original biblical cultural meanings and intentions. Contemporary biblical scholarship has demonstrated that traditional ways of reading Christian texts present many interpretive-hermeneutical problems establishing that definitive claims such as, "the bible says homosexual practice is a sin" is simply not sustainable.
5. This historical outworking of Christian texts has shaped our contemporary social world through Western colonialism and still influences Christian arguments today within more traditional Christian communities. These factors create a bias and a lack of concern for harm caused to sexual and gender minorities. It is a fallacy to claim that sexual and gender minorities, by virtue of this status, can be compared to murderers, rapists of child abusers. Such social forces, ecclesial attitudes, and teaching, and the impact of this on sexual and gender minorities and their families, remain deeply harmful and has been demonstrated to lead to depression, despair,

alienation, and ultimately high levels of suicide among people who find themselves in non-affirming Christian communities.

6.   When Christians have confessed the sin of abuse, torture, murder and ongoing harm, they are now called to find a new life-giving way to welcome, include and bring healing to sexual and gender minority people. Such an affirming response can confidently be rooted in the wider moral logic of the gospel message and the reading of the Bible, so that sexual and gender minorities, together with the whole Christian community, can flourish in lives that give glory to God.

The aim in this chapter is to unpack the last point. What does it look like to embrace sexual and gender minority people so that all can flourish together for the glory of God? Reading and interpreting the Bible is a complex and communal process. The "texts of terror" used against sexual and gender minorities have a long history of causing violence, torture, and brutal killing. This should make us doubt the application of these texts in the way Christians have done and are doing.

Earlier I have outlined how complex the interpretation of these texts is. Frequently, they are pulled out of their historical context and they are pulled out of their rhetorical context. There are serious questions about the accuracy of the translation of some of these texts. I have also shown how diverse the interpretations are. I have described how historic bias colored the reading of these texts. I have shown that there is no certainty about the "traditional" interpretation of these texts. I have also demonstrated that the way these texts are interpreted to judge same-sex erotic experience is different from the interpretive logic applied in other Christian moral arguments. Most of all, in chapter 2, I argued that the larger biblical logic and the centrality of the love commandment and the ministry and the logic of the teaching of Jesus is not adequately considered. For all these reasons, an ideological non-affirmation of sexual and gender minority people in their erotic lives is not a Christian option. By ideological I mean a kind of legal rule or absolutist position.

Nevertheless, I am convinced there is room and need for ongoing discussion on the boundaries of all Christian erotic relationships. There is also room to come to the different forms of affirmation of sexual and gender minorities based in nuanced reading of the Bible. However, there is no room for a complete rejection of all homo-erotic relationships and discrimination against such sexual and gender minorities. Such rejection causes clear and demonstrable harm to people and thus violates the most profound dimension of the gospel of grace.

Reading Our Traditions in the Light of Scriptural Moral Logic

Even as the Scriptural traditions indicate boundaries around sexual expression, they do not label erotic relationships in themselves as essentially sinful. Augustine's conclusion, under the influence of his time, culture and perhaps his Manichean bias, should thus give us cause for cautious critique. Augustine argued, based on the story of the temptation of Adam and Eve in Genesis 3, that "Shame modestly covered that which lust disobediently moved in opposition to the will, which was thus punished for its own disobedience."[512] The way this reading of Genesis 3 is shaped by Roman stoicism and its dualistic notion that rejects erotic relationships as tainted by unmanly passion bends things away from the biblical perspective. Augustine writes, "...for the insubordination of these members, and their defiance of the will, are the clear testimony of the punishment of man's first sin."[513] Augustine still seems to make a subtle distinction between sexual intercourse as intended by God for the purpose of procreation and sexual desire that becomes warped by sin. However, the Roman stoic ideal of the dispassionate rationale male as opposed to the passionate and weak female is not supported by the larger biblical tradition. Such bias does not leave room to recognize the celebration of the beauty and gift of the erotic in holy relationship as expressed in Song of Songs. It is undoubtedly biblical to understand that sexual desire, when it serves human flourishing in its committed cherishment and erotic expression, is part of the goodness of creation and thus gives glory to God.

There is no evidence that the larger Hebrew and Christian traditions ever enthusiastically endorsed same-sex erotic expression. There are some indications that early Christian communities did not always consider such relationships completely unacceptable. The judgmental preaching of Chrysostom is a case in point. Of course, the cultural meaning and the nature of same-sex relationships differ over time, and we have little knowledge of the content of such relationships in different time periods.

Therefore, as important as it is for Christian communities to repent and to stop doing harm, we should take seriously the meaning of the Christian tradition's caution about sexual diversity. If we start reading anti-homoerotic texts from that perspective while keeping the mind all the arguments in this book so far, a liberating clarity emerges. As creatures we are created with a beautiful and healing capacity to cherish and love one another emotionally and bodily. Such embodied love is part of what it is to flourish as creatures of God. How can we read the anti-homoerotic texts of terror in ways that are faithful?

In response, I will return briefly to the key anti-homoerotic texts. First, the Hebrew biblical scriptures contain two prohibitions of Leviticus 18:22[514] and 20:13[515]. The translation and interpretation of these texts in the light of context and culture are still being debated today. If one were to continue to consider these texts as literally applicable today, do these texts, in their historical context, represent a blanket prohibition on same-sex sexual erotic expression for all men? The answer to this is that such universalization is doubtful. These texts, in their biblical context, address Jewish males in a married state within the context of a larger family clan. The argument, advanced by Rabbi Milgrom and Renato Lings, that these two texts specifically address forms of incest within the kinship group cannot be proved beyond a doubt. What we can say with certainty is that these prohibitions in the original classic Hebrew represent a sentence construction that seems to speak specifically to the violation of the marriage bed.[516] Given these factors, the universalization of these texts to all male same-sex relationships is highly doubtful. Almost all contemporary non-affirming interpretations of the Bible rely on insisting that Lev 18:22 and Lev 20:13 must be understood as a universal biblical prohibition of all male homoerotic relationships. The interpretation of all other texts as prohibitions essentially rely on a universalization of the Levitical rule. When this universalization becomes doubtful, it calls into question the contingent interpretations of other texts.

If we combine this well-informed doubt with a consideration of patriarchal culture, the contemporary scientific and social insight into homo-erotic relationships, and the clear evidence of harm, it behooves us to reconsider universal non-affirming positions. Please note that I emphasize "universal non-affirmation" here. Scriptural logic does provide wise guidance for boundaries in all forms of erotic expression.

I am not arguing here that the moral law of the Torah has now become obsolete. Rather, I argue that the guidance of the moral law requires the additional steps of considering the impact of the law of love and its implications for justice and fairness and its implications for the support of human well-being. The patriarchal prohibitions against child abuse, adultery and incest, shaped by the just law of love still remain valid. A married man should not lie with a man as with his wife, yet, the law of love requires that we do not put offenders to death as the text demands. The moral law thus points to the importance of covenant, responsibility, and mutual respect in erotic sexual relationships. We can embrace important moral logic from these texts without buying into the patriarchal cultural context and without feeling compelled to kill people, or without assuming that they apply to _all_ homoerotic relationships.

Reading Romans 1:26-27 renders even more questions. What is being said and what is being prohibited? Even if we were to imagine that Paul meant to say that all homosexual erotic practices, as he understood it, are inappropriate and lustful, should we universalize this perspective to all forms of loving same-sex relationships today? Is he speaking about particular phenomena? Is Paul influenced by the stoic traditions of his time as some would argue? We should also ask, given the trajectory of harm done to sexual and gender minorities, whether this text warrants such harmful behavior? To what extent is Paul shaped by Greco-Roman assumptions on "natural" gender roles? We know from the experience of many sexual and gender minority people that they have never experienced a "leaving behind" heterosexual attraction. Paul clearly did not understand this. We understand today that the reasons for sexual orientation in experience are complex. They include biology, but also other social and developmental factors. Can we truly then lump such people together with how Paul summarizes the problematic behavior:

They are filled with all kinds of wickedness, evil, greed, and vice; they are full of jealousy, murder, fighting, deceit, and malice. They gossip and speak evil of one another; they are hateful to God, insolent, proud, and boastful; they think of more ways to do evil; they disobey their parents; they have no conscience; they do not keep their promises, and they show no kindness or pity for others.[517]

If we understand these words to describe all sexual and gender minorities, we bear false witness against our neighbors. Most of all, the simplistic application of this text to all homo-erotic relationships ignores Paul's rhetorical point. If you set yourself up as judge over the behaviors described in Romans 1, then you condemn yourself not the other (Romans 2:2-

3).[518] Paul offers a rhetorical case for his argument that all have sinned and fall short of the glory of God. In the light of these questions and the rhetoric in the text, it is also important to consider one of the most persuasive arguments around the description of erotic excess in Romans 1. Brownson concludes that the Roman readers of Paul's letter, in light of the excessive language used in Greek (Rom 1:26-27), would inevitably make a connection with the sexual excesses of Emperor Gaius (Caligula) and that, that was most likely what Paul was speaking of.[519]

Whereas none of the questions and perspectives on their own can decisively reframe Romans 1:26-27, their cumulative effect plus the logic of the love commandment requires that we reject blanket condemnations. Most certainly, Paul's negative rhetoric does not make sense when applied to mutually loving, covenanted unselfish erotic relationships. Christians may continue to read Romans 1 in more and less affirming ways. However, all of us ought to consider the additional realities of contemporary knowledge plus the integrity of Christians who are sexual and gender minorities and their experience.

Should we thus simply argue that Romans 1 is outdated and should therefore be ignored? Given my reformed-tradition commitment to take the Bible seriously, I reject a simplistic rejection of the text as outdated. It seems that the text bears witness against the destructive and idolatrous potential of lustful selfish unbridled expression of erotic desire plus the other forms of wickedness it describes. James Brownson describes such lust based in the reading of these texts as "a heart that seeks its own benefit and power."[520] The text still offers serious guidance and pause about unbridled and exploitative erotic behavior.

Are there any positive models for same-sex love in the Bible? Certainly, the Bible bears witness to a deep and physically affirmed love between David and Jonathan, Ruth and Naomi, and Jesus and the beloved disciple. There is no need to claim that these relationships were sexually consummated. Nevertheless, these Scriptural examples provide examples of physically affirming love between people of the same sex.

The Bible is also used to condemn homo-erotic relationships based in an argument of gender complementarity. Augustine's brief discussion of this argument represents a primary source for its influential tradition.[521] The two problems related to this idea have been highlighted previously. One problem is the claim that sexual intercourse is only appropriate in the setting of biologically procreativity. The other problem is the link between gender complementarity and the extreme misogyny of Greco-Roman culture. I now introduce a third problem. The gender complementarity argument assumes that gender as well as sexual orientation are binary categories. It assumes that gender can only rightly be understood as male and female. Thus, this gender binary is reified as both a natural and religious norm. The result is that same-sex erotic experience is considered wrong and should be resisted, changed our sublimated. As noted previously, science has demonstrated that gender is by no means a simple binary. The existence of intersex people is the most obvious challenge to the binary gender assumption. Sexual orientation is also not a reality that can be denied or that is somehow easily changed. In the experience of most sexual and gender minority people, they have never "left behind" "natural" heterosexual desire in favor of homosexual.

But, is there something in this tradition that could still call same-sex erotic relationships into question? Christians will likely continue to disagree on this question. Some will consider same-sex sexual orientation as a creational disorder and thus as an expression of the way sin has warped creation. Others will come to understand same-sex sexual orientation as a variant in God's good creation. I suggest that it is possible to hold versions of both these perspectives without having to do harm and to prohibit loving same-sex relationships.

I disagree with the "creational disorder" theory. It ignores scientific findings and fails to recognize the problem of the patriarchal and misogynistic roots of this idea. However, for those who accept "creational disorder" theory, there remains a perspective that reduces harm and embraces sexual and gender minority people in their whole humanity. The larger Scriptural logic, the prolongation of the ministry and teaching of Jesus into our own context, and the love commandment suggests that a way of transformative grace must be found even where Christians assume that a situation is not perfect and untainted by sin.[522] As noted in Chapter 4, Gabriel Fackre observed in his critique and review of Gagnon's complete rejection of all homoerotic relationships,

However, the church has a history of wrestling with controverted questions, and as a company of forgiven sinners knows of a divine grace that may translate into an exception to a rule as well as to its upholding.[523]

One place where many Christian communities have evolved by incorporating a gracious exception to a rule is in the understanding about divorce. Divorce is never purely a good thing; it is always a failure, and it does harm through broken promises, the hurt of unfaithfulness or an unwillingness to find a way through disagreement. Many Christian traditions continue to regard divorce as tainted by human sin. And yet, Christian communities have also recognized that despite the state of sin and disorder created by divorce, God's grace can bring new life, new relationships, and new healing and welcome to couples and their families. It can be argued that Jesus' discourses in Matthew 19 and Mark 10 suggest that divorce and re-marriage creates an irreparable state of sinful adultery.[524] That perspective argues that the covenantal and relational breach remains. There is no simplistic reboot with a new marriage after divorce… Using this logic, the divorcee always remains in a perpetual state of disorder. If Christians can consider such apparent irreparable perpetual breach as open to God's healing grace, why would the same not be true for sexual and gender minorities? Although this is not my position, I could understand that some Christians may see homoerotic relationships as disordered, but a disorder healed and embraced by God's grace in committed homo-erotic relationships that must be treated with love and affirmation without discrimination. I take Gabriel Fackre's words as truly wise and reflective of such biblical wisdom. It also suggests a way to retain a core element of Christian tradition while also attempting not to do harm.

The Dignity of Human Flourishing

Our understanding of the role and place of the physical and erotic in bringing human wellness engages one of the key patterns of the ministry of Jesus as witnessed in the

Gospels. Consistently and without fail, the Jesus traditions emphasize the importance of human flourishing. Nowhere is this clearer than the way Jesus both affirmed the law and challenged its application when it was detrimental to human flourishing. Love and justice are inseparable. One example of this complexity can be found in the story of the disciples winnowing wheat on the Sabbath. When challenged on not keeping the law (recorded in Matthew 12 and Mark 2), Jesus makes clear that the physical well-being of the disciples is the overriding factor. In fact, he cites Hosea 6:6 to show that mercy is linked to the love of God. According to the Gospel of Matthew, Jesus understands his work as fulfilling the law through the lens of the love of God and neighbor – the love commandment. After emphasizing the importance of the law, Jesus demonstrates his point by referring to the intention of the law as relational harmony and reconciliation (See Matthew 5:17 onwards). In Luke 4:18 (paraphrasing Isaiah 11:2-5), Jesus is recorded as announcing the meaning of his coming reign, it is exactly in the bringing of human flourishing in lifting up the poor and suffering, setting the captives free, healing, and bringing the favor of well-being to humankind that his reign is demonstrated. The coming of this flourishing reign is Good News – the Gospel. This is not a simply a New Testament invention; it reflects the larger logic of the Prophets of the Old Testament and echoes the intention of God's command and wish and blessing for humankind "to be fruitful and multiply" in Genesis 1:28.

The concepts of fruitfulness and growth does of course speak of biological fecundity, but it speaks poetically and metaphorically of so much more. It speaks of humans coming to full potential whether they bear children or not; it speaks of the growth of a creative and beautiful human community. Such a blessing wished upon humankind is God's intention and the most seminal definition of the concept of human dignity. A dignity signaled by the Christian Scriptural claim that we are all created in God's image. The "we" does not only include Christians, it includes every single human being, atheists and murderers, followers of many different religions and even enemies. Within the Christian community we also have this generous and expansive concept of equality of the diversity of people and genders most powerfully expressed in Galatians 3:28.[525] What is particularly interesting about this Galatian verse is its inclusion of slaves, many of whom were eunuchs, who would represent gender diversity that is not simply male or female. To work for the flourishing growth and fruitful community of all people, including gender diverse people, lies at the heart of our understanding of this Scriptural moral logic. This logic is rooted in the Great Commandment of the Love of God and neighbor inextricably linked and in the Christian tradition established by Irenaeus of Lyon in the Latin phrase "*gloria enim Dei vivens homo*"(see also Chapter 2). When we read and interpret texts that appear to work against this logic, we should question our interpretation. Thus, if we seek a Scriptural erotic moral logic in relation to sexual and gender minority people today, human flourishing, and healthy community are touchstones. When we categorically deny sexual and gender minority people a space to flourish as sexual beings we need to reflect deeply on our motivation for denying their dignity and well-being. Nicholas Wolterstorff speaks of this as rights perceived through the lens of Christian Scriptures. These are not simply the "secular" rights of autonomous individuals but the scriptural right we owe to sexual and gender minority people to honor their dignity and to treat them justly. We also need to reflect on the balance of Scriptural

159

witness between the fundamental moral logic and the cultural moral logics encountered. Some people can flourish well without erotic relationships. But these exceptions do not justify a blanket prohibition. As the well-known Christian hymn, "We are One in the Spirit" insists, God calls us to "guard each one's dignity and save each one's pride."

Covenant

So far in this chapter we have established that harm should be prevented, that the Bible does not speak unequivocally against same-sex erotic relationships, and that those who still see a prohibitive dimension in Scripture can lean on God's gracious work to stop harm. We have also established that God's goal for humankind and creation remains full and meaningful flourishing and a moral right to be treated with dignity and justice. I will unpack these affirmations in terms of James Gustafson and David Jensen's concept of covenant which further illuminates the erotic moral logic of Christian faith. I will add to the conversation by linking human dignity, as explored above, to covenant. Gustafson argues that the evolution of Christian moral logic on erotic love has focused on covenanted relationships as the appropriate place for the expression of such forms of love. Christian liturgies of marriage are essentially covenanting liturgies. A covenant between the couple and God is sealed in the presence of a gathered Christian community.

Throughout Christian history, the concept of marriage has been expressed in a variety of cultural forms. Contemporary understandings of marriage in North America are clearly profoundly different that of the early church. Its current perspective is that marriage represents an equal relationship between two people joined in a covenantal relationship in Gods presence.[526] Such a just covenantal structure creates a place for a couple to contribute to the well-being of each other as well as to the well-being of the two together.[527] It is a space of mutual psychological growth, healing relationship building, and even biological healing through touch, cherishment and trust. The potential for recognizing and edifying each other's dignity emerges from this covenantal structure. The publicly recognized and celebrated covenant of two Christians together in marriage supports dignity building wherein trust, mutual confidence, and reliability is constructed. Gustafson notes that such covenantal relationships serve as protection against sin.[528] Similarly, Brownson concludes,

To be sure, the church should continue to stand against those sinful dispositions that motivate the Bible's concerns in sexual ethics, including its discussion in Romans 1. This includes first, a rejection of promiscuity of all kinds and a deep valuing of committed love that cultivates and flourishes in lifelong relationship.[529]

David Jensen also relies on the covenantal tradition to develop a sexual ethic. He states that the idea of marriage is narrower than covenant. Jensen's discussion highlights the problems of idealizing Christian conceptions of marriage and covenant and emphasizes that erotic relationships fosters growth in trust and covenant. His argument serves as a necessary critique of the simplistic argument that love and sex are not the same thing. Indeed, within the theological conception of "good love and good sex," holy love and holy sex, are deeply intertwined. He argues:

160

Sex becomes lovemaking when it cultivates the attentiveness and responsiveness that covenant makes possible. And this gives hope to the body of Christ.[530]

The idea of covenant is thus a broad idea – an expansive frame that supports the growth of mutual trust between people. Erotic sexual expression and the mutual trust it promises to develop within a covenantal relationship generate well-being and ultimately a flourishing community of faith. When erotic sexual desire, no matter its sexual orientation, develops within such a frame, it brings promise.

The Sinful Erotic?

The above discourse represents an ideal. Brownson's warning above incorporates the recognition that Christian erotic discernment requires boundaries. Real people struggle and fail to live up to God's ideal for a flourishing community. Trust is sometimes broken, confidence shaken, and unreliability appears from time to time. In this context the very structure of the covenantal marriage relationships also defines the parameters of sin. Sin ruptures such relationships particularly in the failure of relational integrity. Sin appears when exploitation, harassment, disaffection, resentment and alienation emerge into such relationships. Healthy Christian erotic relationships recognizes the pressures and fissures and seeks to constantly work on what Gabriel Marcel called "creative fidelity."[531] For Marcel, the full engagement of life in creative fidelity is particularly experienced in the expression of love, admiration and friendship. Conversely, seeking creative fidelity requires a turning away from objectification, complacency, self-love, self-satisfaction, and even self-anger to enable each person to embody creative fidelity with a partner. It is this brilliant insight that the Gospel of John reports in the ministry of Jesus when he confronts the Pharisees with their own relational ruptures as they prepare to stone a woman accused of adultery. "Whichever one of you has committed no sin may throw the first stone at her."[532] Jesus refused to participate in self-righteous condemnation. He recognized gospel moral logic will accept that Christian erotic relationships will never be perfect, and grace is always required.

Scriptural moral logic highlights the potential erotic sinfulness. God is not glorified when people selfishly exploit partners and children, where people break covenant commitment, where people dehumanize and objectify others in exploitative ways, where people are focused uniquely on self-gratification. God is not glorified if the love of God does not match the love of our most intimate neighbor. Doing so, represents the sin of lustful desire. Not only is this temptation always with us, but, as Jesus pointed out in the story of the "woman caught in adultery," we all inevitably fall into that sin whether we appear to have good and stable marriages or not. This is what Paul meant in his great rhetoric of Romans summarized in the one stark fact that we are all sinners in need of grace.

Good, celebrated and healing erotic relationships only exist by means of God's grace. It behooves Christians to stop judging sexual and gender minority people and to recognize that God's grace is for all. Covenant faithfulness or "creative fidelity" is always a work in progress no matter what sexual orientation we have.

Loving Gracious Covenant Faithfulness as Erotic Moral Logic

In his commentary on Genesis, Walter Brueggemann identifies a basic relationship pattern between God and God's people. He summarizes how the book of Genesis relays God in God's interaction with humankind in "Sovereign power as patience, faithfulness and anguish."[533] This pattern of sovereignty is expressed in a refrain that Brueggemann frames thus: "When the facts warrant death, God insists on life for his creatures."[534] Clearly, God's glory is thus demonstrated in immeasurable grace that issues in a flourishing creation. God interacts with humankind in a constant faithful process of pastoral accommodation. This process is not a facile unjust pastoral act but, in the frame of our Christian faith, the costly justice of God meted out on the cross. When we deal with the affirmation of sexual and gender people, we are not dealing with a tension between justice, love and doctrine. We are dealing with a call to reflect the glory of God in pastoral grace extended to all in God's community of sinners in justice and love. This quality of pastoral grace is captured by the Hebrew prophets in the concept of *hesed*. In the Good News Bible, the Hebrew word *hesed* is consistently translated as "lovingkindness." There is, however, much more to the Scriptural concept of *hesed*. This lovingkindness involves those elements of suffering patience and anguish that Brueggemann already identified in Genesis. If we are to glorify God in our faithful covenanted erotic relationships, we would have to find the grace to live out our relationships with suffering anguish and patience.

Covenant faithfulness or "creative fidelity" invites us back to one of Gustafson's primary Scriptural guides for moral decision making which he bases in Phil 1:27 and Phil 2:5.[535] Walking in the way of Jesus Christ with sexual and gender minority experiences, places a high demand on our ability to read our keenly held traditions and Scriptural interpretations in the spirit of self-giving and grace. When we might be quick to judge rather than to discern together, this perspective invites us to consider own posture before God and our fellow gender and sexual minority Christians. Walking in the way of the gospel as we discern moral logic moves us to have compassion, kindness and deep concern for the suffering and oppression faced by all sexual and gender minority people.[536] This gracious posture constitutes the boundary for our judgments of others and our treatment of our neighbors. This logic provides no room for simplistic judgment, and harmful behavior. In this logic we always start with our own need for grace before God.

Conclusion: The Boundaries of Moral Discernment in Relation to Sexual and Gender Minority Christians

Regrettably, the many Christian communities throughout history have been sinful in its treatment of sexual and gender minority people. Profound and violent harm was done. This sinful behavior included acts of killing, torture, abuse and selfish exploitation. Such behaviors represented unbridled sinful and selfish passion towards people accused of sodomy or buggery throughout history. As Christians we are directly and indirectly implicated in these sinful acts. In many overt and covert ways some Christians and some Institutions continue to cause harm and to contribute to an atmosphere of disgust, facile judgment, mental distress, and to a culture of violence. In modern times we call these institutional biases, as well as individual biases homophobia. Our appropriate response before God is confession, repentance, and the seeking of reconciliation by making things right. There can be no compromise on this basic appeal of the gospel for faith communities.

How to seek reconciliation and how to work on making things right with sexual and gender minority people will need to take many forms. Our moral discernment of Scripture and Traditions will take a variety of forms. What we cannot compromise is an affirmation of fellow sexual and gender minority Christians and a celebration of the good and blessed grace of God in their relationships. Sexual and gender minority people are not objects or problems; they are part of us. All of us together stand under God's call to glorify God in our relationships. All are called to live erotic lives in the Scriptural logic of human flourishing, unselfish self-giving love, committed covenanted relationships, and "creative fidelity." Together, we are called to rise again in grace, when our love falls into selfishness and lustful exploitation. Whether we see same-sex expressions of covenanted love as a pastoral accommodation in the light of a creational disorder – in the tradition of gender complementarity – or, as a creational variant and thus a different but valid form of Christian love, we need to find ways to welcome and embrace such Christians together with their relationships. Denying and judging such relationships and their worth offends against grace, against the love of our neighbor, and against God's redemptive purpose of flourishing lives for all people. Same-sex covenantal love, rather than offending against the glory of God, has the potential to glorify God in the grace of the Love that will not let us go. Let us stop doing harm.

Bibliography

Augustine, St. 1847. **Seventeen Short Treatises of S. Augustine.** London: Oxford, Henry Parker; F and J Rivington.

Augustine, St. 1866. **The City of God.** In "A Select Library of the Nicene and Post-Nicene Fathers" (Schaff, P. Translator) Vol 2. Edinburgh: T & T Clark.

Alison, J. 1998. The Joy of Being Wrong: Original Sin Through Easter Eyes. Crossroad Publishing Co.

Barth K. 1957. "Die Theologie und die Mission in der Gegenwart" in **Theologische Fragen und Antworten.** Evangelische Verlag, 100-126.

Bartlett, A.W. 2001 **Cross Purposes: The Violent Grammar of Christian Atonement.** Harrisburg: Trinity Press International

Bailey, D.S. 1955. Homosexuality in Western Christian Tradition. London: Archon Books.

Bakke, D. 2003. *The Manly Eunuch* in **Church History.** 72:2 p 389.

Bateson, G., Jackson, D. D., Haley, J. & Weakland, J. 1956. **Towards a Theory of Schizophrenia in Behavioral Science.** New York: John Wiley. Vol 1, 251–264.

Bavinck, J. H. 1960. **An Introduction to the Science of Missions.** Philadelphia: Presbyterian Reformed Publishing Company.

Bosch, D.J. 1991. Transforming Mission: Paradigm Shifts in Theology of Mission. New York: Orbis Books.

Boswell, J, 1980. **Christianity, Social Tolerance, and Homosexuality.** Chicago: University of Chicago Press.

Boswell, J. 1995. **Same Sex Unions in Premodern Europe**. New York: Random House.

Brueggemann, W. 1982. Genesis: Interpretation – A Bible Commentary for Teaching and Preaching. Atlanta: John Knox Press.

Brownson, J. V. 2013. Bible, Gender, Sexuality: Reframing the Church's Debate on Same-Sex Relationships. Grand Rapids: Eerdmans.

Burrus, V. 2003. *The Manly Eunuch* in **The Journal of Religion.** 83:1, 135-136.

Burrus, V. 2000. Begotton no Made: Conceiving Manhood in Late Antiquity. Stanford: Stanford University Press.

Butler, J. 1993. Bodies that Matter: On the Discursive Limits of "sex." New York: Routledge.

Campbell, D.A. 2009. The Deliverance of God: An Apocalyptic Rereading of Justification in Paul. Grand Rapids: Eerdmans.

Carden, M. 2004. Sodomy: A History of a Christian Biblical Myth. New York: Routledge.

Carrasco, R. 1985. Inquisición y represión sexual en Valencia: historia de los sodomitas (1565–1785). Barcelona: Laertes.

Cheng, P.S. 2011. Radical Love: An Introduction to Queer Theology, New York: Seabury Books

Conley, G. 2016. **Boy Erased: A Memoir.** New York: Riverhead Books

Coren, M. 2016. Epiphany: A Christian's Change of Heart and Mind over Same-Sex Marriage. Toronto: McLelland & Stewart.

Crompton, L. 2003. **Homosexuality and Civilization.** Cambridge: Belknap Press, Harvard University Press.

Dall'Orto, G. 1990. "Florence" in Dynes, W.R. (Ed.) **Encyclopedia of Homosexuality, Vol I.** New York: Garland Publishing, Inc. 408-411.

Dall'Orto, G. 1990. "Venice" in Dynes, W.R. (Ed.) **Encyclopedia of Homosexuality, Vol II.** New York: Garland Publishing, Inc. 1364-1367.

DeFranza, M.L. 2015. Sex Difference in Christian Theology: Male, Female, and Intersex in the Image of God. Grand Rapids: Eerdmans.

De La Torre, M.A. 2007. **A Lily Among the Thorns: Imagining a New Christian Sexuality.** San Francisco: John Wiley & Sons Inc/Jossey-Bass.

Douglas, M. 1966. Purity and Danger: An Analysis of Concepts of Pollution and Taboo. New York: Routledge.

Durant, W. & Durant A. 1961. The Story of Civilization VII: The Age of Reason Begins. A History of European Civilization in the Period of Shakespeare, Bacon, Montaigne, Rembrandt, Galileo, and Descartes: 1558-1648. New York: Simon and Schuster.

Dynes, W.R. (Ed.) 1990. **Encyclopedia of Homosexuality Volume I."** New York: Garland Publishers Inc.

Dynes, W.R. (Ed.) 1990. **Encyclopedia of Homosexuality Volume II."** New York: Garland Publishers Inc.

Dynes, W.R. 1990. "Myths and Fabrications." In Dynes, W.R. (Ed.) **Encyclopedia of Homosexuality, Vol II.** New York: Garland Publishing, Inc. 869-872.

Dynes, W.R. 1990. "Philo Judaeus (CA. 20 B.C.-C.A. A.D. 45)" in Dynes, W.R. (Ed.) 1990. **Encyclopedia of Homosexuality Volume II."** New York: Garland Publishers Inc.

Fackre, G. 2002. Book Review: "The Bible and Homosexual Practice". in **Pro Ecclesia**. 11:3, 377-379.

Farley, M. A. 2008. **A Framework for Christian Sexual Ethics.** New York: Continuum.

Fensham, C.J. 2008. Emerging from the Dark Age Ahead: The Future of the North American Church. Ottawa: University of Ottawa Novalis Press.

Ferenczi, S. 1952. "The nosology of male homosexuality (homoeroticism)." In E. Jones (Ed. and Trans.), **First contributions to psycho-analysis.** New York: Brunner/Mazel. (Original work published 1914)

Fone, B. 2001. **Homophobia, A History.** New York: Picador USA.

Fox, L. 2006. **Pagans and Christians.** London: Penguin.

Franklin, K. 1998. "Unassuming Motivations: Contextualizing the Narratives of Antigay Assailants." In **Stigma and Sexual Orientation: Understanding Prejudice against Lesbians, Gay Men, and Bisexuals.** Herek, G.M. (Ed.) Thousand Oaks: Sage Publication Inc.

Gaca, K.L. 2003. The Making of Fornication: Eros, Ethics and Political Reform in Greek Philosophy and Early Christianity. Berkley: University of California Press.

Gambaudo, S. 2013. "Julia Kristeva, 'Woman's primary homosexuality' and homophobia." In **European Journal of Women's Studies.** February, 20 (Issue 1) p.8-20.

Gagnon, R.A.J. 2001. The Practice: Bible and Homosexual Texts and Hermeneutics. Nashville: Abingdon Press.

Cheng, P.S. 2011. Radical Love: An Introduction to Queer Theology. New York: Seabury Books.

Gold, M. (Ed.) 2008. Crisis: 40 Stories Revealing the Personal, Social, and Religious Pain and Trauma of Growing up Gay in America. Austin: Greenleaf Book Group Press.

Goss, R.E. 2002. **Queering Christ: Beyond Jesus Acted Up.** Cleveland: The Pilgrim Press.

Green, M. 2003. Evangelism in the Early Church (Revised Edition). Grand Rapids: Eerdmans.

Grenz, S.J. 1998. Welcoming but not Affirming: An Evangelical Response to Homosexuality. Louisville: Westminster John Knox Press.

Grau, G. 1995. **Hidden Holocaust.** New York: Routledge.

Gustafson, J.M. 1975. **Theology and Christian Ethics.** Philadelphia: Pilgrim Press – United Church Press.

Gustafson, J.M. 2007. **Moral Discernment in the Moral Life: Essays in Theological Ethics.** (Boers, T.A.& Capetz, P.E. Eds.) Louisville: Westminster/John Knox Press.

Haidt, J. 2012. The Righteous Mind: Why Good People Are Divided by Politics and Religion. New York: Pantheon Books.

Harnack, A. 1906. **Die Mission und Ausbreitung des Christentums in den ersten drei Jahrhunnderten** (Erster Band. Zweite neu durchgearbeitete Auflage mit elf Karten.) Leipzig: J. G. Hinrichs'sche Buchhandlung.

Harnack, A. 1908. **The Mission and Expansion of Christianity in the First Three Centuries.** (Trans. Moffatt, J.), Second Expanded Edition. London: Williams and Norgate.

Hays, R.B. 1986. "Relations Natural and Unnatural: A Response to John Boswell's Exegesis of Romans 1" **Journal of Religious Ethics.** 14:1. 184-215.

Helminiak, D.A. 2000. **What the Bible Really says about Homosexuality.** New Mexico: Alamo Square Press.

Herek, G.M. (Ed.) 1998. Stigma and Sexual Orientation: Understanding Prejudice against Lesbians, Gay Men, and Bisexuals. Thousand Oaks: Sage Publication Inc.

Heim, M. 2006. **Saved from Sacrifice.** Grand Rapids: Eerdmans.

Hollander, D. 2005. "Some Remarks on Love and Law in Hermann Cohen's Ethics of the Neighbor" in *Journal for Textual Reasoning*, 4:1 (Nov). Special Issue: "The Ethics of the Neighbor."

Jennings, T.W. Jr. 2005. Jacob's Wound: Homoerotic narrative in the literature of Ancient Israel. New York: Continuum.

Jensen, D.H. 2013. **God, Desire, and a Theology of Human Sexuality.** Louisville: Westminster/John Knox Press.

Jensen, R.M. 2000. **Understanding Early Christian Art.** New York: Routledge.

Johansson, W. 1990. "Law (Major Traditions in the West)" in Dynes, W.R. (Ed.) **Encyclopedia of Homosexuality Vol. 1.** New York: Garland Publishing Inc.

Johnson, J.E. 2013. Divine Communion: A Eucharistic Theology of Sexual Intimacy. New York: Seabury Books.

Johnson, W.S. 2006. Book Review of "The Bible and Homosexual Practice" (Gagnon) and "Jesus, The Bible, and Homosexuality" (Rogers) in **Theology Today**, 63:3 (Oct), 386-394.

Jordan, M. D. 1997. **The Invention of Sodomy in Christian Theology.** Chicago: University of Chicago Press.

166

Jordan, M. D. 2005. Blessing Same-Sex Unions: The Perils of Queer Romance and the Confusions of Christian Marriage. Chicago: University of Chicago Press.

Kaplan, B.J. 2007. Divided by Faith: Religious Conflict and the Practice of Toleration in Early Modern Europe. Cambridge: The Belknap Press of Harvard University Press.

Keener, C.S. 2003. Book Review: "The Bible and Homosexual Practice". In **Union Seminary Quarterly**, 57:1, 166-173.

Keegan, T. 1996. Colonial South Africa and the Origins of the Racial Order. London: Leicester University Press.

Kuefler, M. 2001. The Manly Eunuch: Masculinity, Gender Ambiguity, and Christian Ideology in Latin Antiquity. Chicago: University of Chicago Press.

Kinder, A.G. 1975. Casdiodoro de Reina: Spanish Reformer of the Sixteenth Century. London: Tamesis Books Limited.

Kinnaman, D. & Lyon, G. 2007. UN Christian: What A New Generation Really Thinks About Christianity…and Why it Matters. Grand Rapids: Baker Books.

Kirk, J.R.D. 2011. Jesus have I loved, but Paul? A Narrative Approach to the Problem of Pauline Christianity. Grand Rapids: Baker.

Kreider, A. 2016. **The Patient Ferment of the Early Church.** Grand Rapids: Baker Academic.

Kristeva, J. 1982. **Powers of Horror: An Essay in Abjection.** (Translated: Roudiez, L S) New York: Columbia University Press.

Krondorfer, B. (ed.) 2009. Men Masculinities in Christianity and Judaism: A Critical Reader. London:SCM Press.

Lever, M. 1985. **Les Bûchers de Sodome**. Paris: Fayard.

Lings, K. R. 2009. "The Lyings of a Woman: Male-Male Incest in Lev. 18:22?" in **Theology and Sexuality**. 15:2, 231-250.

Lings, K.R. 2013. Love Lost in Translation: Homosexuality and the Bible. Bloomington: Trafford Publishing.

Loader, W. 2004. The Septuagint, Sexuality, and the New Testament: Case Studies of the Impact of the LXX in Philo and the New Testament. Grand Rapids: Eerdmans.

MacMullen, R. 1984. **Christianizing the Roman Empire (AD 100-400).** New Haven: Yale University Press.

Malyon, A.K. 1982. "Biphasic aspects of homosexual identity formation." **Psychotherapy**. 19. 335-341.

Martin. D.B. 1995. "Heterosexism and the Interpretation of Romans 1:18-32." **Biblical Interpretation.** 3:3. 332-355.

Martin, D.B. 2006. Sex and the Single Saviour: Gender and Sexuality in Biblical Interpretation. Louisville: Westminster John Knox.

Meyer L.H & Dean L. 1998. "Internalized Homophobia, Intimacy, and Sexual Behavior among Gay and Bisexual Men." In **Stigma and Sexual Orientation: Understanding Prejudice against Lesbians, Gay Men, and Bisexuals.** Herek, G.M. (Ed.) Thousand Oaks: Sage Publication Inc.

Milgrom. J. 2000. Leviticus 17-22: Anchor Bible Commentary Volume 3A. New York: Doubleday Books.

Monter, W. 1980/81. "Switzerland." In Licata, S.J & Petersen, R. P. (Eds.) *Historical Perspectives on Homosexuality.* A special edition of the **Journal of Homosexuality** 6:1/2 also published, New York: Haworth Press, Inc. & Stein and Day Publishers. 41-56.

Monter, W. 1990. Frontiers of Heresy: The Spanish Inquisition from the Basque Lands to Sicily. Cambridge: Cambridge University Press.

Newman, P.A. & Fantus, S. 2015. "A Social Ecology of Bias-Based Bullying of Sexual and Gender Minority Youth: Toward a Conceptualization of Conversion Bullying." In **Journal of Gay and Lesbian Social Services** 27, 46-63.

Newman, P.A., Fantus, S., Woodford, M.R., & Rwigema, M.J. 2017. "Pray that God will Change You": The Religious Social Ecology of Bias-based Bullying Targeting Sexual and Gender Minority Youth-A Qualitative Study of Service Providers and Educators." In **Journal of Adolescent Research,** 1-26.

O'Brien, J.M. (Ed.) 2014. The Oxford Encyclopedia of the Bible and Gender Studies. Volume 1. Oxford: Oxford University Press.

Percy, W.A. 1990. "Inquisition" in Dynes, W.R. (Ed.) **Encyclopedia of Homosexuality, Vol I.** New York: Garland Publishing, Inc. 601-606.

Percy, W.A. 1990. "Law, Municipal" in Dynes, W.R. (Ed.) **Encyclopedia of Homosexuality Vol. 1.** New York: Garland Publishing Inc. 689-692.

Percy, W.A. 1990. "Law, Feudal and Royal" in Dynes, W.R. (Ed.) **Encyclopedia of Homosexuality Vol. 1.** New York: Garland Publishing Inc. 685-687.

Percy, W.A. 1990. "Templars" in Dynes, W.R. (Ed.) **Encyclopedia of Homosexuality Vol. II.** New York: Garland Publishing Inc. 1285-1286.

Rogers, J. 2009. Jesus, the Bible, and Homosexuality: Explode the Myths, Heal the Church. Louisville: Westminster John Knox Press.

Ruggiero, G. 1985. The Boundaries of Eros: Sex, Crime, and Sexuality in Renaissance Venice. London: Oxford University Press.

Runia, D.T. 1993. **Philo in Early Christian Literature: A Survey.** Minneapolis: Fortress Press.

Saayman, W. A. & Kritzinger, J. N. J. 1996. **Mission in Bold Humility: David Bosch's Work Considered**. New York: Orbis Books.

Sprinkle, P. 2015. **People to be Loved: While Homosexuality is not Just and Issue.** Grand Rapids: Zondervan Publishing Company.

Stanley, B. 2009. The World Missionary Conference, Edinburgh 1910. Grand Rapids: Eerdmans.

Stark, R. 1996. The Rise of Christianity: S Sociologist Reconsiders History. Princeton: Princeton University Press.

Starkloff, C.F. 2002. A Theology of the In-Between: The Value of the Syncretic Process. Milwaukee: Marquette University Press.

Terpstra, N. 2015. Religious Refugees in the Early Modern World: An Alternative History of the Reformation. New York: Cambridge University Press.

Théry-Astruc, J. 2013. "A Heresy of State: Philip the Fair, the Trial of the Perfidious Templars and the Ponticalization of the French Monarchy." In **Journal of Religious Medieval Cultures.** 39:2. 117-148.

VanderWal-Gritter, W. 2014. Generous Spaciousness: Responding to Gay Christians in the Church. Grand Rapids: Brazos Press.

Vines, M. 2014. **God and the Gay Christian.** New York: Convergent Books.

Vout, C. 2003. *The Manly Eunuch* in **The Journal of Religion History** 27:1, 88-89.

Walsham, A. 2006. Charitable Hatred: Tolerance and Intolerance in England 1500-1700. Manchester: Manchester University Press.

White, H.R. 2015. **Reforming Sodom: Protestants and the Rise of Gay Rights.** Chapel Hill: University of North Carolina Press.

Wink, W. 2002. "Sex and the Bible, To Hell with Gays?" in **The Christian Century.** 119:12 (June), 32-34.

Wolterstorff, N.P. 2013. Journey Towards Justice: Personal Encounters in the Global South. Grand Rapids: Baker Academic.

Young, P.D. 2000. **Recreating the Church: Community of Eros.** Harrisburg: Pennsylvania.

Young, P.D., Shipley, H. & Trothen, T.J. (Eds.) 2015. **Religion and Sexuality: Diversity and the Limits of Tolerance.** Vancouver: UBC Press.

Notes:

Notes from Chapter 1

[1] White, M. 2008. "Rev. Dr. Mel White: Author, Filmmaker, and Former Ghostwriter for Jerry Falwell, Billy Graham, and Pat Robertson." in Gold, M. (Ed.) **Crisis: 40 Stories Revealing the Personal, Social, and Religious Pain and Trauma of Growing up Gay in America.** Austin: Greenleaf Book Group Press. 15-24.

[2] See https://www.youtube.com/watch?v=6Mz5JbkFlok accessed July 6, 2017.

[3]Bailey, D.S. 1955. Homosexuality in Western Christian Tradition. London: Archon Books.

[4] There are many definitions available, this link provides on good example, http://www.vanderbilt.edu/lgbtqi/get-educated/definitions Accessed Aug. 6. 2016.

[5] Farley, M. A. 2008. **A Framework for Christian Sexual Ethics.** New York: Continuum. 130 Footnote 32.

[6] See Margaret Farley's extensive discussion of this in Farley, 2008: 57-63.

[7] In claiming this I realise that I make a case that can be described as "homonormative," that is an approach that follows the "heteronormative" boundaries established in traditional Christian communities. There is great value in also questioning this approach. One of the most creative and interesting conversations on this is represented in Patrick S. Cheng's book, 2011. **Radical Love: An Introduction to Queer Theology,** New York: Seabury Books. These conversations need to ask more fundamental questions about love, relationships and sexual expression in our time and context.

[8] See White, H.R. 2015. **Reforming Sodom: Protestants and the Rise of Gay Rights.** Chapel Hill: University of North Carolina Press.

[9] The influence of St Augustine will be explored in more detail in Chapter 6 and 12 with references to the material introduced there.

[10] Jordan, M. D. 1997. **The Invention of Sodomy in Christian Theology.** Chicago: University of Chicago Press. 29.

[11] The Belhar Confession was written in 1982 in South Africa in response and as a critique of "Apartheid Theology." In 1986 it was adopted by the predominantly black Dutch Reformed Mission Church in South Africa and since then by many Reformed denominations around the world including the Presbyterian Church, USA.

[12] See my discussion of the idea of "Wirkungsgeschichte" and "historically shaped consciousness" at the end of Chapter 4

[13] Aboriginal people prefer to call the continent known as North American: Turtle Island.

Notes from Chapter 2

[14] Conley, G. 2016. **Boy Erased: A Memoir.** New York: Riverhead Books. 336.

[15] See a review of the literature in Newman, P.A. Fantus, S. Woodford, M.R., & Rwigema, M.J. 2017. "Pray that God will Change You": The Religious Social Ecology of Bias-based Bullying Targeting Sexual and Gender Minority Youth – A Qualitative Study of Service Providers and Educators." In **Journal of Adolescent Research,** 1-26.

[16] Gustafson, J.M. 2007. **Moral Discernment in the Moral Life: Essays in Theological Ethics.** (Boers, T.A. & Capetz, P.E. Eds.) Louisville: Westminster/John Knox Press. 39.

[17] Farley, 2008.

[18] De La Torre, 2007. **A Lily Among the Thorns: Imagining a New Christian Sexuality.** San Francisco: John Wiley and Sons Inc/Jossey Bass.

[19] Conley, 2016. 337.

[20] Conley, 2016. 294.

[21] White, 2015. 123ff.

[22] See the reprint of his paper in chapter 1 "Context versus Principles: A Misplaced Debate in Christian Ethics." In Gustafson, J.M. 2007. 1-24.

[23] Gustafson, 2007. 12.

[24] This perspective is in part born out many years of pastoral work where I have encountered gay and lesbian suicides in which Christian attitudes and teaching turned out to be psychologically harmful. It is thus part of my own journey of pastoral moral discernment in community.

[25] I can site many differences, but perhaps the most striking is that very few Christians today would argue that the only form of valid Christian erotic engagement has to be procreative, whereas procreation was the key point about appropriate Christian sexual relationships by the 4th century. Heather White provides a more fulsome discussion of how twentieth century Protestantism, both Mainline and Evangelical, have embraced their own versions of the sexual revolution. See White, 2015. 127 ff.

[26] Margaret Farley points out that the idea of sex as a mechanistic "indomitable biological and psychological drive" has come under scrutiny and that evidence today points to this Freudian assumption as a caricature. Today we understand sexual love as something more complex with a plasticity that goes beyond these mechanistic conceptions. See Farley, 2008. 171.

[27] Young, P.D. 2000. **Recreating the Church: Community of Eros.** Harrisburg: Pennsylvania.

[28] Johnson, J.E. 2013. Divine Communion: A Eucharistic Theology of Sexual Intimacy. New York; Seabury Books.

[29] Cheng, P.S. 2011. Radical Love: An Introduction to Queer Theology. New York: Seabury Books.

[30] Goss, R.E. 2002. **Queering Christ: Beyond Jesus Acted Up.** Cleveland: The Pilgrim Press. See particularly Part 4.

[31] Bosch, D.J. 1991. Transforming Mission: Paradigm Shifts in Theology of Mission. New York: Orbis Books. 58.

[32] Gustafson, 2007. 26.

[33] Gustafson, 2007. 35. I note of course Gustafson's dated non-inclusive language here.

[34] Gustafson, 2007. 36.

[35] Gustafson, 2007. 36.

[36] Farley, 182-186.

[37] Now, the important thing is that your way of life should be as the gospel of Christ requires, so that, whether or not I am able to go and see you, I will hear that you are standing firm with one common purpose and that with only one desire you are fighting together for the faith of the gospel. (GNB)

[38] See the full discussion, Gustafson, 2007. 43 ff.

[39] The attitude you should have is the one that Christ Jesus had: (GNB)

[40] I urge you, then, to make me completely happy by having the same thoughts, sharing the same love, and being one in soul and mind. (GNB)

[41] Wolterstorff, N.P. 2013. Journey Towards Justice: Personal Encounters in the Global South. Grand Rapids: Baker Academic. 109

[42] Farley, 200.

[43] Gustafson, 2007. 44.

[44] Gustafson, 2007. 48.

[45] Gustafson, 2007. 44.

[46] Breuggemann, W. 1982. Genesis: Interpretation – A Bible Commentary for Teaching and Preaching. Atlanta: John Knox Press. 50.

[47] Gustafson, 2007. 36.

[48] Matt 22:27-28; Mark 12:33-34; Lk 10:27-28.

[49] John 14:15 Good News Bible

[50] John 15:10 Good News Bible.

[51] Although, it must also be noted that the story of the "Good Samaritan" also has strong anti-Pharisaic overtones which might be reflective of a Christian bias that developed over time.

[52] "*gloria enim Dei vivens homo, vita autem hominis visio Dei*" also translated as, "For the glory of God is a living human being; and human life consists in the vision of God."

[53] See a fuller discussion of this important insight of 2nd century Christianity in Fensham, C.J. 2008. **Emerging from the Dark Age Ahead: The Future of the North American Church.** Ottawa: University of Ottawa Novalis Press. Chapter 2.

[54] This is particularly clear in the theme of eternal life or, in a more theological translation, "full and meaningful life" in the Gospel of John as summarized in John 10:10.

[55] Micah 6:8 Good News Translation.

[56] Wolterstorff, 2013. 107. See also Dana Hollander's interesting discussion of Herman Cohen's work on the ethics of love in the Jewish tradition. Cohen initially rejected the idea of love of neighbor has helpful to ethics because he observed that responsible ethics did not necessarily result from "love." However, in his reading of the Jewish tradition he showed how love of neighbor in terms of law can and does lead to ethical action. Hollander, D. 2005. "Some Remarks on Love and Law in Hermann Cohen's Ethics of the Neighbor" in *Journal for Textual Reasoning*, 4:1 (Nov). Special Issue: "The Ethics of the Neighbor."

[57] Farley's discussion of the role of Roman misogynist culture and Stoic ideals of passionless sex further supports the argument developed in the second section of this book, see Farley, 30 ff.

[58] Later I will draw on the historical work of Mathew Kuefler and Virginia Burrus to explore the development of manliness and the move, in patristic debates, away from material spirituality, see Krondorfer, B. 2009. **Men Masculinities in Christianity and Judaism: A Critical Reader.** London:SCM Press, 277.

[59] See https://www.ewtn.com/library/PAPALDOC/JP2TBIND.HTM Accessed July 25, 2016.

[60] Farley, 47.

[61] Gustafson, 2007. 490.

[62] Gustafson, 2007. 491.

[63] Jensen, D.H. 2013. **God, Desire, and a Theology of Human Sexuality.** Louisville: Westminster/John Knox Press. 123.

[64] Brownson, J.V. 2013. Bible Gender Sexuality: Reframing the Church's Debate on Same-Sex Relationships. Grand Rapids: Eerdmans. 14 and see Chapter 12 p. 259 ff.

[65] Brownson, 2013. 278-279.

[66] https://www.youtube.com/watch?v=GiD_Lfy2beo&feature=youtu.be Accessed October 25, 2016.

[67] Rom 3:23.

[68] See his full argument in Wolterstorff, N.P. 2008. **Justice Rights and Wrongs.** Princeton: Princeton University Press.

Notes from Chapter 3

[69] See for example the Government of Canada executive summary, http://www.justice.gc.ca/eng/rp-pr/csj-sjc/crime/wd95_11-dt95_11/p0_1.html Accessed May 30, 2016.

[70] In 2013, Stephen Jimenez published "**The Book of Matt**" (Steerforth Press), which referred to other possible factors in the murder including drug use. Jimenez' facts have been called into question. A thoughtful Buzzfeed article examines the matter in more detail and concludes that sexual orientation still played a decisive role in the crime, see https://www.buzzfeed.com/shannonkeating/hate-in-america?utm_term=.ptRQ7or4Y#.wfpbED7lr Accessed July 12, 2017.

[71] Crompton, L. 2003. **Homosexuality and Civilization**. Cambridge: Harvard University Press, 175.

[72] It must be noted that the Synod decision has not been accepted without challenge and that procedural complaints against the decision led to a reversal of the decision in 2016. In 2019 the High Court of South Africa found in favor of the original decision for full affirmation.

[73] https://www.facebook.com/FranklinGraham/posts/1089823717740475
Accessed May 27 , 2016.

[74] Gustafson, J.M. 1975. **Theology and Christian Ethics.** Philadelphia: Pilgrim Press - United Church Press. 99.

[75] Butler, J. 1993. Bodies that Matter: On the Discursive Limits of "sex." New York: Routledge. 225.

[76] Farley, 2008. 63-108.

[77] Douglas, M. 1966. Purity and Danger: An Analysis of Concepts of Pollution and Taboo. New York: Routledge. 3-4.

[78] Structuralism in cultural anthropology argues that there are deeply ingrained structures in all cultures with similar counterparts across cultures.

[79] Farley, 2008. 130, note 32.

[80] Haidt, J. 2012. The Righteous Mind: Why Good People are Divided by Politics and Religion. New York: Pantheon Books. 146.

[81] See for example the conservative columnist John Gray's critique of Haidt's book in the **New Republic** that misses Haidt's nuanced claims https://newrepublic.com/article/102760/righteous-mind-haidt-morality-politics-scientism Accessed May 30, 2016.

[82] Douglas, 1966. 3.

[83] The International Standard Version of the Bible uses the words "detestable" and "repulsive act" to translate the Hebrew word commonly translated as "abomination."

[84] Kristeva, J 1982. **Powers of Horror: An Essay in Abjection.** (Translated: Roudiez, L S) New York: Columbia University Press.

[85] See for example, Gambaudo, S "Julia Kristeva, 'Woman's primary homosexuality' and homophobia." In **European Journal of Women's Studies.** February 2013, Volume20 (Issue 1) p.8-20.

[86] Ferenczi, S. (1952). The nosology of male homosexuality (homoeroticism). In E. Jones (Ed. and Trans.), First contributions to psycho-analysis. New York: Brunner/Mazel. (Original work published 1914)

[87] Malyon, A.K 1982. "Biphasic aspects of homosexual identity. **Psychotherapy.** 19. 335-341. Meyer L.H. & Dean L. 1998 "Internalized Homophobia, Intimacy, and Sexual Behavior among Gay and Bisexual Men." In Stigma and Sexual Orientation: Understanding Prejudice against Lesbians, Gay Men, and **Bisexuals.** Herek, G.M. (Ed.) Thousand Oaks: Sage Publication Inc. 163.

[88] Franklin, K. 1998. "Unassuming Motivations: Contextualizing the Narratives of Antigay Assailants." In **Stigma and Sexual Orientation: Understanding Prejudice against Lesbians, Gay Men, and Bisexuals.** Herek, G.M. (Ed.) Thousand Oaks: Sage Publication Inc. 1-23.

[89] Newman, et al 2017. 1-26.

[90] Newman et al, 2017. 4.

[91] A double bind is an emotionally distressing dilemma when someone receives two conflicting messages from the same source that contradict each other. In psychology and psychotherapy, it is considered as a method of hidden coercion that makes it very hard for the person placed in this bind to identify the abuse of power and to react to it. The term was first coined by Bateson, see Bateson, G., Jackson, D. D., Haley, J. & Weakland, J. 1956. **Towards a Theory of Schizophrenia in Behavioral Science.** New York: John Wiley. Vol 1, 251–264.

[92] Newman, P.A. & Fantus, S. 2015. "A Social Ecology of Bias-Based Bullying of Sexual and Gender Minority Youth: Toward a Conceptualization of Conversion Bullying." In **Journal of Gay and Lesbian Social Services** 27, 47.

[93] Myer & Dean, 1998. 170.

[94] Myer & Dean, 182.

[95] Gagnon, R.A.J. 2001. The Practice: Bible and Homosexual Texts and Hermeneutics. Nashville: Abingdon Press. 4.

[96] Perhaps the most vocal critic is Rene Pommier who points out that if all desire is mimetic (imitational) then how do you explain homosexual desire in a repressive culture where there are no homosexual models to imitate?

[97] See Heim, M. 2006. Saved from Sacrifice. Grand Rapids: Eerdmans; Alison, J. 1998 The Joy of Being Wrong: Original Sin Through Easter Eyes. Crossroad Publishing Co.; Bartlett, A.W. 2001 Cross Purposes: The Violent Grammar of Christian Atonement. Harrisburg: Trinity Press International.

Notes from Chapter 4

[98] Grenz, S.J. 1998. Welcoming but not Affirming: An Evangelical Response to Homosexuality. Louisville: Westminster John Knox Press. Also see Sprinkle, P. 2015. People to be Loved: Why Homosexuality is not just and Issue. Grand Rapids. Eerdmans

[99] Rogers, J. 2009. Jesus, the Bible, and Homosexuality: Explode the Myths, Heal the Church. Louisville: Westminster John Knox Press.

[100] Interestingly enough, Fuller Theological Seminary, in the Fall of 2015, has denied tenure to New Testament professor J.R. Daniel Kirk after the publication of his book **Jesus have I loved, but Paul? A Narrative Approach to the Problem of Pauline Christianity** which contained one chapter that suggested a more open approach to committed loving same-sex relationships.

[101] http://www.nytimes.com/2013/06/21/us/group-that-promoted-curing-gays-ceases-operations.html?_r=0 Accessed June 1, 2016.

[102] http://www.thecanadianencyclopedia.ca/en/article/the-ex-gay-movement/ Accessed June 1, 2016.

[103] See her moving book, VanderWal-Gritter, W. 2014. **Generous Spaciousness: Responding to Gay Christians in the Church.** Grand Rapids: Brazos Press.

[104] http://religionnews.com/2014/10/24/david-gushee-lgbt-homosexuality-matters/ Accessed June 1, 2016.

[105] http://tonycampolo.org/for-the-record-tony-campolo-releases-a-new-statement/#.V08var4w5IE Acessed June 1, 2016.

[106] https://www.youtube.com/watch?v=GiD_Lfy2beo&feature=youtu.be Accessed October 25, 2016.

[107] Coren, M. 2016. **Epiphany: A Christian's Change of Heart and Mind over Same-Sex Marriage.** Toronto: McLelland & Stewart. Coren has since moved his membership to the Anglican Church of Canada.

[108] Gagnon, R.A.J. 2001. The Bible and Homosexual Practice: Texts and Hermeneutics. Nashville: Abingdon. 28-29.

[109] White, 2015.

[110] It has been argued that Joseph's multi-coloured coat, which could be translated as "princess dress" in Hebrew was on exception to that, (See, "Joseph as Sissy Boy," in Theodore W. Jennings Jr. 2005. **Jacob's Wound: Homoerotic narrative in the literature of Ancient Israel.** New York: Continuum, 177 –198) and then of course there are Levitical laws against males dressing in female clothing.

[111] There is Jesus' special relationship with the disciple whom Jesus loved described in the Gospel of John. This relationship included close physical intimacy which is a form of homoeroticism which seems culturally appropriate in Jesus time. The physical intimacy is described as the disciple lying with his head on Jesus' bosom (or breast) at the last Supper, and this disciple being the only one to stick with Jesus right to his death on the cross as he supports Jesus' mother. See, Goss, R.E., 2002. **Queering Christ: Beyond Jesus Acted Up.** Eugene: Resource Publications, Wipf and Stock, 119 ff. and Lings, K.R. 2013. **Love Lost in Translation: Homosexuality and the Bible.** Bloomington: Trafford Publishing, 642 ff.

[112] Clement of Alexandria, **Miscellanies Book III:1.** http://www.earlychristianwritings.com/text/clement-stromata-book3-english.html accessed June 26, 2019.

[113] See Matthew 19:12 and Matthew Keuffler's informative book on the eunuch in Greco-Roman culture and early Christian conceptions of manliness, Kuefler, M. 2001. **The Manly Eunuch: Masculinity, Gender Ambiguity, and Christian Ideology in Latin Antiquity.** Chicago: University of Chicago Press. See also the evangelical scholar Megan L. DeFranza's study on Christian gender conceptions and intersex people. DeFranza, M.L. 2015. **Sex Difference in Christian Theology: Male, Female, and Intersex in the Image of God.** Grand Rapids: Eerdmans.

[114] Gagnon, 2001. 33.

[115] Gagnon, 78.

[116] Fackre, G. 2002. Book Review "The Bible and Homosexual Practice." in **Pro Ecclesia.** 11:3, 377-379.

[117] Gagnon, 33.

[118] Johnson, W.S. 2006. Book Review of "The Bible and Homosexual Practice" (Gagnon) and "Jesus, The Bible, and Homosexuality" (Rogers) in **Theology Today**, 63:3 (Oct), 386-394.

[119] Martin, D.B. 2006. Sex and the Single Saviour: Gender and Sexuality in Biblical Interpretation. Louisville: Westminster John Knox Press. 2.

[120] Martin, 2006; Brownson, J. V. 2013. **Bible, Gender, Sexuality: Reframing the Church's Debate on Same-Sex Relationships.** Grand Rapids: Eerdmans, and the Danish Quaker Biblical Scholar K. Renato Lings who offers a meticulous discussion of biblical themes and texts in Lings, K.R. 2013. **Love Lost in Translation: Homosexuality and the Bible.** Bloomington: Trafford Publishing.

[121] Curiously this connection between Genesis 2 and Romans 1 is not one that played a central role in the emerging anti-homosexual theology of the 4th century.

[122] Brownson, 2013. 26-37.

[123] See Lings full discussion of Genesis 1 and 2, the rib, sexuality and kinship at Lings, 2013, 75-82 and Naomi "clinging to" Ruth 619-626.

[124] https://www.youtube.com/watch?v=GiD_Lfy2beo&feature=youtu.be Accessed October 25, 2016.

[125] Gagnon, 2001. 113.

[126] Gagnon, 114.

[127] https://www.youtube.com/watch?v=GiD_Lfy2beo&feature=youtu.be Accessed October 25, 2016.

[128] Milgrom. J. 2000. Leviticus 17-22: Anchor Bible Commentary Volume 3A. New York: Doubleday Books. 1567

[129] Lings, 2013. 250.

[130] See Lings' balanced and interesting discussion of the David-Jonathan relationship, Lings 2013, 625 ff.

[131] Lings, 2013. 275.

[132] See Gagnon. 2001. 229-289.

[133] See, Lings, 2013. 344 ff. and 567, and 580 ff. see also Brownson's exhaustive discussion about the interpretation issues, Brownson, 2013. 159-161.

[134] https://www.youtube.com/watch?v=GiD_Lfy2beo&feature=youtu.be Accessed October 25, 2016.

[135] Fone, B. 2001. **Homophobia, a History.** New York: Picador USA. 97ff.

[136] See Wolterstorff, https://www.youtube.com/watch?v=GiD_Lfy2beo&feature=youtu.be Accessed October 25, 2016.

[137] Brownson, 2013. 156-158.

[138] Hays, R.B. 1986. "Relations Natural and Unnatural: A Response to John Boswell's Exegesis of Romans 1" **Journal of Religious Ethics.** 14:1. 184-215.

[139] Hays actually provides a wealth of evidence that shows that Paul's conception of "natural" and "against nature" was shaped decisively by his cultural context and arguments in Stoicism. Hays, 1986. 192 ff.

[140] Martin. D.B. 1995. "Heterosexism and the Interpretation of Romans 1:18-32." **Biblical Interpretation.** 3:3. 332-355.

[141] See Lings' full discussion of Romans 1 at Lings, 2013. 564-608.

[142] See Romans 1:29-32.

[143] Campbell, D.A. 2009. The Deliverance of God: An Apocalyptic Rereading of Justification in Paul. Grand Rapids: Eerdmans.

[144] Lings, 2013. 602 ff.

[145] Hays, 1986. 210-211.

[146] Gagnon, 2001. 303-336.

[147] See Sprinkle, P. 2015. **People to be Loved: While Homosexuality is not Just and Issue.** Grand Rapids: Zondervan Publishing Company, in his discussion of *arsenokoites* and the Greek parallels such as *metrokoites* and *doulokoites.*

[148] Hays, 1986. 184.

[149] Martin, D. 2006. Sex and the Single Saviour: Gender and Sexuality in Biblical Interpretation. Louisville: Westminster John Knox.

[150] See Lings' full and very detailed discussion of these vice lists in Chapter 13 of Lings, 2013.

[151] For much more detail see Lings' discussion of these words, Lings, 2013, 529-562.

[152] Gagnon. 2001. 315.

[153] See Helminiak in Lings 2013. 503

[154] Helminiak, D.A. 2000. **What the Bible Really says about Homosexuality.** New Mexico: Alamo Square Press. 115 & Hanks in Helminiak, 2000. 108.

[155] See Harrell as discussed in Lings 2013. 504

[156] See also Brownson's discussion 2013. 273-275.

[157] Keener, C.S. 2003. Book Review: "The Bible and Homosexual Practice". In **Union Seminary Quarterly**, 57:1, 166-173.

[158] Gagnon, 2001. 28-29.

[159] See Stephen Fry's documentary "Out There" on Uganda and http://www.patheos.com/blogs/progressivesecularhumanist/2014/02/ugandan-minister-for-ethics-integrity-says-men-raping-girls-is-natural/ accessed July, 13, 2017.

Notes from Chapter 5

[160] There are many versions of this letter available on the web for example see http://www.ecclesia.org/truth/diognetus.html accessed April 19, 2016.

[161] Bosch, 1991. 48 & 211-212.

[162] Harnack, A. 1906. Die Mission und Ausbreitung des Christentums in den ersten Drei Jahrhundderten (Zweite Neu Durchgearbeitete Auflage mit Elf Karten.) Leipzig: J G Hinrichs'sche Buchhandlung. 127ff.

[163] See Fox, L. 2006. **Pagans and Christians.** London: Penquin; Kreider, A. 2016. **The Patient Ferment of the Early Church.** Grand Rapids: Baker Academic; MacMullen, R. 1984. **Christianizing the Roman Empire (AD 100-400).** New Haven: Yale University Press; Green, M. (1970) 2003. **Evangelism in the Early Church (Revised Edition).** Grand Rapids: Eerdmans; Brown, P.R.L. 1992. **Power and Persuasion in Late Antiquity: Towards A Christian Empire.** Madison: University of Wisconsin Press; Brown, P.R.L. 2008. **Body and Society: Men, Women, and Sexual Renunciation in Early Christianity.** New York: Columbia University Press.

[164] Stark, R. 1996. The Rise of Christianity: S Sociologist Reconsiders History. Princeton: Princeton University Press.

[165] Harnack, A. 1908. **The Mission and Expansion of Christianity in the First Three Centuries.** (Trans. Moffatt, J.), Second Edition. London: Williams and Norgate. 162.

[166] To give just a few examples documented by Harnack, Christians buried pagans who died destitute, they brought food, care and prayers to those in prison, they fed the poor who were not Christian, they ransomed prisoners and occasionally slaves, and cared for those dying of the plague at the risk of their own lives.

[167] Kinnaman, D. & Lyon, G. 2007. UN Christian: What A New Generation Really Thinks About Christianity…and Why it Matters. Grand Rapids: Baker Books. 26.

[168] See Bosch, 1991. 222, Bosch refers here to Newbigin, L. 1986. **Foolishness to the Greeks.** Geneva: World Council of Churches. 100.

[169] Boswell, J, 1980. **Christianity, Social Tolerance, and Homosexuality.** Chicago: University of Chicago Press.

[170] Bailey, D.S. 1955.

[171] Critics of Boswell's work often reject all his arguments based in their judgment that some of his claims overstepped their reach. In essence Jordan shows that the valuable and valid historical data collected by Boswell has been clouded by the kind of questions Boswell tried to answer. Questions that cannot easily be answered based on such data. It is thus the more radical conclusions and applications of the historical data collected that deserves critique. See Jordan, M. D. 2005. **Blessing Same-Sex Unions: The Perils of Queer Romance and the Confusions of Christian Marriage.** Chicago: University of Chicago Press. 132 ff.

[172] Hanks, T.D. 2000. **The Subversive Gospel: A New Testament Commentary of Liberation.** (Trans. Doner, J.P) Eugene: Wipf & Stock. 211-212.

[173] Boswell, 1980. 119-121.

[174] See a full discussion of these mythological associations between animals and human sexuality by Boswell and the strong influence it had on the earliest anti-homoerotic arguments such as those of Clement of Alexandria that became very influential (150-215), 1980. 138-141. Also note a similar discussion in Fox, 2006. 352.

[175] Boswell, 1980. 133.

[176] See Paulinus' poem for Ausonius, Boswell, 1980. 133.

[177] Fox, 2006. 352.

[178] Coleman, P.E. 1980. Christian attitudes to homosexuality. London: SPCK.

[179] See Carl Starkloff's ground-breaking book on this subject, Starkloff, C.F. 2002. **A Theology of the In-Between: The Value of the Syncretic Process.** Milwaukee: Marquette University Press.

[180] Boswell, 1980. 128-131.

[181] Lings, 2013. 110.

[182] Lane Fox notes that the "Alexandrian Rule" took is ethos from the Greek philosophers that saw the only valid sexual activity as that in aid of procreation, see Fox, 2006. 355.

[183] Crompton, 2003. 117.

[184] In a provocative book Kathy L. Gaca has argued that there was a third second century Christian position on sexual ethics that was more supportive of erotic pleasure represented by person called Epiphanes, see Gaca, K.L. 2003. **The Making of Fornication: Eros, Ethics and Political Reform in Greek Philosophy and Early Christianity.** Berkley: University of California Press.

[185] Crompton, L. 2003. 142.

[186] This is a matter of debate, there is a Christian commentator named "Ambrosiaster" who could have been roughly contemporary with Chrysostom, who might be the first to interpret Romans 1 as anti-Lesbian. However, the historicity, and dating of this person and his writing is under dispute.

[187] Chrysostom did not mince words, he described homoerotic relationships as, "monstrous," "Satanical," "detestable," "execrable," and "pitiable." Crompton, 2003. 141.

[188] See Book 4 of Augustine's Confessions.

[189] Crompton. 139.

[190] Fox, 2006. 351-352. It was only by 320 that such marriages led to excommunication.

[191] Harnack. 1908. 87.

[192] Harnack. 1908. 92.

[193] Kreider. 2016. Part 1.

[194] Harnack. 1908. 95-100.

[195] See Jensen, R.M. 2000. **Understanding Early Christian Art.** New York: Routledge. 37ff.

[196] Harnack, 1908. 101-108.

[197] Green, 2003. 24 & 246.

[198] Harnack, 1908. 130.

[199] Harnack, 1908. 135. "In the name of Jesus, his true disciples, who have received grace from him, do fulfil a healing ministry in aid of other men, even as each has received the free gift of grace from him. Some surely and certainly drive out demons, so that it frequently happens that those thus purged from demons also believe and become members of the church. Others, again, possess a foreknowledge of the future, with visions and prophetic utterances. And what shall I more say? For it is impossible to enumerate the spiritual gifts and blessings which, all over the world, the church has received from God in the name of Jesus Christ, who was crucified under Pontius Pilate, and which she exercises day by day for the healing of the pagan world, without deceiving or taking money from any person. For as she has freely received them from God, so also does she freely give."

[200] Harnack, 1908. 135-136.

[201] Harnack, 1908. 147.

[202] Harnack, 1908. 152.

[203] Harnack, 1908. 170.

[204] Harnack, 1908. 175.

[205] Harnack, 1908. 213.

[206] Harnack, 1908. 209.

[207] Harnack, 1908. 213.

[208] Harnack, 1908. 216.

[209] See for example, Torjesen, K.J. 1995. When Women Were Priests: Women's Leadership in the Early Church and the Scandal of their Subordination. New York: Harper Collins.

[210] O'Brien, J.M. (Ed.) 2014. **The Oxford Encyclopedia of the Bible and Gender Studies. Volume 1.** Oxford: Oxford University Press. 35-36.

Notes from Chapter 6

[211] For an excellent and well-documented background study of the anti-erotic shift in Judaism in the century preceding the Christian era and its impact on Christian homophobia see Fone, 2001. 134ff.

[212] Runia, D.T. 1993. **Philo in Early Christian Literature: A Survey.** Minneapolis: Fortress Press. 3-33.

[213] Runia, 1993. 16ff.

[214] Runa, 1993. 23.

[215] Runia, 1993. 320-332.

[216] See Runia 1993. 31 where he describes notes that Billings, unreliably records some other studies in the 17th century including that of Petavius and Allixius.

[217] Lings, 2013. 326.

[218] Lings, 2013. 327.

[219] Lings, 2013. 13 & 327.

[220] Lings, 2013. 309.

[221] Lings, 2013. 313.

[222] Crompton, 2003. 43. One of the possible reasons why so little attention is given to same-sex eroticism in earlier forms of Judaism is that the rabbinical application of the law would have considered many contextual factors. If Jacob Milgrom is correct unmarried same-sex eroticism would not necessarily have been treated as a serious transgression of law.

[223] Dynes, W.R. 1990. "Philo Judaeus (CA. 20 B.C.-C.A. A.D. 45)" in Dynes, W.R. (Ed.) 1990. **Encyclopedia of Homosexuality Volume II."** New York: Garland Publishers Inc. 982.

[224] Lings, 2013. 327.

[225] This is how these relationships were regarded by Philo's in his cultural context, however, earlier classical Greek conceptions of such relationships were focused on an educational mentoring process that was considered exemplary as explored in **Phaedrus**.

[226] Dynes, 1990. 983.

[227] Lings, 2013. 327.

[228] Runia, 1993. 188.

[229] Runia, 1993. 254.

[230] Loader, W. 2004. The Septuagint, Sexuality, and the New Testament: Case Studies of the Impact of the LXX in Philo and the New Testament. Grand Rapids: Eerdmans.

[231] Lings, 2013. 328.

[232] Crompton, 2003. 44.

[233] Dynes, 1990. 983.

[234] See Brownson's full discussion of "nature" 2013. Chapter 11. See also further discussion on the mistranslation of Romans 1:26-27 in Lings, 2013. 608ff.

[235] Franklin, K. 1998 "Unassuming Motivations: Contextualizing the Narratives of Antigay Assailants." In **Stigma and Sexual Orientation: Understanding Prejudice against Lesbians, Gay Men, and Bisexuals.** Herek, G.M. (Ed.) Thousand Oaks: Sage Publication Inc.

[236] Kuefler, 2001. 4.

[237] Burrus, V. 2000. **Begotton no Made: Conceiving Manhood in Late Antiquity.** Standord: Stanford University Press. Burrus, demonstrates the process of social construction of gender through discussion of Paul of Samosatta, Eusebius' "Life of Origen" and the gender arguments of Lactantius (22-35).

[238] Krondorfer, B. (ed.) 2009. Men Masculinities in Christianity and Judaism: A Critical Reader. London:SCM Press. 277.

[239] See reviews in, Bakke, D. 2003. *Church History.* 72:2 p 389, Burrus, V. 2003. *The Journal of Religion.* 83:1, 135-136, Vout, C. 2003. *The Journal of Religion History* 27:1, 88-89.

[240] Burrus, 2000. 4.

[241] Kuefler, 2001. 28ff.

[242] Kuefler, 2001. 29.

[243] Kuefler, 2001. 49.

[244] See also Kuefler's discussion of unmanliness and the love of luxury (2001, 55ff.)

[245] Kuefler, 2001. 80.

[246] Kuefler, 2001. 101-102. See also, Byrne Fone's detailed description of the momentous shift when homophobia is fixed in Christian-Roman law including Justinian's insistence on the death penalty culminating in the banning of all same-sex erotic acts by 544 in Novella 141, Fone, 2001. 173ff.

[247] Kuefler, 2001. 109,

[248] Kuefler, 2001. 109.

[249] Kuefler, 2001. 112.

[250] Kuefler, 2001. 120.

[251] Kuefler, 2001. 140,

252 Kuefler, 2001. 164.

253 Kuefler, 2001. 167.

254 Kuefler, 2001. 173.

255 Kuefler, 2001. 198. We find the actual citation from Augustine on this in his book against the Manicheans. The Literal Interpretation of Genesis IX:5:9. "How much more agreeable, after all, for conviviality and conversation would two male friends live together on equal terms than man and wife?"

256 Kuefler, 2001. 214.

257 Good News Bible.

258 Kuefler, 2001. 223.

259 Kuefler, 2001. 223.

Notes from Chapter 7

260 Runia, 1993. 292.

261 Jordan, 1997. 34.

262 Jordan, 1997. 34, refers to the Latin text of *De civitate Dei* Book 16 Chapter 30 with the Latin, *stupra in masculos* in some English translations it is rendered "unnatural lust."

263 Jordan, 1997. 34. See also Augustine, St. 1847. **Seventeen Short Treatises of S. Augustine.** London: Oxford, Henry Parker; F and J Rivington. 395. "Now if Lot, being so righteous a man that he was meet to entertain even Angels, offered his daughters to the lust of the Sodomites, to the mere intent, that the bodies of women rather than of men might be corrupted by them; how much more diligently and constantly ought the mind's chasteness in the truth to be preserved, seeing it is more truly preferable to its body, than the body of a man to the body of a woman?"

264 Jordan, 1997. 35.

265 Boswell, 1980. 157. See the older translation of the same passage cited in endnote above.

266 Boswell, 1980. 158.

267 Boswell, 1980. 149.

268 See 1 Cor 7:4-6.

269 In Crompton, 2001. 139. (This is from Augustine's **Confessions** Chapter VII:15.) A.C. Outler translated it thus: "Similarly, offenses against nature are everywhere and at all times to be held in detestation and should be punished." Outler's translation of the rest of the text (not cited by Crompton) goes on, "Such offenses, for example, were those of the Sodomites; and, even if all nations should commit them, they would all be judged guilty of the same crime by the divine law, which has not made men so that they should ever abuse one another in that way. For the fellowship that should be between God and us is violated whenever that nature of which he is the author is polluted by perverted lust." See, http://www.ccel.org/ccel/augustine/confessions.vi.html Accessed Aug 7, 2016.

270 Dynes, 1990. "Augustine, Saint (354-430)", 93.

271 Lings, 2013. 31.

272 Jordan, 1997. 33. For an example of the development of the Greek roots of what would become *luxuria* in Latin see Byrne Fone's discussion of Euripides' play *Antiope* where Zetros accuses his brother of effeminacy and cowardice, which later became glossed my *molles* and *luxuria* in the Latin Vulgate, Fone, 2001. 48.

273 Vulgate Gal 5:19: manifesta autem sunt opera carnis quae sunt fornicatio inmunditia luxuria

274 Jordan, 1997. 38.

275 Lings, 2013. 537.

276 Lings, 2013. 338

277 Jordan, 1997. 35-36.

278 Jordan, 1997. 36.

279 Jordan, 1997. 38.

280 Jordan, 1997. 39.

281 See Boswell, 1980. 203.

282 Jordan, 1997. 41. For a detailed discussion of the development of penitential manuals see, Fone, 2001. 188 ff.

283 Jordan, 1997. 42.

[284] See Foucault, M. 2008. The History of Sexuality: The Will to Knowledge. Vol 1. New York: Penguin Books.

[285] Jordan, 1997. 52.

[286] Jordan, 1997. 57.

[287] Jordan, 1997. 66.

[288] Jordan, 1997. 63.

[289] Jordan, 1997. 65.

[290] Jordan, 1997. 95.

[291] Jordan, 1997. 97.

[292] Jordan, 1997. 102.

[293] Jordan, 1997. 105.

[294] Jordan, 1997. 113.

[295] Jordan, 1997. 118.

[296] Jordan, 1997. 121. Most likely these insights came from familiarity with Greek sources, see the discussion of the Pseudo Aristotelian text, *Problemata* in Fone, 2001.86ff.

[297] Jordan, 1997. 120.

[298] Jordan, 1997. 126.

[299] Jordan, 1997. 126.

[300] Jordan, 1997. 128.

[301] Jordan, 1997. 131.

[302] Jordan, 1997. 134.

[303] Jordan, 1997. 143.

[304] Jordan, 1997. 149.

[305] Jordan, 1997. 150.

[306] Crompton, 2001. 188.

[307] Jordon, 1997. 150. Jordan translates *turpis* as wicked it can also be read as shameful or disgraceful.

Notes from Chapter 8

[308] Percy, W.A. 1990. "Law, Municipal" in Dynes, W.R. (Ed.) **Encyclopedia of Homosexuality Vol. 1.** New York: Garland Publishing Inc. 691.

[309] Johansson, W. 1990. "Law (Major Traditions in the West)" in Dynes, W.R. (Ed.) **Encyclopedia of Homosexuality Vol. 1.** New York: Garland Publishing Inc. 682.

[310] Johansson, W. 1990. 683. It must be noted that Thomas' influence was at first weak as his teaching was suspect but slowly gained tracktion.

[311] Johansson, W. 1990. 683.

[312] A statute issued by Emperor Otto I in Rome which prescribes a penalty of strangulation and burning for the sodomitic sin, and a law issued in Jerusalem (around 1129) which prescribed the burning for the sodomitic sin see Percy, W.A. 1990. "Law, Feudal and Royal" in Dynes, W.R. (Ed.) **Encyclopedia of Homosexuality Vol. 1.** New York: Garland Publishing Inc. 686.

[313] Johansson, 1990. 684.

[314] Percy, 1990. 685.

[315] Percy, 1990. 685.

[316] Percy, 1990. 685.

[317] Johansson, 1990. 686.

[318] Percy, 1990. 686 and Fone, 2001. 214.

[319] Percy, 1990. "Law, Municipal." 690.

[320] Percy, 1990. "Law, Feudal and Royal." 687.

[321] Percy, 1990. 687.

[322] Percy, 1990. 692.

[323] Percy, 1990. 692.

[324] Percy, 1990. "Law, Municipal." 690.

[325] Crompton, 2003. 192.

326 Percy, 1990. "Templars" in Dynes, W.R. (Ed.) **Encyclopedia of Homosexuality Vol. II.** New York: Garland Publishing Inc. 1286.

327 Crompton, 2003. 193.

328 Percy, 1990. 1286.

329 Crompton, 2003. 194,

330 Crompton, 2003. 195.

331 Crompton, 2003. 196.

332 Crompton, 2003. 196.

333 See, Théry-Astruc, J. 2013. "A Heresy of State: Philip the Fair, the Trial of the Perfidious Templars and the Ponticalization of the French Monarchy." In *Journal of Religious Medieval Cultures.* 39:2. 117-148.

334 Crompton, 2003. 295.

335 Crompton, 2003. 297.

336 Crompton, 2003. 538.

337 Crompton, 2003. 295.

338 Crompton, 2003. 362.

339 Fone, 2001. 333-334.

340 Crompton, 2003. 363.

341 Crompton, 2003. 264.

342 Cassiodoro de Reina created the influential Spanish translation of the Bible for the Protestant Reformation. For a full discussion of the case and charges against him see, Kinder, A.G. 1975. **Casdiodoro de Reina: Spanish Reformer of the Sixteenth Century.** London: Tamesis Books Limited.

Notes from Chapter 9

343 Crompton, 2003. 286.

344 Durant, W. & Durant A. 1961. The Story of Civilization VII: The Age of Reason Begins. A History of European Civilization in the Period of Shakespeare, Bacon, Montaigne, Rembrandt, Galileo, and Descartes: 1558-1648. New York: Simon and Schuster. 241.

345 Crompton, 2003. 287.

346 Boswell, J. 1995. **Same Sex Unions in Premodern Europe.** New York: Random House.

347 Crompton, 2003. XV.

348 Dall'Orto, G. 1990. "Venice" in Dynes, W.R. (Ed.) **Encyclopedia of Homosexuality, Vol II.** New York: Garland Publishing, Inc. 1366.

349 Dall'Orto, G. 1990. "Florence" in Dynes, W.R. (Ed.) **Encyclopedia of Homosexuality, Vol I.** New York: Garland Publishing, Inc. 409.

350 Dall'Orto, 1990. 410.

351 Dall'Orto, 1990. 410.

352 Crompton, 2003. 251.

353 Crompton, 2003. 252.

354 Crompton, 2003. 252.

355 Crompton, 2003. 254.

356 Crompton, 2003. 258.

357 Crompton, 2003. 260

358 Mt. 7:1 and Luke 6:37.

359 Crompton, 2003. 261.

360 Dall'Orto. 1990. "Venice." 1364.

361 Crompton, 2003. 247.

362 Crompton, 2003. 247.

363 Crompton, 2003. 247-248.

364 Crompton, 2003. 248.

365 Crompton, 2003. 249.

366 Crompton, 2003. 249.

367 See Ruggiero, G. 1985. The Boundaries of Eros: Sex, Crime, and Sexuality in Renaissance Venice. London: Oxford University Press.

368 Labalme, P. 1984. "Sodomy and Venetian Justice in the Renaissance." In **Legal History Review.** 52. 217-254.

369 Crompton, 2003. 250.

370 Ruggiero, 1985. 125.

371 Labalme, 1984. 239.

372 Crompton, 2003. 251.

373 Percy, W.A. 1990. "Inquisition" in Dynes, W.R. (Ed.) **Encyclopedia of Homosexuality, Vol I.** New York: Garland Publishing, Inc. 602.

374 Crompton, 2003. 190.

375 Percy, 1990. 602.

376 Crompton, 2003. 191.

377 Percy, 1990. 603.

378 Percy, 1990. 603.

379 Percy, 1990. 603.

380 The historian Nicholas Terpstra comments, "Over time, the Spanish Inquisition turned its attention beyond Jewish conversos to moriscos, Protestants, and witches, and to sexual 'crimes' like bigamy and sodomy. From 1540 to 1700 there were about 87,000 trials across Spain, with approximately 1,300 executions." See, Terpstra, N. 2015. **Religious Refugees in the Early Modern World: An Alternative History of the Reformation.** New York: Cambridge University Press. 96.

381 The examples below are recorded by Crompton, 2003. 201.

382 Monter, W. 1990. Frontiers of Heresy: The Spanish Inquisition from the Basque Lands **to Sicily**. Cambridge: Cambridge University Press. 280.

383 Monter, 1990. 280.

384 Carrasco, R. 1985. Inquisición y represión sexual en Valencia: historia de los sodomitas **(1565–1785)**. Barcelona: Laertes. 39.

385 Dynes, W.R. 1990. "Myths and Fabrications." In Dynes, W.R. (Ed.) **Encyclopedia of Homosexuality, Vol II.** New York: Garland Publishing, Inc. 869-870.

386 Crompton, 2003. 295.

Notes from Chapter 10

387 Terpstra, 2015. 105.

388 Terpstra, 2015. 76. See, Walsham, A. 2006. **Charitable Hatred: Tolerance and Intolerance in England 1500-1700.** Manchester: Manchester University Press.

389 Terpstra, 2015. 76.

390 Terpstra, 2015. 8.

391 See Calvin's Commentary on Deuteronomy 13:5 as well as Kaplan's discussion at, Kaplan, B.J. 2007. **Divided by Faith: Religious Conflict and the Practice of Toleration in Early Modern Europe.** Cambridge: The Belknap Press of Harvard University Press. 19ff.

392 Terpstra, 2015. 10.

393 Terpstra, 2015. 10.

394 For additional detailed discussion of homophobia in Geneva see Fone, 2001. 324ff.

395 Crompton, 2003. 324. It must be noted that soon after the population numbers Crompton reports the city almost tripled in numbers due to Protestant refugee influx.

396 Monter, W. 1980/81 "Switzerland." In Licata, S.J & Petersen, R. P. (Eds.) *Historical Perspectives on Homosexuality.* A special edition of the **Journal of Homosexuality** 6:1/2 also published, New York: Haworth Press, Inc. & Stein and Day Publishers. 43.

397 Monter, 1980/81. 44.

[398] Monter, 1980/81. 44.
[399] Monter, 1980/81. 45.
[400] Monter, 1980/81. 45.
[401] Crompton, 2003. 324.
[402] Crompton, 2003. 323.
[403] Monter, 1980/81. 45.
[404] Monter, 1980/81. 45.
[405] Monter, 1980/81. 46.
[406] Monter, 1980/81. 49.
[407] Lever, Maurice. 1985. **Les Bûchers de Sodome**. Paris: Fayard. 95.
[408] Crompton, 2003. 462.
[409] Crompton, 2003. 462.
[410] Crompton, 2003. 464.
[411] Crompton, 2003. 463.
[412] Crompton, 2003. 464.
[413] See https://commons.wikimedia.org/wiki/File:Justice_Triumphant.jpg accessed July, 20, 2016.
[414] Crompton, 2003. 466.
[415] Crompton, 2003. 463.
[416] Crompton, 2003. 466.
[417] The title, *Helsche boosheit van grouwelyke zonde van sodomie* (The Hellish evil of the wicked sin of sodomy) the reader who reads Dutch can find it at https://books.google.ca/books?id=RldXAAAAcAAJ&pg=PA61&lpg=PA61&dq=Helsche+boosheit+van+grouw elyke+zonde+van+sodomie&source=bl&ots=4Ibp-Y4E52&sig=g2RUbLy1fTp_3rRbybhlZ-QDxIo&hl=en&sa=X&ved=0ahUKEwjv6MbL_oLOAhUJYiYKHTVrDLgQ6AEIJTAB#v=onepage&q=Helsch e%20boosheit%20van%20grouwelyke%20zonde%20van%20sodomie&f=false accessed July, 20, 2016.
[418] Crompton, 2003. 467.
[419] Crompton, 2003. 467.
[420] Crompton, 2003. 468.
[421] Crompton, 2003. 451.
[422] Crompton, 2003, 452.
[423] Crompton, 2003. 455.
[424] Crompton, 2003. 451-452.
[425] In Crompton, 2003. 529.
[426] Crompton, 2003. 529.
[427] Crompton, 2003. 530. In fact his notes on the topic only became known in the 20th century.
[428] Crompton, 2003. 532.
[429] Crompton, 2003. 455.
[430] Crompton, 2003. 461.
[431] Fone, 2001. 383 ff.
[432] See, http://rictornorton.co.uk/eighteen/ accessed July 21, 2016.
[433] Crompton, 2003. 533.
[434] Crompton, 2003. 366.
[435] "Juden, Zigeuner, Homosexuelle, Sozialisten, Bolschewisten und liberale Sittenverderber" http://www.ibka.org/artikel/ag98/1945.html Acessed July 21, 2016.
[436] https://www.ushmm.org/wlc/en/article.php?ModuleId=10005261 accessed July 21, 2016.
[437] https://www.ushmm.org/wlc/en/article.php?ModuleId=10005261
[438] Crompton, 2003. 533.
[439] Grau, G. 1995. **Hidden Holocaust**. New York: Routledge.

Notes from Chapter 11

[440] Bavinck, J. H. 1960. **An Introduction to the Science of Missions**. Philadelphia: Presbyterian Reformed Publishing Company. 303. We do need to acknowledge that the use of "primitive" here is problematic and communicates some of the blind spots created by Bavinck's own Eurocentric context.

441 Fone, 2001. 395.
442 Fone, 2001. 418;420;541;549.
443 Fone, 2001. 11.
444 Fone, 2001. 565.
445 See White's discussion of the treatment of "sex problems" during World War II, White, 2015. 23-25.
446 See the description of the Newport Incident in Fone, 2001, 567.
447 Fone, 2001. 578.
448 White, 2015.25.
449 Fone, 2001. 590.
450 Fone, 2001. 591-592.
451 Fone, 2001. 596.
452 Fone, 2001. 596.
453 White, 2015. 26-27.
454 Fone, 2001. 598.
455 https://www.history.com/topics/gay-rights/history-of-gay-rights#section_3 accessed July 10, 2019.
456 For a feminist critique of the gay rights movement see, Frye, M. 1983. **The Politics of Reality: Essays in Feminist Theory.** Berkeley/Toronto: Crossing Press.
457 Nevitte, N. 1996. The Decline of Deference: Canadian Value Change in Cross-National Perspective. Toronto: University of Toronto Press.
458 See, McLeod, H. 2007 The Religious Crisis of the 1960's. Oxford: Oxford University Press and Brown, C. G. 2001. The Death of Christian Britain. Understanding Secularization 1800-2001. London: Routledge, and see also Brown, C.G. Religion and the Demographic Revolution: Women in Secularization in Canada, Ireland, UK and USA since the 1960's. Woodbridge: Boydel Press; Taylor, C. 2007. A Secular Age. Harvard: Harvard University Press; Fensham, C.J. 2018. "Towards a faithful Christian community in Canada: A missiological response to religious change" in Paul S. Peterson, The Decline of Established Christianity in the Western World. New York: Routledge. 145-155.
459 Clark, B. & Macdonald, S. 2018. **Leaving Christianity: Changing Allegiances in Canada since 1945.** Montreal: McGill University Press.
460 Fone, 2001. 606 ff.
461 Fone, 2001. 618.
462 **The Social Action Handbook.** The Presbyterian Church in Canada. 39&28. https://presbyterian.ca/wp-content/uploads/gao_social_action_handbook.pdf accessed July 10, 2019.
463 See https://en.wikipedia.org/wiki/LGBT_rights_by_country_or_territory#Timeline accessed July 10, 2019.
464 For a brief description of the history of the Stonewall Riots/Uprising see https://www.theatlantic.com/politics/archive/2013/01/an-amazing-1969-account-of-the-stonewall-uprising/272467/ accessed July 23, 2019.
465 In Fone, 2001. 619.
466 https://www.cnn.com/2019/06/06/us/stonewall-nypd-apology-trnd/index.html accessed July 10, 2019.
467 https://www.thecanadianencyclopedia.ca/en/article/toronto-feature-bathhouse-raids accessed July 10, 2019.
468 White, 2015. 86ff.
469 https://www.latimes.com/archives/la-xpm-1986-06-12-mn-10171-story.html accessed July 10, 2019.
470 https://surviveaplague.com/ accessed July 10, 2019.
471 White, 2015. 20.
472 White, 2015. 1-2.
473 White, 2015. 2.
474 White, 2015. 4.
475 White, 2015. 18-34.
476 Bailey, 1955.
477 White, 2015. 39.
478 White, 2015. 58 ff.
479 White, 2015.48-56
480 White, 2015. 60 ff.
481 White, 2015. 118 & 126ff.

482 For more on the term "culture wars" see https://americanaffairsjournal.org/2017/11/reevaluating-culture-wars/ accessed July 23, 2019.

483 See http://www.nytimes.com/2013/06/21/us/group-that-promoted-curing-gays-ceases-operations.html?_r=0 Accessed June 1, 2016.

484 The landscape of religious affirmation is constantly changing, here is a link to the wike page that tries to keep track of different positions https://en.wikipedia.org/wiki/List_of_Christian_denominations_affirming_LGBT accessed July 16, 2019.

485 There is a potential convergence here with Patrick Cheng's concept of "radical love," however, Cheng's fairly brief discussion of that concept also produces some questions. For example, the radical love that Jesus embodied according to the Gospels did have some boundaries. Jesus clearly challenged those who applied the law in harmful ways to others. Jesus seems to take the position of a kind of preferential option for the poor, marginalized and condemned by those with power and authority. Cheng's definition of sin as "opposition to what God has done for us in Jesus Christ," thus leaves potential room for thus limiting the concept of "radical love" to some degree. See Cheng, 2011. 73.

486 To site this consistent message in the Synoptic Gospels here are passages in the Good News Bible Translation: Mat 4:17 'From that time Jesus began to preach his message: "Turn away from your sins, because the Kingdom of heaven is near!"' Mar 1:15 "The right time has come," he said, "and the Kingdom of God is near! Turn away from your sins and believe the Good News!" Luk 24:45-47 'Then he opened their minds to understand the Scriptures, and said to them, "This is what is written: the Messiah must suffer and must rise from death three days later, and in his name the message about repentance and the forgiveness of sins must be preached to all nations, beginning in Jerusalem.'

487 See the description of V.S. Azariah from India's call for intercultural friendship in Stanley, B. 2009. **The World Missionary Conference, Edinburgh 1910.** Grand Rapids: Eerdmans. 121 ff.

488 See https://en.wikipedia.org/wiki/MS_St._Louis accessed July 18, 2019.

489 Bosch, D.J. 1991. **Transforming Mission: Paradigm Shifts in Theology of Mission.** New York: Orbis Books. See Bosch's discussion from page 4 onwards.

490 Bosch, 1991. 5.

491 Later published in Barth, K. 1957. "Die Theologie und die Mission in der Gegenwart" *Theologische Fragen und Antworten.* Evangelische Verlag, 100-126.

492 Keegan, T. 1996. **Colonial South Africa and the Origins of the Racial Order.** London: Leicester University Press. 83.

493 Stanley, B. 2009. 268 ff.

494 Here Barth deftly uses a rhetorical tool to employ the pejorative dimension of the word heathen and then to associate it with the missioning community itself who was sometimes known to use heathen pejoratively towards those they were ministering to.

495 Barth, 1957. 102.

496 Bosch, 1991. 420;489 and see Saayman, W. A. & Kritzinger, J. N. J. 1996. **Mission in Bold Humility: David Bosch's Work Considered.** New York: Orbis Books.

497 See https://www.rcaanc-cirnac.gc.ca/eng/1450124405592/1529106060525#chp2 accessed July 16, 2019.

Notes from Chapter 12

[498] There are of course things sexual that should be shameful, particularly the selfish expression of sexual desire, the exploitation of others, and the objectification of fellow human beings that dehumanize them. See Jay Johnson's helpful discussion on shame, Johnson, J.E. 2013. **Divine Communion: A Eucharistic Theology of Sexual Intimacy.** New York: Seabury Books. 29-56.

[499] I Cor. 7:9 Good News Bible, Paul also encourages a single life due to his eschatological expectation but does not elevate it to a rule.

[500] An example of Augustine's perspective and his radical dualism between the "animal body" or flesh, and the "spiritual body" can be found in **The City of God** 13:24. Here the sexual arousal of human genitalia become equal to the sinful animal body, "There remains a question which must be discussed, and, by the help of the Lord God of truth, solved: If the motion of concupiscence in the unruly members of our first parents arose out of their sin, and only when the divine grace deserted them; and if it was on that occasion that their eyes were opened to see, or, more exactly, notice their nakedness, and that they covered their shame because the shameless motion of their members was not subject to their will,—how, then, would they have begotten children had they remained sinless as they were created? But as this book must be concluded, and so large a question cannot be summarily disposed of, we may relegate it to the following book, in which it will be more conveniently treated." Augustine, St. 1866. **The City of God.** In "A Select Library of the Nicene and Post-Nicene Fathers" (Schaff, P. Translator) Vol 2. Edinburgh: T & T Clark. 261. Accessed through, http://www.ccel.org/ccel/schaff/npnf102.iv.XIII.24.html Accessed Aug. 5, 2016.

[501] Gustafson, 2007. 491.

[502] Gustafson, 2007, 488.

[503] Many Psychology texts have referred to the ground-breaking work of Rene Spitz (1887-1974) but recently there has been a wealth of study of the link between hormonal balance and physical touch, see for example the popular review in the New York Times, http://www.nytimes.com/1988/02/02/science/the-experience-of-touch-research-points-to-a-critical-role.html?pagewanted=all accessed August 4, 2016.

[504] Gustafson, 2007. 487.

[505] See Spraggon, J. 2003. **Puritan Iconoclasm During the English Civil War.** Rochester: Boydell Press.

[506] Conley, 2016. 336.

[507] Sprinkle, 2011.160.

[508] Sprinkle, 2011.159.

[509] http://www.apa.org/pi/lgbt/resources/therapeutic-response.pdf accessed July 23, 2017.

[510] See Newman and Fantus et al 2015; Newman and Fantus, 2017: Meyer & Dean 1998; Franklin, 1998.

[511] Vines, M. 2014. **God and the Gay Christian.** New York: Convergent Books. 43-57.

[512] Augustine, 1886. 276.

[513] Augustine, 1886. 278.

[514] Thou shalt not lie with mankind, as with womankind: it *is* abomination. (KJV) I am citing the King James Version as it is often the base texts used in condemnation of homoerotic relationships.

[515] If a man also lie with mankind, as he lieth with a woman, both of them have committed an abomination: they shall surely be put to death; their blood *shall be* upon them. (KJV)

[516] In this I accept Lings' argument that a universal prohibition would simply have read, "A man shall not lie with a man." Lings, 2013. 250.

[517] Rom 1:29-31 Good News Bible.

[518] Rom 2:1-3 Do you, my friend, pass judgment on others? You have no excuse at all, whoever you are. For when you judge others and then do the same things which they do, you condemn yourself. We know that God is right when he judges the people who do such things as these. But you, my friend, do those very things for which you pass judgment on others! Do you think you will escape God's judgment?

[519] Brownson, 2013. 156 ff.

[520] Brownson, 2013. 261.

[521] See, Augustine, City of God. Book 14 Chapter 22.

[522] Biblical examples of how grace overrides legalism (not justice) can be found in the story of Peter and Cornelius in Acts 10 as well as in the baptism of the eunuch by Philip despite the Deuteronomic prohibition against eunuchs – Acts 8. Most of all, it is to be found the boundary challenging ministry of Jesus himself.

[523] Fackre, 2002. 377-379.

[524] Of course, such a simplistic reading of the text ignores the socio-cultural concern for the plight of women who could be left destitute if a husband offers a divorce note. It is highly likely that Jesus' perspective included a concern for the plight of powerless and marginalized women under such circumstances. See Miguel De La Torre's discussion of Jesus challenging the idea of women as possessions: De La Torre, 2007.92-93.

[525] Gal 3:28 So there is no difference between Jews and Gentiles, between slaves and free people, between men and women; you are all one in union with Christ Jesus. (GNB)

[526] Developing a theology of marriage is not the aim here, but, it is important to note the diverse meanings and phenomena – traditions - understood as marriage within Christianity. Christian marriage in history by no means represented the best Scriptural understanding of the content of appropriate erotic relationships. See, Coontz, S. 2006. **Marriage, A History: From Obedience to Intimacy, or How Love Conquered Marriage.** New York: Viking.

[527] Gustafson, 2007. 491.

[528] Gustafson, 2007. 491.

[529] Brownson, 2013. 267.

[530] Jensen, 2013. 131.

[531] Gustafson, 2007. 491. There is much more to say about the contribution of Marcel's reflection on "creative fidelity" to our understanding of a Christian moral logic. For one thing, Marcel shows how selfishness in all its forms is the very opposite of such fidelity. In this Marcel's Roman Catholic philosophical perspective is very helpful. See a recent translation Marcel, G. 2002. **Creative Fidelity.** (Translated by Rosthal, R.) New York: Fordham University Press.

[532] John 8:7 Good News Bible.

[533] Breuggemann, 1982. 13.

[534] Breuggemann, 1982. 50.

[535] Gustafson, 2007. 43. Earlier discussed in Chapter 2.

[536] See the reference to Gustafson's observation that we will be sensitive to suffering, injustice and mental and physical suffering in our moral discernment discussed in Chapter 2.

About the author:

Charles Fensham is Professor of Systematic Theology at Knox College, Toronto, School of Theology, University of Toronto. His interests include the integrity of the contemporary Christian public witness. He has previously published, *Emerging from The Dark Age Ahead: The Future of the North American Church,* and *To the Nations for the Earth: A Missional Spirituality.* Charles Fensham is an ordained minister in the Presbyterian Church in Canada, and an active member of the Public Missiology Working Group within the American Society of Missiology.